AF477665

Combating Racial Discrimination

Combating Racial Discrimination

Affirmative Action as a Model for Europe

Edited by
Erna Appelt and Monika Jarosch

Oxford • New York

First published in 2000 by
Berg
Editorial offices:
150 Cowley Road, Oxford OX4 1JJ, UK
838 Broadway, Third Floor, New York, NY 10003-4812, USA

Berg is the imprint of Oxford International Publishers Ltd.

Library of Congress Cataloging-in-Publication Data

A catalogue record for this book is available from the Library of Congress.

British Library Cataloguing-in-Publication Data

A catalogue record for this book is available from the British Library.

ISBN 1 85973 308 5 (Cloth)

Typeset by JS Typesetting, Wellingborough, Northants.
Printed in the United Kingdom by WBC Book Manufacturers, Bridgend,
Mid Glamorgan.

Contents

List of Contributors

Anita L. Allen is Professor of Law and Philosophy at the University of Pennsylvania Law School, Philadelphia, US, having taken this position in July 1998 after serving as Professor of Law at Georgetown University for twelve years. She has published broadly on topics that include rights of privacy, bioethics, race relations, and literature. She has lectured at major universities and colleges all over the US, and in several European and Asian capitals.

Luisa Antoniolli Deflorian is a doctor in law and lecturer in private comparative law at the Faculty of Law, University of Trento, Italy. Her areas of research are judicial precedent as a source of law in the common law systems, EC private law and Community legal process, affirmative actions in Italian, EC and US American law.

Erna Appelt is Associate Professor of Political Science at the University of Innsbruck, Austria. She was the organizer of the international conference Combating Racial Discrimination: Affirmative Action as a Model for Europe? (Innsbruck, Austria 1998). She has published broadly on the field of theory of democracy and women's studies. Recent publication: *Geschlecht – Staatsbürgerschaft – Nation* (Gender – Citizenship – Nation), Campus, 1999.

Melinda Chateauvert teaches in the Afro-American Studies Program at the University of Maryland, US. Her book *Marching Together: Women of the Brotherhood of Sleeping Car Porters* was published in 1999 by University of Illinois Press. As Research Director for the Pay Discrimination Institute, a non-profit legal defence fund in Washington DC, she developed historical and statistical evidence for class action in race- and sex-based wage discrimination cases and continues to work as an expert historical witness for the NAACP Legal Defense Fund and other civil rights agencies.

Frank Cunningham is Professor of Philosophy at the University of Toronto, Canada. He is teaching in the area of social and political philosophy. His books include *The Real World of Democracy Revisited*, Humanities Press, 1994; and *Democratic Theory and Socialism*, Cambridge University Press, 1987.

Nathan Glazer is Professor of Education and Sociology Emeritus at Harvard University, Cambridge, US, and the co-editor of the quarterly *The Public Interest*. Author and editor of many books on ethnicity, among them *Affirmative Discrimination: Ethnic Inequality and Public Policy*, Basic Books, 1975, republished by Harvard University Press, 1987; *Beyond the Melting Pot*, MIT Press, 1989 (with Daniel P. Moynihan); and most recently *We are All Multiculturalists Now*, Harvard University Press 1997.

Lilian Gonçalves-Ho Kang You is Co-Chair of the Equal Treatment Commission in the Netherlands.

Mark Graham lectures at the Department of Social Anthropology, Stockholm University, Sweden. His research interests include immigrants in the Swedish labour market, ethnic discrimination and multiculturalism in Sweden. He is currently completing a book on refugees and Swedish welfare bureaucracies.

Monika Jarosch is a doctor in law and political scientist in Innsbruck, Austria. She was one of the organizers of the international conference Combating Racial Discrimination: Affirmative Action as a Model for Europe? (Innsbruck, Austria 1998). Publications on equal opportunity in Austria and the EU.

Louise Mulder is a member of the Equal Treatment Commission in the Netherlands. She teaches constitutional law at the University of Amsterdam.

John Rex is Professor Emeritus at the University of Warwick, UK. Former Director of the Social Science Research Council's Research Unit on Ethnic Relations, President of the International Sociological Association's Research Committee on Ethnic and Racial Minorities 1974–82, Member of UNESCO International Experts Committee on Race and Racism, 1967. Author inter alia of *Key Problems of Sociological Theory*, 1961; *Race Relations in Sociological Theory*, 1971 and 1982; *Race and Ethnicity*, 1986; and *Ethnic Minorities in the Modern Nation State*, Macmillan 1996.

Dagmar Schiek is Visiting Professor of European Economic Law at Oldenburg University, Germany (since October 1999), teaching German civil law and European and German Labour Law. Her publications include *Lifting the Ban on Women's Night Work in Europe – A Straight Road to Equality in Employment?* 1992; *Sex Equality Law after Kalanke and Marschall* 1998; *Zweites Gleichberechtigungsgesetz für die Privatwirtschaft,* 1995; *Europäisches Arbeitsrecht,* 1998. Current research subjects: European and German equality law (labour law), non-discrimination and private contract law.

Maria Sedlak received her Master degree in linguistics and cultural anthropology from the University of Vienna. Since 1993, she has been participating as a research associate in different international projects, among others she conducted research on racism in Austrian and German political discourse. Presently, she holds a grant of the Austrian Academy of Sciences to pursue her Ph.D. study on emotional communication in psychotherapy.

Maritta Soininen is Associate Professor and lecturer at the Department of Political Science, Stockholm University, Sweden. Her main research interests have been in the field of the political socialization of children and immigrant and refugee policy especially with regard to the Swedish Refugee Reception Programme. She has published on topics like the Swedish corporate model, the prevention of ethnic discrimination, the political participation of immigrants, and *Immigrants in the Political Process,* 1998.

Paul Taylor teaches at the School of Humanities and Social Sciences at the University of Sunderland, Sunderland, UK. Principle areas of research: the effectiveness of equal opportunities policies, particularly within higher education. He has worked on the evaluation of anti-discrimination training activities, a project supported by the International Labour Office. Recent publication: *The Evaluation of Anti-Discrimination Training Activities in the UK*, ILO 1997, (with Powell and Wrench).

Caterina Ventura works as a legal officer in the Department of Foreign Affairs and International Trade, United Nations, Human Rights and Humanitarian Law Section. She has held the positions of investigator, conciliator, legal counsel and policy analyst over the last 15 years in Canadian provincial and federal human rights commissions. She was a consultant to the International Labour Organization project *Combatting* *discrimination against (im)migrant workers and ethnic minorities in the world of work.*

Melissa S. Williams is Associate Professor of Political Science at the University of Toronto, where she teaches political philosophy. Williams's general research interests explore the intersection of ideals of democratic equality and phenomena of social difference. Recent publications: *Voice, Trust, and Memory: Marginalized Groups and the Failings of Liberal Representation*, Princeton University Press, 1998.

Ruth Wodak is Professor of Linguistics at the University of Vienna Austria. She was the winner of the Ludwig Wittgenstein Prize 1996. Many publications in the field of linguistics, cultural anthropology, and women's studies, inter alia: *Language Behaviour in Therapy Groups*, 1986; *The Language of Love and Guilt*, 1986 (with Muriel Schulz); *Power and Ideology*, 1989; *Disorders of Discourse*, 1996; *Gender and Discourse,* 1997; *Communicating Gender in Context*, 1997 (with Helga Kotthoff) *Discourse and Discrimination*, 2000 (with Martin Reisigl); *Semiotics of Racism*, 2000 (with Martin Reisigl).

John Wrench is a senior researcher at the Danish Centre for Migration and Ethnic Studies, University of Southern Denmark. He has researched and published in the area of labour market discrimination and exclusion in the UK and in Europe. Recent publications include *Racism and Migration in Western Europe*, Oxford, 1993 (edited with John Solomos); *Preventing Racism at the Workplace*, Luxembourg, 1996; and *Migrants, Ethnic Minorities and the Labour Market: Integration and Exclusion in Europe*, Basingstoke 1999 (edited with Andrea Rea and Nouria Ouali).

List of Abbreviations

AAP	Affirmative Action Plans
AG	Advocate General
AMS	Labour Market Board
ATF	Action Travail des Femmes
BDA	Bund Deutscher Arbeitgeber (German Employers' Confederation)
BEAA	Bevordering Evenredige Arbeidsdeelname Allochtonen
C.F.R.	Code of Federal Regulation
CCR	(United States) Commission on Civil Rights
CEC	Commission of the European Communities
CRE	Commission for Racial Equality
CUCO	Commission on University Career Opportunity
DGB	Deutscher Gewerkschaftsbund (German Trade Union)
DO	Discrimination Ombudsman
EC	European Community
ECJ	European Court of Justice
EEA	Employment Equity Act
EEOC	Equal Employment Opportunity Commission
EMO	Etnische Minderheden bij Overheid
EO	Executive Order
EU	European Union
FCC	Federal Communications Commission
FEA	Fair Employment Act
FEC	Fair Employment Commission
FPÖ	Freiheitliche Partei Österreichs (Austrian Freedom Party)
GEW	Gewerkschaft Erziehung und Wissenschaft (Union for Education and Science)
HEW	Department of Health, Education and Welfare
ILO	International Labour Organisation
LO	Swedish Trade Union Confederation
LSAT	Law School Admission Test
MBE	Minority Business Enterprise
NAACP	National Association for the Advancement of Colored People

NAC	National Action Committee on the Status of Women
NCARR	National Capital Alliance on Race Relations
OCR	Office for Civil Rights
OFCC	Office of Federal Contract Compliance
OFCCP	Office of Federal Contract Compliance Plans
ÖVP	Österreichische Volkspartei (Austrian People's Party)
RRA	Race Relation Act
SACO	Sveriges Akademikers Centralorganisation
SAF	Swedish Employers' Confederation
SAMEN	Stimulering Arbeitsdeelname Minderheden
SCC	Supreme Court of Canada
SPÖ	Sozialdemokratische Partei Österreichs (Austrian Social Democratic Party)
TCO	Confederation of Professional Employees
UAW	United Automobile Aerospace and Agricultural Implement Workers of America, International Union
UN	United Nations
VBE	Verband für Bildung und Erziehung (Association for Education and Training)

Preface

The European Union considers the fight against racism and xenophobia as one of its important tasks. The European Year against Racism, which the EU launched in 1997, and the establishment of a European Monitoring Centre for Racism and Xenophobia, established in Vienna in 1998, indicate this strong dedication. The European Commission is now considering new legislation to be based on *Article 13 EC Treaty* after the coming into force of the Treaty of Amsterdam in 1999.

The background of this dedication is the conviction that the European nation states as well as the European Union are strictly obliged to guarantee human rights in a comprehensive sense. One aspect of this guarantee is the development of legal instruments that are capable of prohibiting unfair discrimination based on sex, racial or ethnic origin, religion or belief, disability, age or sexual orientation, and promoting the realization of equal opportunities for everybody. Other aspects are the unmasking of racist discourses in all their different forms and the political fight against discrimination and both its blatant and its less obvious but nevertheless very significant effects.

As there is no perfect instrument to deal either with the roots or the effects of discrimination, experts from all over the world have to evaluate existing instruments and develop new ones again and again. European lawyers and politicians also have to realize that democracies outside Europe have their respective experiences with anti-discriminatory policies. This book is intended to examine extra-European experiences as well as European positive action policies and summarize some aspects of the debates in the US and in Canada.

This book is the outcome of the international conference *Combating Racial Discrimination: Affirmative Action as a Model for Europe?* held in Innsbruck, Austria, in September 1998. This conference has been prepared and organized by the Department of Political Science, University of Innsbruck, in cooperation with the European Commission, General Directorate V. We owe special thanks to Odile Quintin, Annette Bosscher, and Sandra Lutchman who were strong supporters of this conference within the European Commission; to Anton Pelinka for advocating antiracist research within the Innsbruck Department of Political Science; to all contributors for their endeavours during the conference and their cooperation when producing this book; to Elisabeth Gensluckner for her research assistance; to Alexandra Weiss for reviewing the bibliography; and finally to Maike Bohn from Berg Publishers for opening up the possibility of publishing this volume.

Erna Appelt and Monika Jarosch, Innsbruck

—1—

Affirmative Action:
a Cross-National Debate

Erna Appelt

Introduction

In Europe as well as in other parts of the world, xenophobia and racism are amongst the unsolved problems of the late twentieth century. Whilst a solid majority of the political elite of Europe is strictly determined to fight against this phenomenon, political and economic problems and trends like globalisation, mass migration and unemployment provoke profound feelings of insecurity reinforcing latent and manifest xenophobic attitudes among European citizens.

At the threshold to the twenty-first century, the European Union (EU) is confronted with contradictory challenges: on the one hand, the political leaders have decided on an expansion of the Union; on the other hand, a consolidation of integration is one of the compelling tasks of the nearer future. The formation of the EU as a political unit, however, faces a number of serious problems, as it is not only the question of an institutional linking-up of the national states. The problems of internal integration are far more complex and involve the 'invention' of a new identity, a 'European identity', which is connected with a symbolic and factual dividing line towards outsiders. This delimitation is of particular signifi-cance in so far as the European national states – unlike various non-European states as for instance the United States, Canada or Australia – never defined themselves as immigration states in the course of their history. So far, the European Union does not understand itself as an open immigration society (Münz, 1996). Many European states can look back on a history of emigration of considerable parts of their own population, and many Europeans have considered emigration to be a matter of course. In sharp contrast to this conviction, for a long time newcomers have been regarded as temporary guest workers, and until today immigration has been interpreted predominantly as something threatening.

As answers to this supposed threat, there have been several brutal attacks upon homes for people seeking political asylum and hostile inroads upon foreigners by right-wing radicals. The number of these xenophobic attacks has not only increased in the 1990s, but these hostilities have been noticed with some understanding, even with a certain consent, by a considerable part of the European population (Eurobarometer, 1998; Institut für Migrations- und Rassismusforschung, 1992; Wrench/Solomos, 1993; Wasmuth, 1996). Not surprisingly, right-wing radical xenophobic parties became popular in several countries of the EU in the last decade. It was this popularity that has caused some parties of the political centre to adopt not only xenophobic rhetoric but also proposals and policies discriminating against people looking for asylum and against 'visible minorities' in general, and often just against third states nationals far beyond any justifiable measure, thus giving legitimacy once more to widespread xenophobic feelings (see Wodak in this volume).

Beyond hostile assaults and attacks upon foreigners, many members of minority groups and immigrants are daily experiencing unfair discrimination. Frequently, they get a less favourable treatment than the majority of the citizens of the Member States, when looking for employment, accommodation, education, and medical welfare. This discrimination threatens to push immigrants and members of discriminated minorities to the lowest level of society, where the different disadvantages within a society intensify each other.

However, racism and xenophobia as well as day-to-day discrimination against persons not regarded as co-nationals have also resulted in a strong appeal for an anti-discrimination policy in Europe in the last decade. Combating racism became a central concern of the European Parliament and the Commission. The formulation of such a European anti-discrimination policy has still to be analysed, against the background of the xenophobic feelings mentioned above and of the rather strong restrictions towards outsiders. Considering the unsolved problem of mass unemployment and the restrictive budget policies in the EU Member States, the chances for an efficient anti-discrimination policy have to be assessed as rather unfavourable. Nevertheless, Europeans have to recognize that migration will be a fact in the nearer future and that the much-contested multiculturalism has become an undeniable reality. The request for the European national states as well as on the European Union to see themselves as multicultural, dynamic immigration societies means nothing other than understanding the changes that occurred in the past decades and those that are also foreseeable for the twenty-first century. Globalisation, the pressure of migration, as well as demographic developments (low birth-rates and simultaneously increasing life expectancy) require an active immigration policy not governed by xenophobia. Thus, an anti-discrimination policy will be on the agenda of the European nation states as well as of the European Union in the next century.

It is the objective of this book to ask what the European Union can learn from extra-European experiences concerning efficient anti-discrimination policies. This concerns above all those policies that do not only forbid and punish discrimination, but that, in addition, take positive measures (positive action) in order to indemnify members of disadvantaged, discriminated, or marginalized groups for these disadvantages and to promote them in such a way that the disadvantages suffered so far can be compensated and that they will become equals in reality. It is the target of such policies to open up the same living and earning opportunities for members of disadvantaged groups as for members of the population that has not suffered discrimination in the long run.

The questions raised here are embedded in their respective political and socioeconomic context; they are, however, also connected with ideas of justice on which our societies are based: discussing the justified claims and rights of citizens and non-citizens, of members of dominant and non-dominant groups, or asking if affiliation with specific groups could establish special claims and rights, concerns the philosophical and legal fundamentals of our societies.

Legal Norms and Conventions

Since the Second World War international organizations have repeatedly acknowledged the principle of non-discrimination.[1] International human rights instruments generally prohibit racism and racial discrimination. Systematic racial discrimination is regularly listed as a gross violation of human rights.[2]

Of particular importance is *The International Convention on the Elimination of All Forms of Racial Discrimination* (1965), which explicitly acknowledges as legitimate measures, that aim to improve the situation of groups and individuals that have suffered discrimination:

Special measures taken for the sole purpose of securing adequate advancement of certain racial or ethnic groups or individuals requiring such protection as may be necessary in order to ensure such groups or individuals equal enjoyment or exercise of human rights and fundamental freedoms shall not be deemed racial discrimination, provided, however, that such measures do not, as a consequence, lead to the maintenance of separate rights for different racial groups and that they shall not be continued after the objectives for which they were taken have been achieved (Article 1.4).

Since the late 1970s the European Parliament, the Council and the Commission have issued several declarations, documents and recommendations in the field of anti-racism (Bell, 1998; European Commission, 1997):

- The Joint Declaration by the European Parliament, the Council and the Commission on Fundamental Rights, 5 April 1977.
- In 1985, the European Parliament agreed to establish a Committee of Inquiry into the Rise of Racism and Fascism in Europe which delivered the so-called Evrigenis Report, including a recommendation of a wide range of measures to be implemented at the national levels and supplemented by European-level action.
- The Joint Declaration by the European Parliament, the Council and the Commission against racism and xenophobia, 11 June 1986.
- In 1988, the Commission submitted a proposal to the Council for a resolution on racism, moving forward from the general principles expressed in the 1986 Joint Declaration and specifying a number of legal developments to be encouraged in the 1986 *Joint Declaration*.
- In 1990, the European Parliament initiated a second Committee of Inquiry, which produced the so-called Ford Report, giving 77 recommendations for action and European legislation to combat racism. As the proposals were not acted upon, the European Parliament stressed the need for legislative action at the European level.
- In 1994, the Corfu European Council agreed in establishing a Consultative Commission on Racism and Xenophobia (the so-called Kahn Commission), consisting of a representative from each of the Member States, two MEPs, a representative from the Commission and an observer from the Council of Europe. The Commission expressed the conviction that an essential prerequisite for effective action by the Community would be an amendment of the Treaty to insert a specific reference to combat racial discrimination.
- Following this recommendation, in December 1995, both the Parliament and the Commission published a Communication on Racism, Xenophobia and Anti-Semitism, underlining that the treaties should be amended in the 1996 inter-governmental conference (IGC) to provide competence for the Community in this sphere.
- Presidency Conclusions of the European Council, 21 and 22 June 1996 in Florence, on the Union's determination to combat racism and xenophobia with the utmost determination.

- Proposal for a Council Regulation, establishing a European Monitoring Centre for Racism and Xenophobia (COM (96) 615 final) of 27 November 1996.
- Declaration of Intent: Europe Against Racism, signed at the launching of the European Year against Racism, The Hague, 30 January 1997.
- Creation of the Monitoring Centre on Racism and Xenophobia, set up in June 1997 by virtue of Council Regulation No. 1035/97.

At last, the repeated demands of the European Parliament, of the Consultative Commission Against Racism and Xenophobia, and of numerous NGOs were successful in so far as the Treaty of Amsterdam introduced the new Article 6a (Article 13 EC Treaty according to new numbering), which reads as follows:

> Without prejudice to the other provisions of this Treaty and within the limits of the powers conferred by it upon the Community, the Council, acting unanimously on a proposal from the Commission and after consulting the European Parliament, may take appropriate action to combat discrimination based on sex, racial or ethnic origin, religion or belief, disability, age or sexual orientation.

Article 6a EC Treaty represents an important step from a policy of confession towards an anti-discrimination legislation. For the first time since the foundation of the European Community in 1957, discrimination is being understood extensively; in addition, anti-discrimination measures are expressly permitted.

However, the new article has to be evaluated as rather weak because it permits but does not demand legislation in the field of anti-discrimination; furthermore, the legislative procedure needs unanimity within the Council after presentation of a proposal by the Commission and after consultation with Parliament. Summing up, the amendment of the EC Treaty introduced by the Treaty of Amsterdam does not open up the way towards making the European Union an open, multicultural immigration society.[3]

Key Terms of the Affirmative Action Debate

As this volume deals with the formulation of European anti-discrimination policies and discusses the possibilities of learning from extra-European experiences, especially from the US affirmative action model, it seems to be useful to clarify some of the key terms of the debate.

Racism

Following a wide consensus the term racism will be defined in this book as follows:

> Racism will be regarded as pattern of thinking and pattern of perception of the members of dominant groups which characterize members of non-dominant groups as different or inferior on basis of real or imagined physical or other characteristics, intending to legitimate inferior treatment, exclusion or violence against, or exploitation of members of non-dominant groups.

This definition corresponds to Article 1 of the International Convention on the Elimination of All Forms of Racial Discrimination (1965), which defines racial discrimination as follows:

> any distinction, exclusion, restriction or preference based on race, colour, descent, or national or ethnic origin which has the purpose or effect of nullifying or impairing the recognition, enjoyment or exercise, on an equal footing, of human rights and fundamental freedoms in the political, economic, social, cultural or any other field of public life.

Equality

Equality is a term that causes considerable confusion in academic and everyday discussions. The term 'equality' – as one of the keywords of the affirmative action debate – is claimed by both supporters and opponents to justify their respective positions. These controversial perspectives could suggest either that the participants in this debate are victims of semantic confusion, or they are using, in bad faith, the notion of equality in a purely ideological manner (Faundez, 1994: 3). However, one of the main sources of the problem lies in the unclear notion of equality. I will therefore supply definitions for the term of equality and the concepts connected therewith, which are to serve at least to avoid unintended misunderstandings.

Today, it is a matter of fact that modern societies are based upon the principle of equality of all human beings. The Constitution of the United States, the Declaration on Human Rights of the French Revolution, the international human rights documents, and the great majority of the national constitutions all over the world declare themselves committed to the principle of equality. However, the concept of equality, seen by itself, does not contain any specific matter. Ronald Dworkin, for instance, maintains that the equal protection clause of the US Constitution anchors the concept of equality without providing any particular conceptions of it (Dworkin, [1977] 1993: 134–5). Thus, the term equality does not give any information about to which goods, claims and burdens human beings are or shall be equal.

It has to be stressed that all modern legal documents and all the subsequent political and moral debates deal with a prescriptive and not with a descriptive equality. Jacobus tenBroek rightly pointed out that the sentence of the Declaration of Independence 'All men are created equal' is a demand and not a description (tenBroek, 1969: 19). However, no conclusions can be drawn from this prescription – or to put it in other words – from this political consensus in which respect equality should be realized.

In order to clarify the possible meaning of equality we have to distinguish two different kinds of equality rights: (1) the right to equal treatment and (2) the right to be treated as an equal. Ronald Dworkin explains the difference between the two legitimate moral and legal claims as follows:

> The first is the right to equal treatment, that means, the right to equal distribution of a chance, a resource, or a burden. For instance, every citizen in a democracy has the right to an equal vote; it is the nerve of the decision of the Supreme Court that a person has to have a vote, even if other and more complex arrangements would better secure the collective well-being. The second one is the right to be treated as an equal, this does not mean the right to receive the same share in a burden or in a utility, but the right to be treated with attention and consideration in the same way as all the others. If I have two children and one is in danger of dying from a disease which causes an indisposition to the other, I do not consider both in the same way, if I throw a coin to decide who of the two is to receive the remaining dose of a medicine. This example shows that the right to be treated as an equal is the fundamental one and that the right for equal treatment has been derived from it. The right to be treated as an equal will implement a right for equal treatment into some circumstances; this will, however, by no means be the case in all situations. (Dworkin, 1977 quoted from Rössler, 1993: 79).

This example makes clear, that the right to be treated as an equal may include the right to certain preferential treatment without violating the principle of equality.

One of the crucial points is the differentiation between formal equality of opportunity and fair equality of opportunity. Formal equality of opportunity requires that laws and quasi-legal devices are not used to deprive subjects of means already in their possession or within their present capacity to obtain in the future (Rosenfeld, 1991: 28). Fair equality of opportunity, on the other hand, requires, according to Rawls, that those with similar abilities and skills should have similar life chances irrespective of the income class into which they are born (Rawls, 1971: 73). Individuals from all economic and social background should be able to develop those skills they are naturally suited for. Thus, fair equality of opportunity demands correction for socially relative disadvantages (Goldman, 1979: 171).

Affirmative Action

The confusion concerning the meaning of affirmative action results to a significant degree from the vast array of often inconsistent practices and policies that fall under that rubric. The following definitions indicate that the term affirmative action does not mean a specific or single political measure; on the contrary, affirmative action indicates different forms of active engagement in promoting equality of groups that have formerly been or presently are the victims of discrimination.

According to Faundez, affirmative action involves treating a subclass or a group of people differently in order to improve their chances of obtaining a particular good to ensure that they obtain a proportion of certain goods (Faundez, 1994: 3).

John Skrentny identifies affirmative action as

> particular practices, policies and laws, on the basis of the extent to which the following unit ideas are present: (1) a requirement that employers see in their everyday hiring and promoting practices group differences and specifically race as real (rather than unreal or irrelevant), (2) an emphasis on counting anonymous minorities in the workforce (rather than treating each individual as an individual), (3) a de-emphasis rather than emphasis on finding individual victims of discrimination, (4) de-emphasis or re-evaluation rather than emphasis or acceptance of previously accepted standards of merit, and (5) an overriding concern with representation, utilization, or employment of minorities, rather than stopping harmful, 'bigoted' acts of discrimination. (Skrentny, 1996: 7–8).

Thus, affirmative action can be defined as attempts to make progress towards substantive rather than merely formal equality of opportunity for those groups such as women or racial minorities that are currently underrepresented in significant positions in society by explicitly taking into account the defining characteristics – sex or race – which have been the basis for discrimination.

Erna Appelt

Affirmative Action in the US and in Canada

The contributions of the first part of the present publication provide an insight into anti-discrimination policies in the US and in Canada. Several scholars investigate the success of and the resistance to anti-discriminatory policies, the institutional and judicial context as well as the sociological aspects of American-style affirmative action. Anita L. Allen argues in her article that US affirmative action has contributed to combating racial discrimination by opening up additional opportunities for work, business and education to members of previously disadvantaged minority groups and to women of all backgrounds. Allen underlines that in the US beyond the demand for compensatory or reparative justice, affirmative action has helped to erase racial subordination, to neutralise the competitive advantages many whites enjoy in education, business and employment, to educate a cadre of minority professionals for service in minority communities, to create minority role models, intellectuals, artists and civic leaders, and finally, to acknowledge society's cultural diversity.

On the background of the Canadian experiences Frank Cunningham asks under which circumstances affirmative action will be supported by members of the majority population. Thus, he analyses the connection between affirmative (positive) action and democracy. Among the goals of affirmative action is to strengthen democracy by enabling people who are marginalized or disempowered to become fully active citizens. However, to be effective, the respective policies require support on the part of those citizens who are already active democratic participants. To the extent that this citizenry is insufficiently motivated to overcome the discrimination that leads to marginalization and does not include the target groups of affirmative action, democratic support will not occur. This creates a dilemma for government agencies or anyone else who wishes democratically to redress democratic exclusions. The intent of Cunningham's paper is to clarify some conceptual issues implicated in this dilemma and to demonstrate the compatibility of democracy and affirmative action.

The contribution of Melissa S. Williams deals with the question if the principle of the equality of persons is best realized through policies of equal opportunity that treat all individuals on the same terms regardless of what social group or class they might belong to, or if it requires policies of positive or affirmative action, which aim to overcome the ongoing consequences of past discrimination through programmes that specifically benefit members of disadvantaged groups. Williams distinguishes among four different types of discrimination: direct or intentional discrimination, statistical discrimination, societal discrimination, and structural or systemic discrimination. She argues that social science evidence sustains the conviction that positive action policies really do increase the number of women and minorities in spheres of education and employment from which they were absent thirty or forty years ago; that their presence has helped to change cultural beliefs about the capacities of these groups; that there is little or no empirical evidence to sustain the claim that positive action increases group stigma or diminishes group members' self-esteem; and that, as it has been practised, positive action seldom entails overriding merit criteria.

Luisa Antoniolli Deflorian underlines that all Western countries have experienced, although at different times, the recognition of minorities' and women's rights as part of the implementation of a general principle of equality, and all of them have gradually moved from a conception of formal equality to one of substantive equality. The shift to a substantive idea of equality, however, has been rather problematic from a legal point of view: it required a step to be taken beyond formal equality and the recognition of the existing imbalance in order to devise legal solutions that would redress it. In her paper Antoniolli examines the legal instruments on which affirmative action is based in the US system and sees the role of the US courts and the federal Supreme Court in particular as being the leading formant that shapes the US legal system.

Melinda Chateauvert considers the historical and sociological justifications for adopting anti-discrimination policies in the US and the use of historical evidence to defend affirmative action policies in the courts. As one revealing example Chateauvert analyses the question of who is allowed to participate in the construction of the transportation infrastructure, which is at the heart of the debate over minority contracting programmes. Under current US guidelines issued by the Department of Transportation, this multi-billion dollar industry is supposed to set aside a small percentage of its annual contracts to minority- and woman-owned firms. However, the US Supreme Court's decision in *Richmond v. Croson* severely limited the scope of this programme. The new guidelines, issued to comply with *Croson*, were recently challenged by a conservative legal foundation in the State of Maryland. In order to demonstrate persistent racial discrimination against African American entrepreneurs Chateauvert, as an historian for this case, examined how the state and local jurisdictions had awarded construction contracts prior to the adoption of minority contracting.

The Canadian example being presented by Caterina Ventura illustrates that equality is not a static concept, and therefore methods to achieve it cannot remain unchanging. Canada has progressed from the most basic level of human rights protection dealing with the intentional, isolated incident of discrimination where the complete onus for redress was on the victim to the creation of human rights commissions which responded to individual complaints, to the development of the theory of systemic discrimination to constituting the Charter and the substantive equality theory – all of which still lay the onus of ameliorating the situation on the individual or advocacy groups, and finally, to employment equity – where it is recognized that it is more effective if the onus is passed on to the employers who have the ability to make the changes to avoid discrimination. The judiciary's pronouncement that differences in treatment are sometimes necessary to allow individuals to compete on an equal footing, provides the basis for the implementation of affirmative action programmes. In Canada, in order to achieve equality, accommodation of disadvantaged groups through affirmative action programmes is considered as necessary.

The contribution of Nathan Glazer focuses on the question of what Europe can learn from the thirty-year experience of the US with affirmative action. Glazer argues that Europe, in sharp contrast to the US, does not have a lower caste or anything like it. Europe does have an immigrant problem and a second-generation immigrant problem. However, there are different categories of immigrants in each country, and their problems are different. Thus, the problem of defining the categories eligible for positive action would be difficult and disruptive. Glazer admits that positive action covers a huge range of policies, and many of these may not be very controversial and can be defended as part of the general effort that we see in all European countries to raise the skills and qualities of labour. But positive action also suggests the possibility of what Glazer names 'hard affirmative action'. That kind of affirmative action is controversial in the US and – according to Glazer – would be best avoided.

The European Union – an Ethnic Mosaic

There are some considerable differences between ethnic and racial conflicts in the US or in Canada on the one hand and in Europe on the other hand. Already a very superficial view of Europe makes it obvious that almost all European states have encountered a number of ethnic conflicts that often have historic roots, frequently being the result of the homogenizing strategies of nation states. Thus, the EU can be seen as an ethnic mosaic, and the range of problems is correspondingly wide; ethnic conflicts are rooted in many different problems resulting, *inter alia*, from violations of self-determination and the refusal of equal opportunities, and these are often connected with the problem of socioeconomic backwardness of so-called autochthonous minorities.

'Old' Ethnic Minorities – 'New' Migrant Communities

In the last decades these 'old' ethnic conflicts have been set over by problems and conflicts due to mass migrations to which the European states have given different political answers. In fact, most European states have drawn a line between, on the one hand, so-called autochthonous minorities that may frequently enjoy substantial rights or even some form of regional autonomy and, on the other hand, minorities of recent immigrant origin[4] (Bauböck, 1995: 8).

During the history of the formation process of the European nation states, the overwhelming majority of the ethnic minorities were subjected to a forced cultural and linguistic homogenization and an assimilation under strong political and social pressure. In contrast with these ambitions, a long-term integration of migrant workers has not been intended in the last decades. For the admitting countries, labour migration has primarily had the function of meeting the demand for low-paid and unskilled workers, and migrant workers are mostly referred to the lowest segment of the labour market. As the factor motivating the migration of the majority of guestworkers has been the improvement of their economic situation, collective claims for self-determination have been of no importance or of minor importance. However, these claims become important, when the integration process fails.

Besides the differentiation between 'old' ethnic minorities and 'new' migration minorities or communities,[5] we have to consider the fact that some minorities are referred to as 'visible minorities'. 'Visible minorities' are first targets of discrimination and have to be protected by measures that are able to prohibit violent attacks, racism and other discrimination. In our context, we have to underline that the visible minority status cuts divisions across citizenship status and produces new graduations of inequality. Thus, even those people with full and formal citizenship rights can suffer disadvantages in the labour market on the grounds of colour (Wrench, 1996: 4). Apart from the 'visible minorities', minorities like 'gypsies', and 'travelling communities', and others who do not fit into the scheme of our modernised, homogenized world, are particularly threatened and affected by unfair discrimination and violent attacks.

In this connection, particular attention has to be paid to the fact that female migrants and female members of all minorities often suffer multiple discrimination. They are over-represented in atypical work and in the informal economy: employed as cleaners, houseworkers, in the service sector, as unpaid workers in family businesses, and as domestic workers. In brief, they are concentrated in insecure jobs with high work intensity and little employment protection, with either part-time or long working hours. With little prospect of receiving training or further skills on the job and without access to training, black and migrant women have very little hope of moving up the employment ladder (European Parliament, 1995: 62).

Variations in Immigration Policies

In connection with the research topic of the present publication we have to stress some differences between the immigration policies of Western European states on the one hand and countries like the US, Australia or Canada on the other hand. The US, Australia and Canada have consciously used immigration as part of the process of nation building and have, in the long run, been forced to revise their concepts of national identity and their institutional structures to take account of the growing cultural diversity of their populations. Western European countries never aimed to change their demographic and cultural composition through immigration, but that has in fact happened, and the current debate on national identity and citizenship should take account of this by moving away from monocultural myths (Castles, 1993: 29). According to Castles and many other scholars, one of the major challenges confronting the advanced industrial democracies of Western Europe is the acceptance and integration of postwar migrant workers and political refugees and their families, especially those from the Third World.

Positive Action – European Style

In the second part of this book some experts from the EU Member States examine European experiences in the field of anti-discrimination policies and the implementation of different positive action measures in the UK, in the Netherlands and in Sweden will be presented. They also raise the question of whether positive action in favour of women can be a model for anti-discrimination policies in the field of racial discrimination.

Analysing the British example, Paul Taylor mentions three main types of positive action being lawful under current UK legislation: encouragement measures to attract applicants; pre-entry training to increase the pool of potential applicants; and in-service training to increase the potential for career advancement. Taking lawful positive action in the UK relies strongly on the principle of proving that underrepresentation exists, and this can often act as one of the first hurdles that employers have to overcome. The motivations for undertaking positive action can vary tremendously and may be a result of a combination of factors. Taylor underlines that positive action only offers one alternative route to compensate for previous discrimination: it provides a way of dealing with the consequences of discrimination rather than dealing with the causes.

In the Netherlands, Lilian Gonçalves-Ho Kang You and Louise Mulder argue in their paper, positive action policies relating to ethnic minorities focuses mainly on the four principal immigrant groups: the Surinamese, the Turks, the Moroccans, and the Dutch Antilleans. Whereas immigration from Surinam and the Dutch Antilles has been historically linked to the colonial past, more and more immigrants were attracted to the Netherlands in the decades after the Second World War to meet the demand for unskilled labour. According to the authors, equal opportunity and recruitment procedures being free from direct or indirect discrimination is not enough to promote ethnic diversity on the shop floor. It requires greater involvement on the part of management and employees, not just through tolerance, but by accepting and acknowledging cultural differences. The authors argue that positive action measures do not in themselves diminish the disadvantaged position of ethnic minorities in the job market in a substantial way; therefore positive action must be seen in the broader scope of promoting the proper functioning of a multicultural society, which includes the promotion of ethnic diversity on the shop floor.

Maritta Soininen and Mark Graham examine policies that have been pursued in the Swedish labour market in the 1990s in order to increase ethnic diversity in the workforce and to counteract ethnic discrimination in the context of the Swedish institutional framework consisting of the welfare policy-making model. Since the beginning of the 1990s, there has been consistent high unemployment, which has been tackled by an expanded labour market policy. Increasingly, targeted measures for disadvantaged groups, including immigrants, have been introduced. Soininen and Graham analyse the fact that egalitarian ideals in Sweden have been class based: class inequalities attract attention and the class based corporate policymaking model attempts to find means to remove their worst expressions. Other types of inequality have not provoked the same kind of attention. This has tended to exclude questions of ethnic inequality including ethnic discrimination from the labour market agenda. There is pressure for this to be changed in the 1990s.

The contribution of John Rex analyses the different meanings of the term 'integration' and the different political concepts of assimilation on the one hand and of multiculturalism on the other hand. Rex argues that there clearly is a need for action to be taken if immigrants of various kinds are to obtain their full rights as citizens, however a strong commitment to affirmative action in the narrower sense could divert attention away from the problems many migrants are facing in European societies. In the US a radical case was argued for affirmative action on the grounds that the fact of slavery and its consequences left the descendants of slaves in a structurally distinct position from other members of the excluded and the so-called 'underclass'. The question in Europe, according to Rex, *is* whether the position of incoming minorities rests upon an equivalent historic wrong.

Analysing 'racism at the top', Ruth Wodak and Maria Sedlak argue that racism can present and manifest itself in different masks and guises: blatantly, aggressively, and explicitly, or covertly in the mode of positive self-presentation and legitimization. They argue that exclusion and racism cannot be attributed to the populist and extreme right only; they are not marginal phenomena. Exclusion lies at that core of everyday politics in Western Europe today, and the mainstream parties are equally involved in restrictive and discriminatory practices, that are legitimized on moral and humanitarian grounds. Wodak and Sedlak use the 'Critical Discourse Analysis' as one way of combating racism, claiming that discourse is a central means of the production and reproduction of racism, because communication is the instrument of political debate and the means through which beliefs and prejudices become manifest. Thus, the detailed analysis of the possible range of variation of linguistic realizations of racism is an important political task as it allows us to identify racist practices which would otherwise be covert.

Dagmar Schiek scrutinizes the achievements of EC sex equality law in order to avoid failures that may have hampered their efficiency in other fields of anti-discrimination law. Schiek considers the interrelation between gender and 'race' discrimination and focuses on the necessity of addressing adequately both forms of discrimination, and especially discrimination of ethnic minority women on both grounds in legal frameworks. The contribution of Schiek covers two different aspects of EC anti-discrimination law: the legal concept of sex equality as mirrored in the jurisdiction of the European Court of Justice (ECJ) with specific attention to the group dimension and the asymmetric dimension of sex discrimination, and the question of how double discrimination can be addressed. Schiek stresses that there is a need for a 'European' equality policy. She also suggests that EC non-discrimination policy must not be restricted to an individual litigation approach. According to Schiek this policy should be driven by an asymmetric and substantive approach to equality. This policy should comprise individual and group related legal remedies. The empowering aspects of legal action against discrimination should not be underestimated.

Finally, John Wrench summarises the outcome of the *European Compendium of Good Practice* which has been one of the follow-ups of the Joint Declaration on the Prevention of Racial Discrimination and Xenophobia and Promotion of Equal Treatment at the Workplace, signed in 1995 by EU workers' and employers' organizations. Wrench sees one of the problems in furthering action against discrimination across the EU in the differing conceptions of and assumptions about racism and discrimination that exist in different European countries. Wrench observes a common attitude of 'no problem here', an attitude that is, however, expressed uncommonly, each manifestation being culturally and historically specific to each member state. The *European Compendium of Good Practice* is not a survey, but a collection of case studies that act as examples of some of the practices at work. Therefore, it cannot be taken as providing an overview of the current state of action on this issue across the EU. Nevertheless, it does give us some indication of the character of this action. However, it seems to be rather significant that sometimes national researchers had to look quite hard to find their case studies of good practice for the Compendium.

Conclusion

What can the Europeans learn from the international debate about anti-discrimination policies? Nowadays, the legislators and constitutional court judges of many countries in different parts of the world are convinced that *equal opportunities* are a value worth striving for and cannot be achieved by means of non-discrimination alone, when permanent and strong discrimination exists. The principle of non-discrimination is too weak, whenever continuous disadvantages have occurred and if discrimination has not been brought to an end.

The legislators of more and more countries are considering that certain forms of systematic disadvantages have not been targeted against individuals as such but against individuals as members of specific groups. Therefore, special measures are required to end this form of discrimination. Within the framework of anti-discrimination strategies, the fact of belonging to disadvantaged groups has to be regarded as relevant and worth receiving consideration: if affiliation with a certain ethnic group is the reason for disadvantages, the fact of this affiliation has to be taken into account; if legitimate claims and rights have been systematically violated because of the characteristic 'colour of the skin', it is necessary to take the characteristic 'colour of the skin' into consideration in order to bring this unfair and unjust situation to an end. Affirmative or positive action considering these affiliations and characteristics has nothing to do with reverse discrimination, but has the intention of ending unjustified, unfair discrimination. There is a general consensus that taking into account of such characteristics or of group affiliations must exclusively serve the institutionalisation of real equal opportunities.

In several countries, so-called quotas, timetables, goals and targets have been introduced as means for ending systematic discrimination. These measures can be regarded as *pragmatic answers* to a problem, not solved or hardly solved by other measures to end unjust treatment of members of groups that experience permanent discrimination. On basis of the today's legal situation and the rulings of the Supreme Court of the US, as well as of the European Court of Justice, it is legally neither admissible to give preference to less qualified persons over higher qualified persons, nor are rigid, merely numerical quotas admissible.

Special promotion measures should provide equal opportunities for those groups that have been systematically excluded or systematically disadvantaged. Thus, interpreting special promotion measures for the systematically disadvantaged as a violation of the principle of equality means nothing else but defending claims for domination or unjustified advantages. A violation of the principle of equality exists only if it can be proved that the target of certain measures is not the removal of existing illegitimate discriminations and disadvantages but the establishment of new unfair discrimination. This means that positive action programmes are admissible and advisable as long as they serve the realization of the principle of equality. If they serve another purpose and pursue another intention, they become illegitimate.

Members of which groups should be involved? Without any doubt, the principle of equality strictly interpreted results in the conviction that special political consideration is due to all those whose legitimate rights and claims have been systematically violated, who have been or who are still exposed to systematic disadvantages, or whose claims to substantive equal opportunities have been infringed. However, in European societies, unlike in the US, 'race' is not the most important cleavage; the situation in Europe seems to be much more complex: widespread hostility to members of 'visible minorities' overlaps with discrimination against ethnic minorities and migration minorities.

In most European countries one of the crucial points is fair admission to citizenship: in societies, in which the second or third generation of immigrants still have the status of aliens – a non-citizen status – anti-discrimination measures appear to be putting the cart before the horse; to achieve citizenship in a formal way should be the first step (Heckmann, 1992: 233). On the other hand, this answer falls short, firstly, because citizenship status represents only one problem: racism and discrimination are often targeted against co-nationals with 'minority characteristics', and secondly, because we have to understand that integration is a process of mutual recognition. A long-standing affiliation with a society implies mutual obligations: it implies rights for the immigrants and obligations for the majority. Where there is a permanent violation of the principle of equality, both citizens, and denizens should profit from measures in favour of disadvantaged groups. According to Bauböck, the targeted groups of integration policies should be defined broadly and include immigrants (the foreign-born population), aliens (non-citizens), and minorities of immigrant origin (Bauböck, 1995: 46).

If European societies increasingly develop into multicultural societies, the politics of diversity, including policies like promoting proportional employment, must be worked out. However, if educational opportunities or housing facilities for disadvantaged groups are not considerably improved, proportional employment will not be a meaningful goal. Affirmative or positive action is above all advisable when structural and racial discrimination occurs jointly and when other structural .measures do not lead to an ending of systematic disadvantages. Compared with non-discrimination (criminal) laws, structural and person-targeted promotion measures do have the advantage that they are future oriented; that high procedural costs can be saved; that frequently they can be performed on a voluntary basis; and that models can be worked out, bringing advantages both for employees and employers.

Generally, voluntary programmes are to be preferred to mandatory ones as a higher standard of consent can presumably be achieved. However, in cases of stubborn refusal compulsory measures may be politically necessary and advisable. Special attention should be given to the fact that person-targeted promotion measures do frequently give rise to counter- and circumventory strategies. Here, strengthening public support is playing an enormous role. Without this support these policies are very likely to be boycotted. Recent experience has shown that positive or affirmative action programmes are successful, if they are unanimously backed by the enforcing authorities. Particularly in recent history, there are convincing examples to show that social acceptance of the prohibition of discrimination can be pushed through from top to bottom.

Finally, it has to be underlined that positive action programmes have to be evaluated continuously; it is necessary to check who is actually profiting from these measures and whether those most strongly disadvantaged can or cannot improve their situation. Positive or affirmative action programmes can be important steps towards bringing unjustified discrimination to an end. This requires the introduction of independent institutions and tribunals, which must have investigation and evaluation rights and which should have the right to file actions (Ventura, 1995: 46; Wrench, 1996: 153).

Notes

1. Inter alia: UN Convention on Human Rights (1948); European Convention on Human Rights (1950); United Nations Conventions relating to the Status of Refugees (1951); Convention of the International Labour Organization concerning Discrimination in Respect of Employment and Occupation (1958); UNESCO Convention against Discrimination in Education (1960); European Social Charter (1961); International Convention on the Elimination of All Forms of Racial Discrimination (1965); International Covenant on Civil and Political Rights (1966); International Covenant on Economic, Social and Cultural Rights (1966); European Charter for Regional or Minority Languages (1992); Declaration and a Plan of Action on combating Racism, Xenophobia, Anti-Semitism and Intolerance of the Council of Europe's (1993); European Commission against Racism and Intolerance (ECRI); Framework Convention for the Protection of National Minorities (1995) (Commission of the European Communities 1992).
2. For many years, combating discrimination against migrants has also been one of the central concerns of ILO (Wrench/Taylor, 1993; Zegers de Beijl, 1997).
3. In particular, several NGOs have voiced the criticism that the amendments to the treaties have not resulted in regulating access to European citizenship to third-state citizens at Community level.
4. Canada and Australia, on the contrary, officially recognize minorities of immigrant origin as ethnic minorities entitled to specific attention and assistance in public policies.

5. Bauböck distinguishes between *ethnic communities* and *ethnic minorities*. The first of these labels refers to their internal cohesion and sense of collective identity, the second one to their position in the wider society (Bauböck, 1994: 8).

Part I
The Extra-European Debate

Can Affirmative Action Combat Racial Discrimination? Moral Success and Political Failure in the US

Anita L. Allen

Introduction

The nations of Europe are home to a diverse range of peoples. European diversity, like North American diversity, can be understood to include differences of 'race', ethnicity, culture, language, national origin, citizenship, ancestry, and religion. Diversity has many causes, some remote in history, such as colonialism; and others recent or ongoing, such as labour migration. In addition to the varieties of population diversity just mentioned, sex and sexual orientation are sources of meaningful social diversity within modern Western nations.

Diversity of all types can enhance the cultural lives of contemporary societies. But in nations with heterogeneous populations, some groups, especially women and minorities, suffer from economic disadvantages. Government aid programmes in heterogeneous nations may favour persons belonging to racial majorities. Employers may deliberately or inadvertently subject unpopular minority groups to systematic discrimination, by limiting their employment to low-paying jobs with few opportunities for promotion to higher paying jobs. This has been true of the US, where 'affirmative action' policies have arisen alongside comprehensive civil rights statutes to fight the problem of economic disadvantage traced to discrimination (Cashman, 1990). The major, direct beneficiaries of affirmative action have been non-white minorities and women of all population groups. A vital question to consider is whether, if minority groups and women in the nations of Europe face wrongful discrimination and economic disadvantage, American-style affirmative or 'positive' action should be implemented in Europe (Faundez, 1994).

In the US, 'affirmative action' refers to an act, policy, plan or programme designed to remedy the effects of wrongful discrimination (Allen, 1996).

Americans have primarily adopted affirmative action to redress the injustice of discrimination based on 'race', ethnicity, or sex. Affirmative action to redress discrimination based on national origin, language, religion, disability, or sexual orientation is also practised. In recent years, some policymakers have stressed the goal of diversity rather than the goal of correcting injustice as the primary goal of affirmative action (Goldberg, 1997; Sher, 1997). Affirmative action for the sake of diversity assumes that employment, business, and education are improved by participation from members of varied population groups and both sexes.

The US government adopted affirmative action as part of its national public policy in the 1960s, in an effort to increase opportunities for blacks ('African-Americans'), formerly termed 'negroes' and 'coloreds'. Affirmative action policies soon embraced the disadvantages experienced by all women, and all members of certain significant minority groups. Government affirmative action policies targeting blacks were also aimed at Native Americans ('Indians'), and Americans of Asian, Pacific, Alaskan and Spanish-speaking backgrounds. The private sector began to implement affirmative action programmes in the US in the 1960s as well, responding to changing civil rights attitudes and the threat of government coercion (Belz, 1984).

Although many Americans now accept the importance of addressing the aftermath of slavery, legally enforced racial segregation, immigration, and prejudice, some forms of affirmative action have grown to be controversial (Cahn, 1995; Carter, 1991; Erzorsky, 1991; Fullinwider, 1980; Sowell, 1975; Steele, 1998). The most controversial forms of affirmative action award employment (for example jobs and promotions), business opportunities (for example government contracts), or education (for example admissions to selective public and private colleges and universities) on a preferential basis to white women or members of specific governmentally recognized minority groups – the so-called African-Americans, Asian and Pacific-Americans, Hispanic-Americans and Native Americans.

Affirmative action can contribute to combating racial discrimination by opening up additional opportunities for work, business and education to members of previously disadvantaged minority groups and to women of all backgrounds (Erzorsky, 1991; Mosely/Capaldi, 1996). To the extent that it has increased opportunities for women and minority group members, affirmative action has been a moral success in the US (Lawrence/Matsuda, 1997; Bowen/Bok, 1998). Unfortunately, affirmative action has been something of a political failure. Republican politicians began to turn their backs on affirmative action in the early 1980s (Belz, 1984; Capaldi, 1985).

In the 1990s, a conservative public-policy law firm in Washington DC, the Center for Individual Rights, began a campaign of advertising and lawsuits to discredit affirmative action policies by describing them as 'reverse discrimination' violative of the constitutional rights of whites to equal treatment (Bronner, 1999).

What is Affirmative Action?

A civil rights policy pertaining employment, business and education in the US, 'affirmative action' most often denotes 'race'-conscious and result-oriented efforts undertaken by private entities and government officials to correct the unequal distribution of employment opportunity and education that many attribute to a history of slavery, segregation, and racism (Horne, 1992; Spann, 1993). For most of its history, the US excluded women of all 'races' from most forms of employment outside of the home and public life. Varied practices to benefit racial minority group members and women of all backgrounds are termed 'affirmative action'; they include:

- preferential employment, including recruitment, hiring and promotion;
- preferential schooling, including college and university recruitment and admissions;
- special programmes for women and/or minorities designed to better educate students and train workers;
- 'set-aside' programmes, reserving a percentage of business opportunities for women and/or minorities;
- political empowerment measures, including efforts to create political districts in which a majority of the eligible voters are racial minority group members capable of electing minority candidates to state, local and federal offices.

Measures of these types may be wholly unfamiliar to Europeans, and I will therefore describe them in greater detail below, starting with preferential employment.

Employment is one of the most important contexts for affirmative action in the US. In employment, affirmative action has meant hiring what might be termed a 'racially balanced' workforce that includes a proportionate or 'representative' number of Americans of African, Latino, Asian or Native American ancestry, using the distribution of minority groups in the national or local population to gauge adequate representation. Balanced workforces may result from affirmative action preferences.

Preferential hiring can be a form of affirmative action, but not all affirmative action in employment involves significant preferences. For example, more broadly advertising job openings in newspapers circulated in black neighbourhoods do not necessarily afford blacks employment advantages over other groups.

Affirmative action on the basis of 'race' involves preferential hiring when a person's 'race' results in employment for which 'race' is not otherwise a genuine job-related qualification. 'Race' is arguably sometimes a legitimate criterion for employment. For example, law enforcement advantages may result from hiring black and Hispanic police officers to work with youths in black and Hispanic urban communities. At their best, affirmative action preferences award employment opportunities to qualified minority candidates over similarly qualified whites. Everyone agrees that affirmative action ought never lead to preferences that favour unqualified persons over qualified persons solely for the purpose of filling preestablished racial quotas (Greenawalt, 1983; Goldman, 1979).

Education is another important context for affirmative action in the US, although it appears that 'positive action' is not proposed for the distinctly different European systems of education. Public and private educators in the US have focused on 'desegregation', 'integration', 'diversity' or 'multiculturalism to address a history of racially segregated schooling' (Berry/Blassingame, 1982; Boxhill, 1984). Most public schools in the US (especially in the southern states) remained strictly segregated by 'race' until the late 1960s, even though the Supreme Court outlawed legally enforced racial segregation in public primary and secondary schools in the famous case of *Brown v. Board of Education* in 1954 (Drake/Holsworth, 1996). At some schools, affirmative action policies have led administrators to allocate financial resources to recruiting and retaining minority students with special scholarships, curricula, and social programmes. At others, it has led to admissions procedures that de-emphasize standardized test scores and other traditional qualifications (Thernstrom, 1997).

Any distribution of public benefits on the basis of 'race' for remedial purposes arguably fits the definition of 'affirmative action'. Thus, 'minority set-aside' requirements that reserve a percentage of government (public) contracts for minority-owned businesses are definable as affirmative action. The concept also reaches special efforts made by public and private scientific, humanistic and arts organizations to disburse a share of their grants, awards and prizes to members of once-neglected minority groups or white women. The concept even reaches redistricting to aggregate minority voters into districts that remedy a history of inadequate political representation. Although blacks and other minority group members have sometimes been elected to high local and national office by white majorities, such election is still unusual, giving rise to the argument that democratic participation by minorities must be enhanced by affirmative action interventions.

Meeting numerical objectives, including 'ratios', 'goals' or 'quotas', on a 'timetable' has served as a concrete guideline for measuring the progress of affirmative action (Spann, 1993; Johnson, 1992). The terms numerical 'goals' and 'quotas' are sometimes used interchangeably to denote optimal percentages or numbers of persons belonging to specific groups targeted to serve in specific capacities. 'Numerical goals' has been used to connote flexible guidelines for group inclusion; and 'quotas', by contrast, to suggest rigidity.

Some of the controversy about affirmative action in employment and education stems from the belief that, to achieve preordained quotas, unqualified and significantly less-qualified minority group members and/ or women are sometimes hired over better-qualified whites (Glazer, 1998; McGary, 1977–78). Employers and school administrators commonly select minority-group members for employment or admissions over others who achieved higher scores on examinations; but they do so in contexts in which lower test scores are not thought to be disqualifying. For example, a number of the most elite US law schools regularly may admit blacks who score in the 80th percentile over whites who score on the 90th percentile on the Law School Admissions Test (LSAT) to ensure that their study bodies include a number of the best and brightest blacks in the applicant pool (Bowen/Bok, 1998; Thernstrom, 1997). Historically speaking, very few blacks score in the 90th percentile; and yet black graduates of these schools typically go on to very successful, useful careers as lawyers, judges and business people. Some employers who have discovered that exclusive reliance on standardized employment tests would result in virtually all white work forces use a practice called 'race norming' to scale test results and ensure employment to top-scoring minorities and top-scoring whites alike.

Behind the practices of preferring minorities to whites or others with higher test scores is the belief that standardized tests do not always accurately reflect the knowledge, skills and competence of minorities (Erzorsky, 1991). It is sometimes argued that standardized tests contain a cultural bias; or that minority group members underperform out of stress and expectations of failure. It is also argued that objective tests can be only one important part of a more complicated process of determining who should be included in one's workplace or school. Test scores may fail to reveal, for example, who is most motivated for success and best suited overall for a particular work team. Moreover, for some employers and schools, human diversity reflecting the diversity of a region or the nation is valued inherently or for its practical business advantages. A big-city retailer might expect to do better attracting a larger share of the market to its stores if the men and women hired as salespeople reflected the local population; but it might also feel an obligation as one of its region's major employers to offer opportunities broadly to a diverse segment of the workforce.

The History of US Affirmative Action

The US Congress introduced the term 'affirmative action' into American law in 1935 in the Wagner Act by requiring 'affirmative action' of employers guilty of discrimination against workers on the basis of union membership. In June 1941, President Franklin D. Roosevelt issued Executive Order 8802, a precursor of affirmative action policies in the arena of 'race' relations. Intended to boost the wartime economy and reduce severe black unemployment, the Order mandated 'special measures' and 'certain action' to end 'discrimination in the employment of workers in the defense industries or government (occurring) because of "race", creed, colour, or national origin'. White House discussions of employment policy during the presidency of General Dwight D. Eisenhower included consideration of mandatory 'affirmative action'. A few years later, in March 1961, President John F. Kennedy issued Executive Order 10925, calling for the design of 'affirmative' remedies for employment discrimin-ation and establishing a President's Committee on Equal Employment Opportunity to expand and strengthen efforts to promote full equality of employment opportunity across racial lines.

The sweeping Civil Rights Act of 1964 outlawed all racial discrimin-ation in employment, education, housing, public accommodations and voting. As a result of this Act, whites could no longer lawfully exclude blacks from restaurants, theatres, cinemas, retail stores, hotels, transporta-tion, and recreational facilities. Title VII of the 1964 Act banned discrimin-ation by employers of twenty-five or more employees, labour unions and employment agencies; it also created the Equal Employment Opportunity Commission. The Act outlawed federal aid to racially segregated schools, and banned unequal application of the requirements of voter registration. The Voting Rights Act of 1965 went even further in protecting the franchise, restricting literacy tests and authorizing federal election oversight in the states.

Finally, in 1965, at the height of the black civil rights movement, President Lyndon B. Johnson's Executive Order 11246 established affirmative action as the centrepiece of national employment policy. The Order aimed at 'the full realization of equal employment opportunity' and required that firms conducting business with the federal government and these firms' suppliers 'take affirmative action to ensure that applicants are employed, and that employees are treated during employment, without regard to their "race", creed, colour, or national origin'. Subsequently Executive Order 11375, implemented by Labor Department Revised Order No. 4, required that government contractors set 'goals' and 'timetables' for employing 'underutilized' minority group members. The Labor Department developed official regulations that defined 'affirmative action' as 'a set of specific and result-oriented procedures' undertaken with 'every good faith effort' to bring about 'equal employment opportunity' (Allen, 1996). Coordinator of President Johnson's civil rights and affirmative action policies, Vice President Hubert Humphrey declared in 1965 that the US had 'neglected the Negro too long' and that 'government, business and labor must open more jobs to Negroes (and) must go out and affirmatively seek those persons who are qualified and begin to train those who are not' (Allen, 1996).

Beginning in 1967, the federal agency formerly known as the Department of Health, Education and Welfare (HEW) required colleges and universities receiving federal funds to establish affirmative action goals for employing female and minority faculty members. In 1972, the Department issued guidelines for federally supported colleges and universities requiring both non-discrimination and efforts to recruit, employ, and promote members of formerly excluded groups 'even if that exclusion cannot be traced to particular discriminatory actions on the part of the employer'. The HEW guidelines distinguished affirmative action 'goals', which its directives required as indicators of probable compliance, from 'quotas', which its directives prohibited. The HEW guidelines stated that schools were not mandated to lower their scholarly standards or hire less-qualified minority applicants. Ultimately, the Equal Employment Opportunity Commission established that result-oriented affirmative action was required of all employers within its jurisdiction, not just federal contractors or educational institutions receiving federal funds.

Political support for the federal government's affirmative action initiatives was initially strong and broad based. Some maintained that affirmative action using numerical goals, quota and time tables was a necessary complement to the 1964 Civil Rights statutes. A century after the formal abolition of slavery, African Americans as a group remained substantially poorer, less well educated and politically less powerful than whites as a group (Wilson, 1987; Mosley, 1992). Legally enforced segregation had intensified black inequality. Native Americans and other minority groups also lagged behind.

The leadership of the National Association for the Advancement of Colored People, the Congress on Racial Equality, the NAACP Legal Defense Fund, and the National Urban League quickly endorsed affirmative action (Finch, 1981). Diverse sectors of the economy promptly responded to Washington's affirmative action programmes. For example, in 1966, the City of New York, the Roman Catholic Church in Michigan, and the Texas-based retailer Neiman-Marcus were among the organizations announcing voluntary plans requiring that their suppliers and other contractors take 'affirmative' steps toward hiring African Americans (Allen, 1996).

The Benefits of Affirmative Action

Reflecting ties to the civil rights movement, the stated goals of affirmative action range from the forward-looking goal of improving society by remedying distributive inequities, to the backward-looking goal of righting historic wrongs (Erzorsky, 1991; McGary, 1977–78). Affirmative action on behalf of African Americans often was, and often is, defended by scholars as compensation or reparations owed to blacks by whites or a white-dominated society (Boxhill, 1984; Thomson, 1977). In particular, it is argued that after two centuries of legally enforced slavery, racial segregation, and racism, African Americans now deserve the jobs, education, and other benefits made possible through affirmative action. Beyond compensatory or reparative justice, goals ascribed to affirmative action include

- promoting economic opportunity for minority groups and individuals;
- erasing racial subordination;
- neutralizing the competitive advantages many whites enjoy in education, business, and employment;
- educating a cadre of minority professionals for service in underserved minority communities;
- creating minority role models, intellectuals, artists, and civic leaders; and finally,
- acknowledging society's cultural diversity (Erzorsky, 1991; Boxhill, 1984; Greenawalt, 1983; Goldman, 1979).

Europeans considering positive action policies for their nations based on American-style affirmative action policies are advised to consider the beneficial results of thirty years of affirmative action in the US, and the justice of those results (Bowen/Bok, 1998; Lawrence/Matsuda, 1997; Glazer, 1998). Affirmative action has not abolished all poverty, racism and sexism, nor has it ended all segregation in housing, education or social life. Affirmative action, a supplement to the basic civil rights law of the US, could never have been intended to eliminate those problems entirely. Problems of drug use, teenage pregnancy and crime bar and undercut some affirmative action gains for the poorest of the poor. Dwindling government welfare support for poor women with children and the lack of a national health insurance scheme also undercut the potential benefits of affirmative action. People without adequate healthcare and childcare will not be reliable workers.

Although too many domains of American life, such as the US Senate and the leadership of major corporations, remain virtually all white and all male, affirmative action has done some good. Affirmative action in employment and education is directly responsible for the dramatic increase in the number of highly competent minority physicians, lawyers, judges, public servants, professors, and business people found in the US today, compared with thirty years ago. While segregation by 'race' remains a problem in housing and education, workplaces are more integrated than in the past. Integration offers basic employment and career opportunities to motivated minority group members and opportunities for enlarging multicultural understanding for everyone.

Why the Controversy?

Europeans should embrace positive action modelled after American-style affirmative action, only after careful examinations of how and why affirmative action came to be so controversial barely ten years after its inception as public policy. The affirmative action practised in employment, education and other fields in the US has excited intense political, intellectual and legal debate. The debates centre on the charge that 'race'-conscious remedies designed to end invidious discrimination against one group will amount to invidious 'reverse discrimination' against another (Newton, 1973; Greene, 1989; Sher, 1997; Glazer, 1998).

The political popularity of affirmative action during the Lyndon B. Johnson administration subsequently yielded to controversy. During the presidency of the pro-affirmative action president Democrat Jimmy Carter, disagreements over the legality, morality and efficacy of affirmative action strained African Americans' relationships with labour unions and conservatives within the Republican Party. Some white liberal Democrats who had supported the civil rights movement of the 1960s became increasingly suspicious of government-backed racial quotas and the simmering resentment among white workers in the 1970s and 1980s.

Presidents Ronald Reagan and George Bush campaigned on express opposition to affirmative action 'quotas'. President Reagan spoke out against affirmative action's numerical goals and quotas, and this became one of the cornerstones of his public policy agenda on issues affecting African Americans. High-profile conservatives defended the ideal of a colourblind society and characterized blacks as overly dependent upon welfare, affirmative action, and other government programmes attributed to liberal democrats. In this period the media lavished attention on affirmative action policies at the expense of other critical issues affecting blacks, including unemployment, health, hunger, and homelessness (Daniel/Allen, 1988). Consistent with the Reagan agenda, however, the federal government lessened its enforcement of civil rights policies. Moreover, a number of Supreme Court – and lower federal court – cases curbed affirmative action in employment and other key fields (Kull, 1992; Rosenfeld, 1991; Rossum, 1980).

In the 1990s many were prepared to attribute significant gains for blacks to affirmative action, including an increase in black employment and promotion at major corporations, in heavy industry, in police and fire departments, and in higher education (Erzorsky, 1991; Lawrence/ Matsuda, 1997). Yet, in the 1990s persistent critics converted 'affirmative action' into a virtual pejorative, along with 'preferential treatment', 'reverse discrimination', and 'quotas'. Symbolic of the era, President Clinton abruptly withdrew the nomination of Lani Guinier to head the Civil Rights Division of the Justice Department after her critics, who branded the Yale-educated lawyer the 'quota queen', derided her support for certain affirmative action policies as radical extremism.

The NAACP and the National Urban League, two powerful black organizations, maintained official support for affirmative action and the civil rights laws. Other leading minority group organizations and women's groups did the same. Minority group members have not all agreed that affirmative action is a good thing worth fighting for. Some prominent African American scholars have questioned affirmative action on the grounds that it is incompatible with a 'colourblind' civil rights policy and optimal anti-poverty policy (Loury, 1988; Sowell, 1984). Other African Americans have sometimes criticized affirmative action on pragmatic grounds (Carter, 1991; Steele, 1994; Wilson, 1987). Some are disappointed that affirmative action policies aid the middle class, leaving the problem of dire rural and urban poverty without a remedy (Sowell, 1983; Goldman, 1979). Others argue that racial preferences are inherently demeaning to minorities, and stereotype certain 'races' as inferior in skill and intellect to others. Critics say racial preferences are demeaning or dispiriting to minorities; that they compromise African Americans' self-esteem or self-respect (Sowell, 1975). Minorities complain of having to cope with the resentment among white Americans resulting from minority preferences. As an antidote to simmering white (and other groups') resentments, William J. Wilson (1987) has proposed promoting 'race' neutral 'universal policies' aimed at the health and employment problems of the poor rather than merely promoting affirmative action for racial minorities (Kahlenberg, 1996).

The problem of white resentment and unsettled expectations has become a major topic of discussion, and is thought by some to be a practical obstacle to the continuation of affirmative action programmes. Legal opponents of affirmative action have argued that racial preferences are illegal under laws that include the Civil Rights Act of 1964 and the equal protection clause of the Fourteenth Amendment of the US Constitution. Politically conservative opponents of affirmative action have advanced the additional argument that affirmative action wrongly assumes that persistent minority economic inequality stems from slavery, segregation and racism, when the central cause of inequality is a pervasive breakdown in work, family and community values in minority communities.

Supporters of affirmative action for blacks have offered pertinent replies to all of these arguments (Erzorsky, 1991). To the contention that affirmative action does not help the poorest blacks, a reply has been that affirmative action nonetheless enhances the lives of some deserving blacks. To the argument that affirmative action lowers esteem for blacks and blacks' self-esteem, a reply is that blacks were always held in very low esteem in the US and are vulnerable to low self-esteem due to inferior education and employment. To the argument that affirmative action is racially divisive and breeds resentment, a reply is that one group of citizens (blacks) should not be deprived of the benefits of affirmative action simply because of another group's (white) resentment, unless that resentment can be shown to stem from genuine racial injustice. Finally, to the finger-pointing argument that black's problems result from lapses in blacks' individual responsibility, one reply is that communities of poverty, drugs, and violence result as much from decades of private and public decision making concerning legal, economic, and social policy as from individual choices.

Among libertarian philosophers it is sometime argued that employers have a moral right to choose their own workers, using whatever criteria they wish. A more common libertarian argument is that social and economic benefits should be distributed on the basis of colourblind principles of entitlement, merit and personal fault. In liberal academic and intellectual circles, opponents of affirmative action have questioned the coherence of the idea that blacks as a group are entitled to merit or deserve affirmative action as compensation or reparations for past wrongdoing (Sher, 1997). Genuine corrective justice, some philosophers say, is both causal and relational. That is, when an injury occurs, the person who caused that injury must personally pay his or her victim. The ex-slaves wronged by slavery are dead, as are the people who wronged them. It is therefore illogical, the argument continues, to hold all current whites responsible for the evils of slavery that were perpetrated by the remote ancestors of some whites against the remote ancestors of some blacks. Against the argument that African Americans standing to benefit by affirmative action were never in bondage to whites and may have led lives free of egregious discrimination, some philosophers defend affirmative action as a moral right of persons belonging to groups that have been uniquely harmed in the past by public law and that are disproportionately poor or otherwise disadvantaged today. Black, Hispanic, Asian, Hawaiian, and Native Americans fit this description. Admitting that white citizens are not personally at fault, these advocates of affirmative action observe that all white citizens benefit from the system of racial privilege that continues to pervade American institutions (Thomson, 1977). Whites have a competitive advantage over racial minorities that society may fairly seek to erase through affirmative action.

Constitutional Issues

In the US, the federal courts have authority to decide the constitutionality of state and federal laws. The Supreme Court, whose judges are appointed for life tenure by the President of the US with the consent of the Senate, is the highest federal court. Affirmative action has been challenged frequently in the federal courts. However, the question of the constitutionality of racial quotas and other affirmative action measures has no simple answer.

Between 1969 and 1998 alone, the Supreme Court decided about two dozen major cases relating to the legality of diverse 'race'-conscious remedies. A number of these cases validated specific affirmative action measures; but several important cases related to education, employment, minority business opportunity and voting did not. The ultimate constitutional status of the use of racial preferences is therefore unclear, and will remain unclear until an appropriate case or controversy is successfully brought before the Supreme Court on appeal. The Supreme Court is not required to hear most cases submitted to it, and appears to avoid affirmative action cases that might force a politically explosive determination.

Paramount in affirmative action cases that reach the federal courts are the implications of Title VII of the Civil Rights Act of 1964 and other civil rights statutes enacted by Congress. The principle of equal protection embodied in the Fifth and Fourteenth Amendments of the Constitution is critical when plaintiffs contest affirmative action by governmental entities. The Supreme Court has established that the Constitution prohibits discrimination on the basis of 'race' by state and federal government, as a denial of equal protection of law. The Court's equal protection jurisprudence presumes that racial classifications are potentially invidious, giving rise to the need for 'strict scrutiny' — a stringent, virtually impassable, standard of judicial review — when challenged. The constitutional conundrum posed by affirmative action is whether the provisions of the Constitution that presumptively ban state and federal government discrimination on the basis of 'race' and entail the need for strict scrutiny review, nonetheless permit the use of the 'race'-conscious remedies to end racial discrimination. Whether framed by constitutional or statutory questions, affirmative action cases commonly involve procedural complexities relating to assigning the burdens of proving or disproving that the absence of minorities or women in an institution is the result of unlawful discrimination.

A brief chronological overview of the Supreme Court's affirmative action cases involving 'race' reveal the difficulty of assessing the constitutional status of racial preference policies in the US. The Supreme Court endorsed 'race'-conscious numerical requirements to achieve school desegregation in *United States v. Montgomery County Board of Educ.* (1969) and *Swann v. Charlotte-Mecklenburg Board of Educ.* (1971). These were unanimous decisions. In a different context, the Court again endorsed 'race'-conscious remedies in *United Jewish Orgs. v. Carey* (1977). Over Fourteenth Amendment and other constitutional objections, the Court upheld a New York redistricting plan that explicitly attempted to increase the voting strength of 'non-white' voters — Blacks and Puerto Ricans — seemingly at the expense of a community of Hasidic Jews, viewed as whites under the plan. Chief Justice Burger dissented from the judgement of the Court, stressing his discomfort with putting the 'imprimatur of the State on the concept that "race" is a proper consideration in the electoral process'.

In 1977, the Court established a limitation on affirmative action that it would reiterate in subsequent cases. *International Bhd. of Teamsters v. United States* (1977) held that a disparate impact on minorities alone does not make a seniority system illegal under Title VII; *Firefighters Local Union No. 1784 v. Stotts* (1984) overturned a District Court's injunction prohibiting the city of Memphis from following its seniority system's 'last hired, first fired' policy during layoffs. In *Wygant v. Jackson Bd. of Educ.* (1986), Justice Thurgood Marshall dissented from a ruling of the Court invalidating the provision of a collective bargaining agreement between a school board and the local teachers' union that would have preserved minority representation in teaching staff in the event of layoffs.

Two cases involving affirmative action in law and medical school admissions evidence the Court's judgement of limited constitutional tolerance for affirmative action plans involving numerical quotas: *De Funis v. Oregaard* (1974) and *Regents of the Univ. of California v. Bakke* (1978). The more definitive of the two, the *Bakke* case, struck down the special admissions programme of the Medical School of the University of California at Davis that included a 16 per cent quota for 'blacks, Chicanos, Asians, and American Indians'. A twice-rejected white applicant to the school challenged its admissions programme both under Title VII of the Civil Rights Act of 1964 and the equal protection clause of the Fourteenth Amendment. Although the Court struck down admissions quotas in this case, it went on to endorse diversity as a constitutional goal for higher education.

The high Court reconciled Title VII with voluntary affirmative action programmes in *United Steel Workers v. Weber* (1979). The *Weber* case upheld an employer's affirmative action plan that temporarily required a minimum 50 per cent African-American composition in a skill-training programme established to increase African-American representation in skilled positions. *Johnson v. Transportation Dept.* (1987) would go on to hold that Title VII permits affirmative consideration of employees' 'race', gender or disability when awarding promotions.

A year after the *Weber* case, in *Fullilove v. Klutznick* (1980), the Court upheld a provision of the congressional Public Works Employment Act that mandated that 10 per cent of federal funds allocated for local public construction projects go to 'minority business enterprises', statutorily defined as at least 50 per cent owned by citizens who are 'Negroes, Spanish-speaking, Oriental, Indians, Eskimos, and Aleuts'. The provision had been challenged under equal protection principles. Justice Marshall, concurring in the judgement in *Fullilove* argued that 'Congress reasonably determined that 'race'-conscious means were necessary to break down the barriers confronting participation by minority enterprises in federally funded public works projects'.

Title VII permits affirmative action that includes numerical goals, and may permit courts to order it. In *Local 28 of the Sheet Metal Workers' Int'l Ass'n v. EEOC* (1986), the Supreme Court upheld a court-ordered membership plan for a trade union found guilty of racial discrimination violating Title VII. The plan included a membership goal of 29 per cent African-Americans and Latinos. The Court was again willing to permit a numerically based affirmative action remedy in *United States v. Paradise* (1987). There the Court validated a temporary affirmative action plan ordered by a lower court that required a one-for-one promotion ratio of qualified whites to qualified blacks in the Alabama Department of Public Safety. The Department had been found guilty of discrimination in 1972, but had failed to adopt a promotion procedure that did not have a disparate impact on blacks. Justice William Brennan wrote an opinion arguing that the affirmative action order was a narrowly tailored means to achieve a compelling government purpose, and therefore met the requirements of strict scrutiny imposed by Fourteenth Amendment equal protection.

Like the *Bakke* case, *Richmond v. J.A. Croson Co.* (1989) successfully attacked an affirmative action plan reserving specific numerical percentages of a public benefit for minorities. The invalidated 'minority set-aside' plan required prime contractors with the City of Richmond to 'subcontract at least 30 per cent of the dollar amount of the contract to one or more Minority Business Enterprises'. Justice Thurgood Marshall dissented from the judgement in *Croson*, warning that the Court's ruling threatened all affirmative action plans not specifically enacted by Congress as had been the plan in *Fullilove*.

Metro Broadcasting, Inc. v. FCC (1990) upheld two 'race'-conscious Federal Communications Commission (FCC) programmes designed to enhance programme diversity. The 'race'-conscious set-asides were challenged under equal protection principles by a 'non-minority' broadcasting company that had lost its bid to acquire a broadcasting license to a minority-owned company. Programming diversity, a goal both the FCC and Congress linked to ownership diversity, was found to be derived from the public's First Amendment interest in hearing a wide spectrum of ideas and viewpoints, a sufficiently important interest to justify the 'race'-conscious policies. Justice O'Connor and three other justices dissented from what they considered excessive deference to Congress and a refusal to apply strict scrutiny to an instance of 'race'-conscious thinking grounded in racial stereotypes.

Decided by the slimmest majority and largely on First Amendment grounds, *Metro Broadcasting* leaves standing the basis for Justice Marshall's concerns about the future of affirmative action. So, too, does *Shaw v. Reno* (1993). This case held that white voters stated a legitimate Fourteenth Amendment equal protection claim against North Carolina for creating a gerrymandered voter redistricting plan 'so irrational on its face that it could be understood only as an effort to segregate voters' on the basis of 'race'. In an attempt to comply with the *Voting Rights Act*, North Carolina had created a redistricting plan with two irregularly shaped 'majority-minority' (majority Black and Native American) districts. In reversing the lower court, the Court invoked the ideal of a colourblind society.

The ideal of a colourblind society continues to vex proponents of 'race'-conscious remedies to discrimination (Schwartz, 1988; Eastland/ Bennett, 1979; Livingston, 1979). The greatest consistency in the evolving law of affirmative action is that, at any given time, its precise contours will mirror the mix of perspectives then present on the Court concerning the deepest purposes and meaning of the 1964 Civil Rights Act and the Fourteenth Amendment of the Constitution. A series of rulings in the spring and summer of 1995 cast considerable doubt on the allowable scope of affirmative action. Notably in the case of *Adarand Constructors v. Pena* (1995) the court ruled, five to four, that the federal government's affirmative action programmes must be able to meet the same strict standards of constitutional review as had previously been applied by the Court to state and local programmes.

No clear mandate from the Supreme Court has enabled political opponents of affirmation to score victories. In 1997 California voters endorsed Proposition 209 and thereby enabled the elimination of affirmative action in its public universities and colleges (Chavez, 1998). In *Hopwood v. Texas* (1998), a federal district court in Texas declared the University of Texas Law School's admissions policies unconstitutional because they included affirmative action for minority individuals. On the other hand, the other federal courts continue to uphold affirmative action measures. In *Boston Superior Police Federation v. Boston* (1998), a federal appeals court upheld a 'race'-conscious promotion in the Boston city police department to address the department's history of racial discrimination.

Conclusion

The US is enjoying a cycle of prosperity and multicultural awareness generated by its diverse and industrious population. Still, competition for the best jobs and business opportunities, along with colourblind interpretations of the constitution, has made affirmative action more controversial than it should be. It is uncertain whether the expanding number of racial, cultural, and linguistic minorities in the US will make it more or less likely that affirmative action programmes will flourish without undue controversy in the future. I fear that the large number of minority groups seeking legitimate recognition will make affirmative action seem impractical, if it is to apply to white women and all minorities; and unfair if white men feel they are the only group ineligible for 'preferences'. One must hope that affirmative action is not excised from public policy before its ability to benefit all who need it has been fully tested.

Controversy over the use of racial and sexual preferences in the US may suggest grounds for caution by Europeans. That there is political opposition to affirmative action in the US, however, does not entail that there would be similar political opposition to 'positive action' policies in Europe (Jones, 1991). A significant portion of the controversy in the US over affirmative action relates to higher education school admissions policies. European countries have more uniform systems of government-supported education through the university level. Educational opportunity is more equitably distributed. European countries also have robust traditions of social welfare, contrasting sharply with the extremes of individualism seen in the US. Finally, since the Second World War, Europeans have exhibited heightened concerns about justice and equality for minorities. These are generalizations, of course, and do not apply to all Europeans in every nation. Nevertheless, the point remains that policies controversial on one side of the Atlantic need not be seriously controversial on the other. The positive potential of positive action deserves recognition. Admittedly, some aspects of European society may make positive action in the form of employment and government assistance offered to minorities on a preferential basis a hard political sell. European nations with restrictive citizenship requirements and populations with hostile attitudes towards immigrants may resist positive action proposals. Yet one must hope that Europeans will not dismiss positive action proposals to end discrimination – and to enhance equality and diversity in the economic sector – without full investigation and debate.

—3—

Positive Action and Democracy
Frank Cunningham

Introduction

Among the goals of positive action is that of strengthening democracy by enabling people who are marginalized or disempowered to become fully active citizens. However, to be effective, positive action programmes require support on the part of citizens who are already active democratic participants. To the extent that this citizenry is insufficiently motivated to overcome the discrimination that leads to marginalization and does not include the target groups of affirmative action (hence the need for the programmes), democratic support will not be forthcoming. This creates a dilemma for government agencies or anyone else who wishes democratically to redress democratic exclusions. The intent of this paper is to clarify some conceptual issues implicated in this dilemma and to demonstrate the compatibility of democracy and positive action. I shall begin by explicating the dilemma's premises.

The main reasons that positive action is required for a healthy democracy are as follows:

- positive action enlarges the numbers of those who can effectively engage in democratic participation by providing educational, economic, and social means for such participation to people previously denied them;
- because positive action addresses categories of people and is meant to function on a large scale, it makes available pools of active citizens and political leaders from a broad range of a society's demographic groups;
- in turn, this helps to promote active commitment to the society as opposed to resentment on the part of the previously marginalized, and to nurture a culture of civic virtue within people from privileged groups by removing some sources of intolerance, namely, stereotypical attitudes bred of economic and cultural ghettoization;

- exclusions that are systemic and typically involve downward spirals require the deliberate and programmatic measures positive action undertakes. Putative counterexamples do not involve the categories of people most severely excluded, especially 'visible minorities' and women.

Controversial aspects of these claims are addressed in some other contributions to this volume. Key terms, such as 'democracy', also stand in need of definition; this task will be addressed below. First I shall refer to some experiences in my native Canada, which, while local, illustrate a general point about democracy and positive action.

In response to pressure beginning in the 1970s on the part of social movements and especially of the well-organized National Action Committee on the Status of Women (NAC), Canada's Federal Government enacted legislation in 1986 to promote what it called 'employment equity' for four systemically disadvantaged groups – women, aboriginal people, 'visible minorities', and the disabled – in selected public and private sector institutions (see Ventura in this volume).[1]

Notwithstanding the obligation this placed on my own workplace, the University of Toronto's departments and faculties remained dominated by white able-bodied males. Debates about positive action in the University are carried on without reference to the equity legislation, about which few know, and administrators who wish to ignore or circumvent its terms are able to do so with ease. In this respect the University is similar to the other public and private sector institutions, which, in principle, are similarly committed to positive action. I do not mean to suggest that there has been no progress at all in Canada. Under a more ambitious Federal plan instituted at the same time as the Contractors Program, some gains, especially for middle-class women, have been made that almost certainly would not have been made without it, and a stronger version of the Employment Equity legislation is in the process of being implemented. However, as the Human Rights Commission itself notes, the promise of positive action to make major inroads in combating systemic discriminations, especially regarding 'visible minorities' has not developed (Human Resources Development of Canada, 1997).

Reflecting on this experience, two questions pose themselves: how could the law of the land be so easily ignored? And, given widespread non-compliance, how could the legislation have been passed in the first place? With respect to the second question, some maintain that the legislation only resulted from the concerted efforts of the NAC. On a conception of democracy beginning with James Madison and reaching full development in the 1950s in the theories of the power-political or 'pluralist school' in the US, political policy in a democracy is the result of efforts by its most effective interest groups to exert pressure on elected officials. One may agree that interest-group responsiveness constitutes a low level of democracy, but when this is the main way that policy gets affected, a large measure of support by a public beyond those actively engaged in interest group organizations is still required even if it is passive support, misleadingly characterized by the pluralists as public apathy. The Canadian legislation was, I believe, made possible by a general public attitude that agreed with the social movements that people from the targeted groups were unfairly disadvantaged and that something should be done to rectify this.

At the same time two attitudes combine to militate against public support for positive action beyond non-binding entreaty: an impersonal belief that preferential hiring, promotion, or university admission are unfair to members of non-targeted groups and make for inferior assign-ments of position and a self-regarding fear that one's own opportunities are diminished by the programmes. Popular agreement with the under-lying concern behind positive action facilitated passage of laws promoting it, while counteracting values and fears have prompted legislative bodies to leave loopholes in the laws and enforcement agencies to be at best timid in carrying out what meaningful legislation there is. No doubt one reason for this is that not all officials charged with enforcing the legislation are committed to it, and resources for monitoring compliance are limited. But these are the sorts of things that are subject to correction in response to public pressure. Hence, relative government inaction is an indication that sufficient popular support for positive action is lacking.

Democracy

'Democracy', as I use the term, refers to the efforts of people whose activities mutually affect one another to take collective action in ways which each hopes will yield his or her preferred outcomes and which are reversible by future collective action (so people are prepared to tolerate outcomes they do not prefer). The main alternatives to democracy are warfare, autocracy, and submission to tradition or to luck. One feature of democracy thus characterized is that it is not something a collection of people either entirely possesses or entirely lacks, but it is a matter of degree. Crudely put, the more people there are in some shared circum-stance who participate in collective action with a realistic expectation of at least sometimes contributing to an outcome preferred by them and/or the more aspects of people's lives which are subject to such actions, the more democratic the circumstance is.[2]

Collective action, like individual action, involves decision making, and some democratic theorists limit democracy simply to participation in a specified decision procedure, such as casting ballots in majority votes. Were democracy no more than this, then only the most blatant forms of exclusion, such as earlier electoral laws in North America denying women or blacks the vote, would be democratically discriminatory, and positive action programmes intended to enhance democracy would have little place once this discrimination was eliminated. The relative paucity of women or blacks in elected positions and the continued marginalization of issues of special concern to them in legislative agendas now, long after they acquired the right to vote, well illustrate that 'democratic participation' should not be so narrowly construed.

Elections for parliamentary representatives or referenda on specific issues are moments in extended processes. To have a realistic expectation of making a difference in these processes it must be possible not just to caste a vote but to have input to such matters as who runs for office and on what platforms or what issues are put to a referendum. Robust democratic participation requires being able to help keeping elected officials honest and ensure that mandated policies are carried out. These levels of participation are achieved with difficulty, even for relatively privileged people, requiring as they do economic resources, free time, education and the possession of relevant information, and access, both formal and informal, to people and institutions in positions of political influence.

Regarding democracy in this way also explains how public resistance to duly enacted laws might sometimes be itself democratically justified. Legislators often like to think that a law passed by an elected parliament must be democratically supported until or unless replaced by future legislative voting. However, quite aside from the facts that not all those affected by legislation have the opportunity to vote for legislators and that few voters have input to political party nominations, full democratic support for legislated policies would require public understanding of the ways they will be carried out and of their likely impact. This consideration bears on the question shortly to be addressed of whether positive action should be imposed by legislative bodies. When and to the extent that a legislature is democratically elected, such an approach does carry some democratic legitimacy, but it is a mistake to think that therefore nobody has cause for complaint on democratic grounds.

Yet another consequence of regarding democracy as a matter of degree pertains to criticisms of societies that call themselves democratic yet are democratically deficient. Were democracy an all-or-nothing affair, the presence in countries like my own of categories of people denied the means for full and effective political participation would render them entirely undemocratic; so democratic action against discrimination internal to such countries would be impossible. On a conception of democracy where it admits of degree, by contrast, one can acknowledge that the presence of such people makes a society less democratic than it would be without the exclusions, while still recognizing a measure of democratic popular control. A practical implication of this recognition is to direct attention to the task of identifying prodemocratic policies, institutions, and attitudes and to nurture them, while simultaneously working to diminish the society's anti-democratic dimensions.

The circumstances that admit of more or less democracy, to make another definitional observation, are not limited to formal government but obtain whenever people share ongoing situations where their actions affect one another. It is therefore appropriate to ask about the degree of democracy of a city, a country, a region of a country, a region of the world, or, indeed, of the entire world, a university, a neighbourhood, a union, a political party, a family, and so on. To recognize this characteristic of democracy is to resist those conceptions where democracy is limited to relations between citizens and a government. Non-citizens within a country obviously have a stake in the country's future. Refusal to recognize as undemocratic denial to non-citizens of effective means for participating in collective action with citizens thus involves an excessively narrow view of democracy.

Similarly, the geographic boundaries of democracy are both narrower and broader than those of a state. This means that democratic politics are appropriate at a local level, where they might be more effective than in larger ventures and help to build toward them. Thus, while attempts at positive action on a large scale at my university have had limited success, the unilateral efforts of some individual departments have made more progress. I attribute this to the fact that these followed protracted discussion and debate within the departments. Though still not as robust as one might desire, the positive action programmes self-imposed by these departments have had more success than in the university as a whole, due, I submit, to their democratic support.

In making these comments I do not wish to endorse those critics of positive action who, while professing agreement with its aims, insist that it is best done only locally. Contexts of democracy overlap, and one might say that they do so vertically as well as horizontally. Democracy-promoting measures like positive action are best advanced when pursued simultaneously at a local and at an encompassing global level; so it is not being recommended that global efforts be set aside, but that they and local initiatives be pursued in tandem. Moreover, when dealing with populations which are mobile between educational institutions or work places, failure to advance on a global front creates a disincentive to take local action, as a locale with vibrant positive action programmes could find itself overburdened.

As between non-governmental, voluntary initiatives and governmental ones, the latter are sometimes singled out as special because they carry with them the threat of state force. It is for this reason that some champions of positive action favour a 'top down' approach for its effectiveness, while others oppose this as objectionably statist. On the orientation suggested in this paper, government legislation is indeed a special case, but not because it carries a threat of sanction. For one thing, not all formally encoded laws are enforced, as the example of the Canadian Contract Compliance experiences shows. Also, from the point of view of an individual the sanctions of non-governmental, 'voluntary' rules can sometimes be more threatening than state sanctions, for instance when the latter involve little more than a fine or warning, while extra-state sanctions might exclude people from participation in an organization important to them.

With respect to positive action, I see state-sanctioned legislation as special for two reasons. Not all the interests of citizens are immutable or even very clearly fixed in their own minds. Rather, popular political values in a (more or less) democratic environment both form public policy and are formed by it in an interactive way. The state embracing a policy is one way that it is legitimated and made a priority in the public mind; so governmental initiative helps to form public values while at the same time following them. This task admittedly requires demanding leadership skills, but it is easier to accomplish in practice than abstract theory might suggest. The task is pursued in a democratic fashion when government enacts policies that extend and make concrete values that are already widely held in a population, thus drawing out implicitly held existing norms rather than trying to impose policies on people with values hostile to them. The second special role of state action with respect to positive action is one common to all matters of public goods that, even when long-range aims are agreed upon, they can be defeated when individual participants fear short-term disadvantage. Obliging all employers to adopt positive action policies is thus like obliging them to adopt environmental or work-place health safeguards.

In addition to admitting of degree and being of broad scope, democracy as here conceived is a contextual matter. On this 'contextualist' approach no one procedure by means of which collective democratic decisions are made is privileged. Rather, depending on circumstances, sometimes majority voting or the delegation of authority to representatives will be the most democratically effective, and at other times direct participation in efforts to achieve consensus will be preferable. Sometimes democratic decision making should be bound by formal rules, while other times it is best governed by informal conventions. Conceived this way, most current theoretical debates over what 'true' democracy is — for instance, between liberal and participatory democrats or between pluralist and deliberative democrats — should be regarded as controversies over how progress in democracy is best achieved and regress avoided. Or they might be conceived of as differences over what is realistic and desirable as a goal of democratic decision making — for instance, to negotiate a compromise among conflicting parties or to overcome conflict by reaching consensus — and this, too, may vary by context.

One consequence of this feature of democracy is that one need not forego striving to build a public consensus in favour of strong positive action campaigns that set targets proportionate to the numbers from a target group in the population or in an available job or educational pool even while compromising with critics of positive action by setting lower targets. If the feasibility of negotiation or of consensus building is a matter of context, it should not be assumed either that consensus can never be reached or that compromises are carved in stone. Another consequence of the contextual feature of democracy is especially pertinent to debates over the democratic credentials of positive action.

Democracy is often simply identified with majority rule determined by voting where each person casts a vote equal to that of every other participant. But in circumstances where some people stand to be greatly affected by the outcome of a vote while this would only slightly affect others who are nonetheless eligible voters, weighted voting is sometimes justified on democratic grounds. This might seem puzzling, because democracy came into existence in opposition to overtly anti-egalitarian organization of political society and is founded on the principle of the equal moral worth of individuals and their resulting entitlement to equal participation in public affairs. A contextualist viewpoint on democracy removes puzzlement.

The justification for weighted voting (or reserved legislative seats) is not that some people are deemed more important human beings than others, as in feudal societies but that, to accord people equal respect and appropriate participation in decisions affecting them, it is sometimes necessary to adjust democratic decision-making procedures to take account of their special circumstances. This same observation pertains to a challenge sometimes levelled against positive action for being anti-democratic because it involves special treatment. In distinguishing between 'equal treatment' and 'equity', where the latter attends to special needs ignored in the former, proponents of positive action are in keeping with democracy concretely undertaken (Gould, 1996; Williams, 1998; Young, 1990).

Positive Action and Systemic Discrimination

'Positive action', as I use the term, refers to any policy aimed at offsetting or undoing systemic discrimination. Individuals suffer 'systemic discrimination' when:

- educational, employment or other such options they reasonably consider or might reasonably consider important to lead an enjoyable and fulfilling life are denied them on an ongoing basis;
- just in virtue of their membership in a group where the group is defined by reference to characteristics which do not justify this denial; and
- where their exclusion depends on broad social, legal, cultural, or economic circumstances rather than on the individual prejudices of others (though exclusion often both feeds and is reinforced by prejudice).

Systemic discrimination is sometimes also labelled 'structural', 'indirect', or 'institutional'.

Positive action is often identified with preferential treatment, but since positive action policies include such things as anti-discrimination education, provision of special facilities for members of discriminated against groups, campaigns to eliminate stereotyping in schoolbooks or the media, or any other proactive measures that go beyond just prohibiting discrimination, this identification is mistaken. Still, in my subsequent comments I shall usually have in mind preferential policies, recognizing that they, themselves, admit of several forms. Because such policies constitute the strongest and most contentious forms of positive action, successful defence of them will also defend weaker forms. In addition, the most deeply entrenched and detrimental forms of systemic discrimination – especially evident with respect to racism – require the most vigorous responses. It may well be that in order to garner popular support for positive action it is best to begin with its less ambitious forms. However, if preferential treatment is entirely ruled out as an option, those who favour proactive measures to combat systemic discrimination will find themselves in the position, should the weaker forms fail, of either giving up or shifting to policies once rejected by them, thus making it even more difficult to win wide public support.

The characterization of 'positive action' given above links it to the specific goal of overcoming or diminishing systemic discrimination. This is not the only goal that positive action can serve. Positive action campaigns in the city of Toronto to include people of South and East Asian communities in its police force, for instance, have yielded clear advantages to the city by making law-abiding citizens from those communities more comfortable with the police and denying law breakers from the communities the advantage of police ignorance of their languages and cultures. Hence, 'positive action' could refer just to policies that aim at changing the distribution by demographic group of people in occupational and related stations, where various justifications could be given for specified distributions. Though there is nothing objectionable about this broad definition, I prefer to tie positive action directly to the aim of combating systemic discrimination. This is the most common and important use of positive action programmes, and systemic discrimination often skews otherwise desirable distributions of people through occupations.

More salient to democracy than the specific aims to which positive action is definitionally linked is that it is a goal-directed conception having to do with the broad contours of a society. Very often debates over the value of positive action are conducted as theoretical contests between alternative conceptions of justice (distributive versus acquisitory) or of rights (group versus individual) ideologically deployed by people locked into rival camps. As a result, endorsing or rejecting positive action is a way of declaring how one stands on already fixed political or theoretical positions, and the goals it might further are lost sight of. By focusing instead on problems that positive action policies are supposed to address, these policies may be reconceived as potential democratic projects. If widespread recognition can be achieved that systemic discrimination both exists in a society and is detrimental to it, then a collective decision to address this problem by means of positive action becomes a live and practical option.

Conceiving of positive action as an option for democratic projects does not in any way ensure that it will be chosen by a populace. An alternative solution often proffered to social problems arising from discrimination is to pass and enforce anti-discrimination laws with respect to such things as employment or university admission and trust in free competition to yield a demographically representative distribution unless putative group-related deficiencies in natural talent impede this. But placing debates about the relative merits of this approach and the more proactive ones of positive action on the terrain of democratic problem solving focuses the debates in ways that taking abstract stands does not.

The free competition approach has been tried in many local circumstances with notable lack of success, as in the case of blacks in the US or Aboriginal peoples in Canada. Possible explanations for this consistent with a free educational or job-market approach are that more time is needed, or that anti-discrimination laws are not enforced, or that talent in the respective groups is lacking. Positive action proponents ought to take such explanations seriously and debate them, but such debate will be differently conducted depending on whether or not advocates on both sides are approaching them as ways of testing solutions to agree upon society-wide problems.

It might be argued that transposing deliberations over positive action from ideological terrain to that of democratic problem solving runs afoul of the dilemma with which my remarks were introduced: the democratic problem solvers will be those who are able and disposed to engage in democratic processes and thus involve few people excluded from effective democratic participation. A feature of systemic discrimination contributing to optimism that this impediment can be successfully confronted is that such discrimination does not depend upon individual prejudice. To the extent that discrimination does not result from individual bigotry, calling attention to other circumstances that engender it can help to gain support for positive action policies provided there is a realistic expectation that the policies can successfully counteract such circumstances.

If, in addition, one assumes a politically active population mainly of prodemocrats, another consideration that mutes the dilemma is suggested. On the definition of democracy given above, a society free of systemic discrimination will be more democratic than otherwise. Why should people who enjoy a large measure of effective input to collective decision making (in part because they do not suffer systemic discrimination) want to broaden democracy by extending this privilege to others? Some extra-democratic reasons are evident. A society in which there is a permanent underclass will be an unpleasant place to live: disaffected compatriots and either continuing welfare expenses or walled cities and high policing and prison costs.

But there are also the specifically democratic advantages referred to in my introductory observations. Let me expand on the advantage regarding a virtuous civic culture. Democratic theorists are almost all in accord that democracy in a pluralist society (which is now nearly all the globe's societies) requires a political culture favouring toleration and mutual respect. Prodemocratic citizens who recognize this fact will accordingly wish to promote and maintain such a culture. However, cultural attitudes are not like tap water in a basin that can be easily contained and turned off and on at will. Attitudes on the part of relatively advantaged citizens of hostility or indifference toward the disadvantaged are difficult to reverse at the boundary between the two groups and are prone to generate an ethic of mean-spirited selfishness. This in turn severely impedes the sort of toleration required for democracy.

It is true that large-scale positive action programmes typically require state intervention in private affairs, and one need not be a neoliberal to agree that such intervention carries with it anti-democratic bureaucratic risks. But if systemic discrimination leads, as it sometimes has, to widespread malcontent and violence, it, too, can engender state intervention of a sort, moreover, that is more democracy threatening than enforced positive action policies.

The Dilemma 'Solved' and Further Problematized

To summarize: the dilemma of democracy and positive action admits of solution if such action is undertaken as a democratic project aiming to strengthen democracy itself in a potentially self-building process, appealing to democratic impulses on the part of relevant populations as well as to self interest, pursued in both local and global forums, and conducted in ways that appropriately seek either compromise or consensus, or pursue both simultaneously. As in the case of all theoretical approaches to real social problems, this is not exactly a 'solution' but a recommendation for a way of conceiving of a problem.

The advantages I claim for the approach are to situate positive action on the terrain of democratic politics and to remove impediments to practical solutions based on faulty assumptions: that a society in which systemic discrimination exists is entirely undemocratic or, conversely, that systemic discrimination is not anti-democratic as long as formal decision-making procedures are available to everyone; that positive action is at odds with a democratic notion of equality; that those who do not suffer systemic discrimination have no reasons to support positive action; that negotiation of conflict is not a democratic failing, or, again conversely, that democracy is nothing but such negotiation; and other such assumptions. I wish now to turn to two challenges to efforts at combating systemic discrimination democratically: the problem of the proudly prejudiced and the unavoidability of economic concerns.[3]

The Proudly Prejudiced

The solution to the dilemma assumes that within democratically empowered parts of a population there exist prodemocratic sentiments and that systemic discrimination is not primarily a matter of ill will. However, one feature of systemic discrimination is that it reinforces itself by engendering or exacerbating prejudice. When prejudicial attitudes come to be partially definitive of someone's identity and when they are intensely held (Nazis, white supremists or misogynistic sexists grotesquely exemplified both possibilities), discrimination is condoned, or as in the grotesque cases actively promoted, without concern for democratic constraints or the long-term consequences for democratic practice and culture. These observations suggest two scenarios that challenge democratic responses to systemic discrimination: (1) those who harbour intense prejudice are in a minority, but they have disproportionate control over government, education, the media, and major private-sector enterprises and hence are able to impede effective democratic activity to dismantle discriminatory structures; (2) overridingly strong prejudice motivates the majority.

The first scenario calls for concerted political action, especially by people active in social movements who champion positive action acting in concert with sympathetic political parties or people within political parties. Important to such endeavours in my view are some lessons about social-movement activism and democracy suggested by reflection on socialist politics around the First and Second Internationals. In agreement with the broad sense of democracy endorsed in this paper, socialist theorists and activists, especially in the Marxist tradition but not confined to it, correctly saw concerted activity by workers as itself a form of democratic activity – that is, as activity by those sharing a common situation to affect it by joint action. However, this activity was carried on in a militantly sectarian manner: democracy was class relativized in such a way that anything that was not seen to serve the interests of workers was viewed as in league with a pernicious, 'bourgeois' form of democracy opposed to true, 'proletarian democracy'.

Sectors of the population from outside the working class and working people who were primarily concerned to combat racism, sexism, national chauvinism, or religious discrimination were labelled class enemies or victims of bourgeois ideological manipulation, with the result that building majority alliances was foreclosed, and the initial democratic impulse of socialism was turned on its head. A lesson to be learned from this experience (not learned within the variety of socialism that autodestructed from 1989) is that such things as social-movement coalitions and networks have the potential to mobilize majorities against prejudiced, minority domination but only if they are themselves democratically pursued, that is, in mutual respect among those who would directly profit from positive action and between them and those from relatively privileged groups who might be won over either on moral grounds or in consideration of long-term self interest.

Scenario (2) is even more challenging. In their books, *The Sexual Contract* and *The Racial Contract,* Carole Pateman (1988) and Charles Mills (1997) argue that modern societies are organized in accord with a tacit agreement on the part of men, in the one case, and 'white' people, in the other, to subordinate women and non-whites. Of course, men do not constitute a majority, and, on a global scale neither do white people, but men are so close to being a majority that if nearly all of them were allied to keep down women, scenario two would be approximated, and whites do constitute a majority within many countries.

On degrees of democracy approach, a situation where a majority oppresses a minority is not only morally objectionable, but also democratically deficient. This is because while, other things being equal, majority rule is more democratic than minority rule, majority rule where the rights of minorities are protected is more democratic than majority rule where they are not (Oppenheim, 1971). This means that government agencies or elected officials who are committed to democracy need not assume that prejudicial attitudes on the part of a majority commits them to acquiescence in continuing discrimination. If such agencies and officials are sincere democrats they should see it important on democratic grounds to resist the effects of persisting prejudice through enforcement of anti-discrimination legislation and to attack prejudicial attitudes themselves by means of vigorous educational campaigns. Nor need prodemocrats in government or anywhere else assume that majority prejudice is immutable.

Notwithstanding the advantage of the sexual and racial contract theses for highlighting the way that those who profit from prejudice are oblivious to its pernicious and unfounded nature, I doubt that such things as sexism and racism are so universally and strongly held that inroads cannot be made against them. One ray of hope, recognized by Pateman and Mills, is that male or white 'traitors' sometimes join or even initiate anti-discrimination efforts. This raises the question of where these traitors come from. Presumably, they are not freaks of nature or super-heroic saints; hence there must be something potentially shared by others that leads them to break the oppressive contracts.

Another lesson from the erstwhile socialist experience is especially apt for those in workplaces, voluntary association, and social movements who wish to dismantle prejudice. One way that this socialism perpetuated sectarianism was by positing a notion of the worker as homogeneously constituted by fixed, working-class interests, forgetting that any worker is also of some gender, ethnicity, (attributed) 'race', nationality, sexual orientation, and so on, and that addressing work-related concerns are not always such a person's first priority. The same observation applies to any other category of people, including men and whites, who, even while, qua male or white, harbouring prejudicial attitudes toward women and 'visible minorities', may also identify with them in other aspects (as workmates, fellow country people, in religious affiliation, and so on).

I take it that prejudice is crucially sustained by the combination of stereotyping and lack of empathy. Joint activity in shared undertakings has the potential to break these two attitudes down, but only if those engaging in them do so as equals. The impetus for insisting on such equality typically comes from those in positions of subordination, for example when women demand ordination in a church or black workers campaign for representation in union leadership. Success in such ventures, though by no means guaranteed, is facilitated by the fact that it strengthens the Church or the union. I cannot sociologically prove the hypothesis that when or to the extent that people jointly engage in activities important to them and do so on a basis of equality, this reduces prejudice by calling into question stereotypical attitudes and engendering empathy, but if the hypothesis is on the right track, we have an example of how local-level democratic activity can further anti-discrimination causes even in the face of widespread prejudice.

Economic Resources

So far I have addressed democracy and positive action as capable of being treated independently of the economic organization of societies. Both capitalist and socialist or social-democratic societies admit of degrees of democracy, and positive action programmes are not linked to any one political-economic orientation. However, there is one respect in which I do not think economic questions can be set aside, and it is a very large respect. At my university, as at other workplaces, discussions about proactively recruiting women and minority group members began in the 1970s. At that time there were some voices of opposition, using now familiar arguments such as that academic appointments should be blind to anything but pure scholarly ability. Regarding women, there were also some arguments that are less in vogue today: that women were incapable of serious thought or that they would not fit in with the male society of the workplace. Those who advanced these arguments were few in number and most of them were more annoyed than deeply opposed to the proposals.

Today the opposition voices are more in number and much more passionate in their opposition notwithstanding the fact that blatantly discriminatory values of earlier times have waned. Casting about for an explanation I can only conclude that the difference between the two epochs is the economy. In the 1970s Canadian educational establishments in particular were booming. We currently face a situation where in all but a very few academic disciplines, qualified people seeking employment far exceed available positions. With all manner of business and public sector employers also down sizing, this situation is general. In circumstances like these it is unrealistic to expect people who do not directly profit from a positive action programme and whose already slim employment prospects would be made worse to set aside self interest and support positive action.

The point is not that hard economic times create prejudice (though it may also through time do this, too), but that even unprejudiced members of groups not targeted by positive action find it difficult to support policies that will worsen their own prospects. Democracy probably could not survive if people saw it in exclusively self-interested terms (because they would be too willing to support anti-democratic measures whenever they thought this would benefit them), but neither could democracy survive if it demanded self-sacrificing altruism. Required, as John Stuart Mill and several other theorists have noted (Krouse, 1983), is a balance between self interest and public spiritedness in approaching democratic politics. At the very least, economic insecurity taxes public spiritedness, and if, in addition, increasing competition for scarce resources breeds a culture of mean-spirited greed and selfishness, civic minded attitudes can atrophy altogether.

The conclusion I draw is that serious campaigns for positive action cannot be divorced from political-economic campaigns to reverse a global trend toward concentration of enormous wealth in a very few hands leaving insufficient resources for adequate distribution among the rest of a population. State and sub- (or super-) state agencies that enact positive action legislation without also taking effective action to reduce unemploy-ment and to enhance educational opportunities will either be acting in bad faith with respect to systemic discrimination, or they will be unwittingly laying a basis for the legislation to be ignored or rescinded. Champions of positive action who are content to view their campaigns simply as programmes for achieving a fair distribution of shrunken employment and career resources, will find the programmes of limited value even when implemented. They will also find them difficult to implement, at least with democratic support. But, as I have been urging in this chapter, positive action requires democracy as much as democracy requires positive action.

Appendix

This appendix responds to a request of participants at the conference in Innsbruck, 1998, for counterarguments to standard objections to positive action. I thus sketch the general lines along which I believe four of these objections can be met.

- *Objection.* Positive action is unnecessary, because enforcement of legislation prohibiting discrimination in admission, hiring or promotion is sufficient.
- *Reply.* Anti-discrimination legislation, important though it is, does not address the problem of underrepresentation due to systemic discrimination. One example of such discrimination is that the conditions of study or employment in many institutions require educational or prior work experience that members of a disadvantaged group, being confined to economic and educational ghettos, lack. Another example is the absence of role models, which creates downward spirals where people from disadvantaged groups lack the confidence to prepare for entry to professions.
- *Objection.* When positive action involves preferential treatment it is objectionably discriminatory against those from non-targeted groups.
- *Reply.* Any selection criterion will be advantageous for some people and disadvantageous for others. If an enterprise decided that it required some employees fluent in a certain foreign language or if a university decided to admit more people qualified to pursue science programmes and fewer into arts programmes, these decisions would enhance the chances of employment or admission for some and diminish it for others. Such decisions constitute objectionable discrimination only when they are arbitrary or otherwise unjustified. The debate over reverse discrimination, then, should mainly address the justifications for adopting strong positive action policies. One justification is that

proactive policies can contribute to the society-wide task of removing morally objectionable and socially harmful systemic barriers to full substantive equality of opportunity. Another justification is that public or private sector institutions will better serve a public that includes people from disadvantaged groups if members of those groups hold positions of responsibility in the institutions.

- *Objection.* The only acceptable consideration for admission, promotion, or employment should be whether applicants merit a post in virtue of being able to perform the skills proper to it.
- *Reply 1.* The ability to understand and communicate with people from disadvantaged groups is sometimes itself an important skill for occupying a post in an institution that interacts with such people, and this skill is more likely to be possessed by individuals from those groups than by others.
- *Reply 2.* One need not sacrifice skills in order to implement positive action. For example, posts might be kept open until applicants from a target group with the requisite skills are found. Or people might be enrolled in special training programmes from which they 'graduate' only when or if they have demonstrated proficiency in the required skills.

These two replies also apply to an extension of the objection according to which preferential admission or hiring inhibits selecting the very best candidate. There is nothing to prevent implementing strenuous training programmes with demanding standards for success or setting high criteria in a job search. Defenders of positive action also point out that criteria of 'the very best' often include such abilities as fitting in with the pre-existing culture of a workplace or having useful business or government connections and thus contribute to systemic discrimination.

- *Objection.* When they involve preferential treatment, positive action programmes must classify and count people by racial, gender, ethnic or other categories. In addition to being difficult to accomplish, such exercises call attention to differences thus exacerbating social fragmentation and prejudicial attitudes.
- *Reply 1.* Positive action does not apply to all groups of people in a society, but only to those subject to evidently debilitating systemic discrimination in significant numbers, and it is only required while the discrimination persists. In the most glaring cases, which are especially prevalent regarding racial discrimination, preferential treatment can be undertaken without formal counts in confidence that

progress toward appropriate representation will be made. More systematic programmes are indeed facilitated by estimating numbers of people, but only within targeted groups. While such estimates will be approximate and include anomalies, absolute precision is not required in the cases that are sufficiently widespread to be recognized as candidates for proaction.

- *Reply 2.* It is because members of a group subject to systemic discrimination are already informally identified and singled out in being excluded that the positive action policies are justified. It is not the collection of data by group that causes prejudicial group differences, but previously existing social attitudes and structures of disadvantage. Indeed, by not taking counts by 'race' it would be impossible to know to what extent racial discrimination occurs. Governments express little concern about counting by national origin for immigration purposes, by gender for a large variety of reasons, or even by 'race' regarding some medical concerns. Therefore, the objection cannot be to counting per se but to the purposes for which classification and counting are intended. Let the debate, then, explicitly focus on those purposes.

Notes

1. It should be noted that, contrary to an assumption I have found among many Europeans who look to the Canadian example, this legislation is different from Canada's constitutionally enshrined policies in support of multiculturalism as none of the five target groups of employment equity constitutes an ethnic minority. Another caveat concerns the term 'visible' and other such terms below, which are placed in quotation marks to indicate recognition that racial categories are socially constructed (Goldberg, 1993: chapter 3; Zack, 1997).
2. This informal definition aims to retain the idea that democracy involves popular sovereignty without commitment to the problematic concept of a 'general will'. Needless to say, this discussion compresses a large topic (Cunningham, 1987: chapter 3; 1994, essay 3).
3. I do not mean to suggest that these are the only challenges. Another vexing problem is that of 'false consciousness', when significant numbers of people from groups subject to systemic discrimination either fail to recognize that they are thus disadvantaged or oppose

government policies in their favour. This problem was grappled with in the women's movement, especially in its early days, and poses the problem of whether 'democratic paternalism' can ever make sense. I do not address this problem in the present paper because I consider it a moot point regarding racism, very few of whose victims are content with their situation.

In Defence of Affirmative Action: North American Discourses for the European Context?[1]

Melissa S. Williams

Is the principle of the equality of persons best realized through policies of equal opportunity, which treat all individuals on the same terms regardless of what social group or class they might belong to? Or does it require policies of positive or affirmative action,[2] which aim to overcome the ongoing consequences of past discrimination through programmes that specifically benefit members of disadvantaged groups?

These questions have been hotly debated in North America for three decades. I have come to believe that policies of positive action, broadly defined, are an important component of a broad commitment to combating deeply entrenched patterns of social, economic, and political inequality in democratic societies. Principles of equal opportunity and non-discrimination are not, by themselves, sufficient to overcome these deep-rooted structures of inequality, which are reproduced from one generation to the next even in the absence of overt or intentional discrimination.

Before launching into the reasons for my conviction on this point, we might pause to ask how well suited the concepts of equal opportunity and positive action are to the European context. Consider, first, the target groups of both equal opportunity and affirmative action policies in the US and Canada. All of these groups (women and ethnic or 'racial' minorities) are comprised principally of legal citizens. Moreover, the immigrant populations that are covered by these policies are, for the most part, permanent residents, and their children born on North American soil will automatically become citizens. Thus, the background assumption of both equal opportunity and affirmative action policies is that virtually all of the long-term residents of the territory are or should become full and equal members of society, and should have equal access to key social, economic, and political institutions. Although the ideal of equal access remains unrealized, there is at least rhetorical agreement upon that ideal.

Clearly, this assumption is also at work in countries like the UK and the Netherlands, which have adopted positive action policies. But immigration, employment, and non-discrimination policies of many European countries do not appear to reflect even rhetorical agreement upon the goal of the full and permanent membership of immigrant minorities. The paradigm of guest worker status may be waning, as immigrants who originally settled in Europe under guest worker policies are gradually being admitted to a greater array of rights of membership (Soysal, 1994). Yet to the extent that employment and residence laws restrict long-term immigrants' access to housing and to employment beyond low-skilled labour (Wakolbinger, 1995: 16), the discourses of equal opportunity and positive action may be politically premature, however morally compelling they are. The existence of a distinct class of foreign workers who are largely confined to low-paying jobs and who have limited security for either their residence or their employment stands in stark tension with the ideal of full and equal membership that stands in the background of equal opportunity and positive action discourses alike.[3] Some European countries lack strong policies of non-discrimination toward ethnic minorities (Wrench, 1996), a clear precondition for enforceable policies of positive action.

A related concern is that positive action policies appear to assume that the society is a 'closed system'. That is, they suppose that society has a fairly stable population base (in which it is possible to distinguish clearly between members and non-members) and a more-or-less fixed set of employment and educational resources, which should be distributed among the population without systematic bias. Yet in recent years populations in Europe have been in flux, a dynamic that results not only from the rise of immigration from non-European countries but also from European integration.[4] The relative fluidity of European populations may serve to blur the distinction between the members and non-members of any given European society. To that extent, it also blurs the distinction between disadvantaged persons who (as members) are owed an obligation of equal treatment, and disadvantaged who (as transients) can make valid claims of humanitarian relief but cannot claim benefits that attach to permanent membership. The fluidity of populations in Europe also raises the necessity for the European Union (EU) to be involved in positive action programmes. Beside this, there are some disadvantaged populations in Europe – notably the Roma or Gypsy people – for which a pan-European policy of positive action would be appropriate.

My point here is not that North American policies toward disadvantaged minorities are morally superior to those in Europe. On the contrary,

European immigration policies have tended to guarantee basic welfare rights to immigrant populations that are far more substantial than welfare rights in the US in particular. My purpose, rather, is simply point to some assumptions that may not travel well across systems.

The Limits of Difference-Blind Equality

Equal opportunity doctrine prescribes two basic principles for distributing social positions. First, the agents and mechanisms of distribution should follow a strict principle of non-discrimination by ensuring that morally arbitrary characteristics like sex or 'race' play no role in the allocation of benefits (see, for example Rawls, 1971: 73–4). Second, only those attributes relevant to the good at stake should play a role in the decision. Thus, hiring criteria must constitute 'bona fide occupational qualifications' under equal employment opportunity law.

The doctrine of equal opportunity is a clear moral achievement. But if a central goal of democratic society is to overcome group-based barriers to full and equal participation in key social, economic and political institutions, equal opportunity principles are not enough. In order to see why, it is helpful to distinguish among four different types of discrimination: direct or intentional discrimination, statistical discrimination, societal discrimination, and structural or systemic discrimination.

Direct or Intentional Discrimination

This is the least misunderstood form of discrimination; its agents are usually quite conscious of it as they perpetrate it. It consists in the exclusion of an individual from a social benefit solely because of group-based characteristics (such as 'race', sex, ethnicity, sexual orientation, religion) to which the agent of discrimination attaches stigmatic meaning.

Statistical Discrimination

Statistical discrimination leads to the rejection of candidates from particular social groups, not because the agent of discrimination consciously disdains the group, but because patterns of behaviour are viewed as characteristic of the group and as liabilities for the institution in question. Women job candidates, for example, have often been regarded sceptically by employers who fear that they will become pregnant and take maternity leave, which imposes costs on employers. In the US, some employers have assumed that there is a higher rate of absenteeism among minority than among white employees, and they therefore view minority job applicants with a more sceptical eye. Often the employer's assumptions about statistical tendencies in a particular group are incorrect, which shows that there is a fine line between statistical discrimination and direct discrimination based on unfavourable group stereotypes. But even when the assumptions are borne out by the evidence, statistical discrimination treats individuals not on their merits but on the basis of group characteristics, and so violates the liberal principle of equality.

Societal Discrimination

Societal discrimination also arises not from any conscious prejudice on the part of the agent of discrimination, but from the agent's (putative) social knowledge about group differences and social group relations. Specifically, societal discrimination is based on the knowledge that even if the employer or admission officer is free of hostility or prejudice toward a group, the broader society is not free of negative attitudes. However, the success of an enterprise may well depend on easy-going, unstrained interactions between the employee and the public, as well as among employees. Where the employer knows that there is a strong social prejudice against an ethnic minority, s/he may be reluctant to hire a member of that minority group for a position that involves regular contact with the public, as in many sales positions. Where a job requires close coordination with co-workers (as in many assembly-line, construction and fire-fighting jobs, for example), and many members of the existing workforce have racist and sexist beliefs, an employer may be reluctant to hire a woman or minority job candidate, and may try to rationalize this decision with the belief that it is for the person's 'own good' that he or she should not be subjected to the hostility of co-workers.

Structural or Systemic Discrimination

The concept of structural inequality or systemic discrimination comprises those sources of group-patterned disadvantage and inequality that are neither a consequence of the voluntary choices of individual members of the disadvantaged group nor a product of particular social agents' bias against the group. In short, the category of structural discrimination includes sources of group bias in the social system that cannot easily be charged to the account of direct discrimination, statistical discrimination, or societal discrimination.

It is possible to break down the concept of structural discrimination into several types or categories. The first – and closest to the types of discrimination mentioned above – is sometimes labelled 'indirect discrimination' (see, for example, Wrench, 1996). These obstacles to equal employment opportunity are embedded in recruitment practices and work requirements that (often inadvertently) function disproportionately to exclude minority groups from the workplace. A recent study of European recruitment practices, for example, showed that many firms recruit new employees through their family connections to current employees. Because there are few minority employees in the workforce, this method of recruiting functions as a barrier to minority recruitment (Wrench, 1996: 48). Work requirements, especially those concerning employees' physical appearance, may be neutral but will in fact function to exclude some minority members from positions.

'Past-in-present' discrimination is among the most pervasive and pernicious sources of structural inequality, particularly in the areas of education and health care. It occurs where '"neutral" practices in an institutional area . . . have differential negative impact on minorities because of past intentional discrimination in the same institutional area' (Hill, 1988: 366). In places where educational achievement is strongly associated with family income, and future employment opportunities are determined by educational achievement, then patterns of group-structured economic inequality are likely to persist wherever a group has been systematically confined to low-paying jobs, as has been the case for workers of non-European origin in most European countries. These restrictions create intergenerational patterns of group-structured inequality that are not likely to disappear for at least a generation after restrictions have been lifted.

Structural inequality may also take the form of 'side-effect' discrimination (as Hill calls it), in which the links between social spheres mean that discrimination or inequality in one sphere will generate inequality in another social sphere. As Susan Okin argues, persistent patterns of gender inequality in income and occupational status are precisely the result of 'inequality from sphere to sphere' (Okin, 1989). To take one component of this dynamic, inequality in the division of domestic labour, including child rearing, quickly translates into inequality in the world of paid employment, where the structure of work assumes that the worker is a man who has a wife to manage domestic and child-rearing responsibilities. As long as such norms persist women will continue to bump up against the 'glass ceiling', a palpable structural barrier to gender equality in the workplace even where there is no overt discrimination against women.

Low levels of political participation and office-holding among minorities are, in many cases, another example of side-effect discrimination. Practices that keep minority workers in low-paying and low-skill jobs also make it more difficult for them to gain access to political processes. The close relationship between socioeconomic status and political participation is well established; any practice that confines a minority group to low-paying jobs will, therefore, probably produce relatively low levels of political participation as well. This is true even where minorities are not explicitly prevented from full participation, as of course many are. To the extent that poor access to political institutions frustrates policy changes that could enhance minorities' social circumstances and employment opportunities, the relationship between income and political participation can generate a vicious cycle of exclusion.

If they are taken seriously by enforcement authorities, strong policies of non-discrimination can be effective tools for combating direct, statistical, and societal discrimination. This is not to say that such policies are easy to undertake, particularly in periods when xenophobia is on the rise. A strong policy of equal employment opportunity would simply not accept the argument that social hostility toward a group makes employees from that group a liability for employers, even if there were an element of truth to this argument. Indeed, some practices that fall under the category of structural discrimination — for example standards of merit or occupational qualifications that indirectly discriminate against minorities or women — are vulnerable to challenge under anti-discrimination policies, as North American legal practice has borne out.

Yet most forms of structural discrimination are not amenable to change through anti-discrimination principles alone. Where there are close relationships between minority status, low educational attainment, low-income and low-skilled occupations, and poor housing and health, and where these patterns persist intergenerationally, group-structured inequality may respond only to group-focused policies that take positive action to overcome barriers to full participation.

The concepts of systemic inequality and structural discrimination are integral to the defence of positive action. Both the concept of structural discrimination and the practices of positive action entail moving beyond a narrowly individualistic conception of social relations and of moral responsibility. Acknowledging the existence of structural discrimination means acknowledging that unjust inequalities exist, but that blame for their existence cannot be assigned to any specific, identifiable individuals. Embracing the policies of positive action means accepting the notion that a democratic society, as a whole, collectively bears the moral responsibility for eradicating unjust institutions. It is telling, I think, that critics of positive action either ignore the phenomenon of structural inequality altogether, or deny that the political community bears any moral responsibility for combating it.[5]

Positive Action for Whom?

Positive action policies are always focused on identified groups, which have a strong moral claim to benefit from such policies. In general, these groups, which have a strong case for group recognition in general, and positive action in particular, are marginalized ascriptive groups. As I use the term, 'marginalized ascriptive groups' have four characteristic features: (1) patterns of social and political inequality are structured along the lines of group membership; (2) generally, membership in them is not experienced as voluntary; (3) generally, membership in them is not experienced as mutable; and (4) generally, there are negative meanings assigned to group identity by the broader society or the dominant culture.

The first feature of marginalized groups points to the fact of structural (or systemic) inequality – the fact that the dynamics of social, economic, and political processes reliably reproduce patterns of inequality in which members of these groups lie well below the median of the distribution of resources. Although conscious acts of discrimination may contribute to the reproduction of group-structured inequality, the concept of structural inequality refers to the fact that patterns of inequality may be reproduced by social practices even without intentional discrimination.

The last three features of marginalized groups warrant my use of the term 'ascriptive' to characterize these groups. In the sociological literature, the term 'ascriptive' signifies that a person's role or status in society is a product of unchosen characteristics such as sex, 'race' or age rather than a result of his or her actions. It thus stands in contrast with achievement of roles and statuses, which are based on what an individual has actually done. On the level of individual interactions, a member of an ascriptive group will often be treated by others on the basis of attributes they ascribe because of 'race' or gender or kinship ties, rather than attributes actually displayed (Theodorson and Theodorson, 1969: 17, 353, 416; Marshall, 1994: 19, 510).

It is important to note that while the identities ascribed to individuals may include allegedly natural behaviours, nothing in the concept of ascriptive groups as such supports the claim that any essential identity attaches to individuals because of their possession of ascriptive traits. Rather, the term merely signifies the fact that cultures assign social meaning to the possession of certain traits, and that individuals who possess those traits will be treated differently from those who do not possess them. The traits that carry ascriptive meanings often vary from one culture to the next. For example, class might be an ascriptive trait in some societies but not in others (or in some social contexts but not in others). It is also important to emphasize that the traits – and so the meanings they carry – are neither chosen voluntarily by the individuals who bear them, nor can they be (readily) changed by them. For these groups, the social meanings attached to the traits they possess are negative and help to reinforce (and provide a rationalization for) structural patterns of material inequality. Taken together, these aspects of marginalized ascriptive group identity mean that an individual may occupy certain social roles and statuses, and face dimmer prospects of success than others, because of personal characteristics over which s/he has no control.

The marginality of these groups, then, is doubly constituted by their disadvantaged position in the distribution of social, economic and political resources and by the fact that their ascriptive traits carry stigmas or other social meanings that limit individuals' agency. To borrow Nancy Fraser's helpful conceptual framework, members of these groups are burdened simultaneously by cultural injustices and economic injustices, by injustices of recognition and injustices of distribution (Fraser, 1997: chapter 1). Indeed, patterns of structural inequality frequently result from the interaction of these two forms of injustice.

The mutually reinforcing dynamics of material and cultural inequality clearly affect many immigrant groups, particularly those whose presence in the host country arose from foreign worker programmes aimed at filling employment categories that native citizens regarded as undesirable. To the extent that members of the majority are already inclined to bigotry and resentment against immigrants, they are encouraged by the fact that immigrants are often doing the work that they disdain. Such resentment becomes all the more intense during hard economic times, when the members of the majority hit bottom and resent immigrants for competing for scarce jobs. Both dynamics tend to create relations of hostility between majority and minority communities, leading the immigrant community to turn inward rather than fighting a losing battle for inclusion and respect. Such dynamics can also radicalize immigrant communities, encouraging them to define themselves in opposition to the majority rather than attempting to fit in as quietly and peacefully as possible. Thus, it does not take long for racism or other forms of bigotry to produce the dialectic of inclusion/separation that also tends to characterize the relationship between the dominant majority and groups that have been oppressed over a long history, such as African-Americans. These dynamics produce relations of mutual distrust, which severely undermine the prospects for shared citizenship and leave the minority community vulnerable to the majority's neglect or violation of their interests.

History plays an important role in the project of defining the groups whose moral claims are strongest, for several reasons. It is not accidental that the groups that are most profoundly disadvantaged in contemporary society have also been the subjects of legal exclusions from citizenship and state-sponsored discrimination. The causal connection between marginalized group identity and state-supported discrimination runs in both directions: the cultural stigmas that dominant groups have historically attached to marginalized group identity helped to sustain discriminatory practices; and those discriminatory practices have themselves been causally connected to the ongoing group-structured patterns of distributive inequality. The more egregious the historical forms of domination, and the deeper the history of inequality, the more firmly entrenched are patterns of both distributive and cultural inequality likely to be. Moreover, contemporary cultural injustice toward members of a marginalized group can often take the form of a public failure or refusal to acknowledge the injustice of a group's historical experience. Finally, the concept of structural inequality that constitutes a part of my definition of marginalized groups itself contains a temporal dimension, for it is difficult to determine whether patterns of group-structured inequality are both systemic and unjust unless they are reproduced over time (Williams, 1998: 16–8).

The temporal dimension of systemic inequality complicates the project of identifying the groups that should benefit from group-based programmes such as positive action. In particular, it makes it difficult to assess to what extent immigrant groups should be the targets of such programmes. Although immigrant communities are often overrepresented at the bottom of socioeconomic strata – as is the case, for example, for Pakistani immigrants to Britain, Algerians in France, and Turks in Germany – it is also true that these populations were not economically well off at the time of their immigration. It is therefore difficult to disaggregate causal factors in trying to account for persistent patterns of low socioeconomic status among immigrant groups, particularly when there is a continuing influx of relatively poor immigrants into the host country. In other words, although there may be sources of structural discrimination that perpetuate group-structured inequality intergenerationally, this would not be apparent simply from aggregate data showing that an immigrant group occupies a relatively low socioeconomic stratum over time. In addition to such aggregate data, it would be necessary to have data showing how second-

and third-generation immigrants fare relative to first-generation immigrants. If by the third generation there is not a significant improvement in the socioeconomic stratum of an immigrant group, it is reasonable to assume that at least one of the forms of discrimination is at work. If group-structured inequalities persist intergenerationally even after strong anti-discrimination policies have been legislated and enforced, it is highly probable that some form of structural discrimination exists.

In European societies whose anti-discrimination laws do not cover non-citizens, and where immigrants face barriers to citizenship into the third generation, it does not seem far-fetched to suppose that both direct and structural discrimination contribute to the relatively low socio-economic stratum of some immigrant groups. Once direct discrimination begins to create intergenerational patterns of disadvantage, it may be difficult to reverse these patterns quickly by anti-discrimination policies alone.

Beyond Formal Equality of Opportunity: the Varieties of Positive Action

When people criticize positive action policies, they usually have in mind the practice of 'preferential treatment', wherein individual candidates for employment or for university admission are given some preference over other candidates if they are women or members of a disadvantaged ethnic or 'racial' minority. As I will discuss below, critics of preferential treatment argue that it entails a sacrifice of the merit principle, which holds that individuals should be rewarded for their innate and developed abilities and talents, not for the fact that they happened to be born into this group rather than that one. They regard policies of preferential treatment for women and minority candidates as an undeserved reward for a birth-given trait, which compromises the performance of social and economic institutions by sacrificing high performance standards for the political goal of appeasing disgruntled groups.

But there is much more to positive action than preferential treatment. Indeed, many of the varieties of positive action are natural extensions of policies of equal opportunity and non-discrimination. Policies aimed at combating the exclusion of disadvantaged groups from full social participation stand on a continuum from formal policies of non-discrim-ination to preferential treatment, and it is useful to sketch some of the key points along this continuum. There is not a sharp divide between policies of equal opportunity and positive action; rather, taking equal opportunity seriously as a moral goal leads naturally toward positive action to overcome systemic racism and sexism. Let me briefly review some of the points on this continuum.

Active rather than Passive Equal Opportunity Policies

There are many jurisdictions where equal opportunity legislation is on the books, but where state authorities do not have strong enforcement mechanisms in place. The active enforcement of non-discrimination laws requires some monitoring agency with responsibility for keeping track of employers' hiring practices, accessible grievance processes for candidates who suspect they were discriminated against on grounds of sex or ethnicity, and a reliable system of redress for those who have suffered discrimination.

Bona Fide Occupational Qualifications

As I have already discussed, formally 'neutral' hiring policies may actually be biased toward certain groups because they include eligibility criteria that are not relevant to job performance and that some groups are more likely to meet than others. Policies and grievance procedures that recognize such criteria as a form of impermissible discrimination constitute a form of positive action against unjust exclusion.

Active Recruitment from Disadvantaged Groups

A policy of formal equality of opportunity does not, by itself, increase the representation of women and minorities in areas where they have traditionally been excluded. Employers' recruitment devices may be unconsciously biased against female and minority candidates. Even when non-discrimination requirements make clear that positions must be advertised in easily accessible public sources, and even where employers conform conscientiously to those requirements, personal connections and word-of-mouth publicity often have a tremendous impact on who applies for and is seriously considered for a job. These informal personal and social networks of recruitment are likely to include people who are demographically similar to the employer or recruitment officer. To compensate for the obvious group biases of such social networks, recruitment practices should include active efforts to find highly qualified women and minority candidates who would not be inclined to apply for positions without some special encouragement. Active recruitment policies include: advertising in publications that are aimed at the groups in question (women's newspapers, minority newspapers); using existing networks to get word-of-mouth information about the existence of qualified women and minority candidates; and actively contacting the institutions that train qualified candidates (vocational schools, universities, professional schools) to solicit the names of possible women and minority candidates.

Group-targeted Education and Training Programmes

Even stringently enforced non-discrimination requirements do not achieve genuine equality of opportunity in societies where individuals' life chances have been constricted by poverty or by membership in stigmatized social groups. A procedure that purports to treat all individuals alike will probably result in the success of the advantaged and the failure of the disadvantaged given equal levels of talent and ambition. Some positive action programmes attempt to address the problem of background inequality directly by providing special education or training programmes for disadvantaged groups.

None of these forms of positive action gives weight to a candidate's group identity at the stage of admissions or appointment. None of them involves any compromise with the principle of merit. To the contrary, all are aimed at removing obstacles to the recognition of appropriately qualified women and minority candidates. Yet all involve more than formal equality of opportunity; all involve some form of affirmative or positive action toward the goal of eliminating unfair disadvantage.

Preferential Treatment as a Species of Positive Action

The logic of preferential treatment follows the same logic as the preceding modes of positive action: that we cannot overturn long-standing and deeply entrenched patterns of inequality without active effort. Advocates of preferential treatment go a step further by arguing that non-discrimination, even if combined with the above forms of positive action, will not be sufficient to overturn these patterns in a reasonable amount of time. Preferential treatment rests on the view that non-discrimination policies would make disadvantaged citizens wait too long for unjust patterns of inequality to be reversed. Indeed, because of the intergenerational consequences of poverty and cultural marginalization, it is not clear that non-discrimination policies alone would ever reverse systemic inequality for marginalized groups.[6]

It is also important to recognize that policies of preferential treatment themselves admit of a great deal of variation, and that many forms of preferential treatment involve little or no tradeoff between the principle of merit and the goal of equality. Preferential treatment for disadvantaged groups, like positive action in general, can take different forms and follow a variety of decision rules, for example:

1. *The 'other things being equal' rule*
   When there are two candidates, one female or minority and the other male or white, and both are equally well qualified, one should choose – other things being equal – the woman or minority candidate. This policy requires absolutely no compromise with the merit principle. It is also vulnerable to the objection that other things are seldom equal, and that the subjectivity of judgements of qualification (including judgements about how well a person will 'fit in' with the existing institutional culture) is likely to benefit candidates from relatively advantaged groups.
2. *The high threshold of qualification rule*
   Among a pool of candidates who far surpass the minimum level of competence, choose the woman or minority candidate over the male or white candidate even if the latter has marginally better qualifications.
3. *The minimum threshold of qualification rule*
   Among a pool of candidates who meet the minimum level of competence, hire the woman or minority candidate over the male or the white candidate even if the latter has significantly better qualifications.

Positive action practices do not only vary according to the balance they strike between the merit principle and the goal of increased presence for women and minorities. They also vary in their approach to the question of numerical goals. Any of the merit-based decision rules can be combined with any of a variety of numerical goals for female and minority representation. These also stand on a continuum.

1. *Tokenism*
   Ensure that at least one woman or one minority member is selected.
2. *Proportionality to the recruitment pool*
   If women constitute only 20 per cent of the total population of qualified applicants for a position, then aim to fill 20 per cent of positions with women.
3. *Proportionality to the total population*
   If minorities constitute 25 per cent of the total population, aim to fill

25 per cent of positions with minorities, even if they constitute a smaller percentage of the recruitment pool. This policy obviously expresses a more ambitious positive action policy than the preceding one.

Further, each of these numerical goals can be pursued either as a target or as a quota – as an aspiration of the appointment policy, or as a rigid requirement. Finally, these numerical goals can aim either at marginal equality (of x number of positions to be filled in a given year, 25 per cent will be minorities), or at global equality (of x number of positions in an institution, only women will be hired until 50 per cent of positions are held by women, and thereafter half of all new positions will be awarded to men, half to women).[7]

Although critics of positive action often suggest that it means hiring unqualified women or minority candidates instead of qualified male or white candidates, that is a caricature of preferential policies. None of these policies sacrifices the merit principle altogether. Indeed, if preferential treatment programmes did lead to the selection of candidates who are simply unequipped to handle the challenges of their position – if students admitted under these policies failed out of programmes at a high rate, or if positive action professional school students regularly failed the bar exam or the medical board exams, or if people hired under these policies regularly failed to perform their jobs competently – then the policies serve very little constructive social purpose. Setting women and minorities up for failure is not a good way to overcome systemic discrimination.

Once we take the elimination of structural discrimination as a valid social goal, we may begin to question conventional, difference-blind criteria of merit. The problematic character of conventional standards of merit becomes clearer when we turn to address some of the more common critiques of positive action.

Objections to Positive Action

Positive Action Constitutes Reverse Discrimination and Punishes Innocents

Given democratic societies' commitment to the ideal of individual equality, any policy that allocates benefits on the basis of group membership is suspect. The strong critic of positive action would reject even those versions of it that do not trade off group equality against the merit principle, since those programmes do undertake a redistribution of resources based on group membership. But preferential treatment receives the strongest criticism: that preferences for 'racial' minorities are morally indistinguishable from active discrimination against them. Preferential treatment, critics argue, simply reverses the direction of racial discrimination, and now benefits minorities at the expense of whites rather than benefiting whites at the expense of minorities.

This argument is politically ascendant in North America. Yet it is based on a series of conceptual errors. Consider first the critics of positive action who argue that it punishes innocents (for example whites who are not racists and who had no role in creating the structures that marginalize others) or rewards non-victims (such as minorities who come from middle-class backgrounds and so have not suffered severe inequality). Despite the fact that structural discrimination often has its roots in historical injustice, the strongest argument for positive action, in my view, rests on its capacity to combat the unintentional reproduction of unjust inequalities. It rests most soundly on a forward-looking, not a backward-looking conception of democratic equality. The aim of preferential treatment is not to assign blame for past wrongs, but to ensure that past wrongs do not continue to generate injustice in the present and in the future.

The second conceptual error of the 'reverse discrimination' argument turns on its understanding of merit (see especially Young, 1990: chapter 7). These critics assume that there are clear and objective standards of merit, such as standardized tests and grade point averages, which ought to be the sole criteria according to which candidates are chosen. But as a matter of fact, many institutions used far more nuanced judgements of merit in making their selections. For medical school, for example, admissions committees might well pay attention to a student's interpersonal skills as well as his/her academic record in choosing between him/her and another student with a comparable record. They might also attend to applicants' geographic roots as part of an effort to make sure that certain areas receive adequate medical service. It is not difficult to see how, within such a process, a candidate's ethnicity might be highly relevant to the committee's decision. There are many circumstances in which a candidate's group identity might be a directly relevant component of her overall qualifications, if membership in a group would enable him/her to serve members of that community more effectively. The social purposes served by training minority candidates is not only that it improves service delivery to minority communities, but also that in doing so it helps to reduce their social and cultural marginalization.

If it is true that positive action policies do ameliorate structural inequality, then the arguments about 'reverse discrimination' appear in a very different light. In the absence of programmes aimed at overcoming barriers to equal participation, we can expect that members of marginalized groups will not be able to compete effectively with members of relatively privileged groups, even where formal equality of opportunity is in place. In the absence of positive action, then, members of relatively privileged groups are effectively shielded from the competition of members of marginalized groups. The obverse of unjust negative bias is unjust privilege. The concern with 'reverse discrimination' expresses settled expectations and a sense of entitlement to scarce social goods. It recognizes an increase in vulnerability that comes from having to compete with those who were not in the competition pool before. It undermines the sense of security that comes from having group ownership over scarce social resources. The consequence of dismantling unjust inequality is that unjust privilege will fall. That consequence is never popular with the privileged. In order to accept it, they must both acknowledge the injustice of their privilege and accept a world in which that privilege disappears. Neither comes easily to the human psyche.

I do wish to make clear that I am not rejecting the principle of procedural equality for individuals as an important element of justice. It certainly has its place in the construction of fair democratic institutions.[8] Let me just reiterate that the problem with difference-blind proceduralism (like equal opportunity doctrine) in a world that contains structural discrimination is that it will reproduce unjust inequalities. Tempering the merit principle with a group-conscious policy aimed at overcoming structural injustice does not entail an abandonment of the principle of individual equality; it aims to realize that principle in a manner that is sensitive to both history and context.

Positive Action Intensifies Intergroup Conflict

The second major category of objections to positive action policies rests on the claim that they exacerbate rather than alleviate intergroup hostility. There are two basic species of this argument. The first is that by conferring benefits on the basis of group identity, positive action reinforces the very group classifications whose relevance they aim to eradicate. The presupposition of this argument is that if only we treated individuals as individuals, and not as members of this or that social group, then group identity would soon become irrelevant as a source of inequality. Policies that give explicit recognition to group identity, critics argue, recreate group difference and create incentives for individuals to assert group-based claims. It is illogical, they suggest, to use group classifications in public policy when the explicit aim of such policies is to ensure that individuals' life chances are not limited by their membership in these groups. Difference-blind policies, on this view, are the only rationally consistent strategy for eradicating group disadvantage.

The fallacy in this argument is the supposition that difference-blind policies will lead to difference-neutral social practices and processes. As I have argued above, the concept of structural discrimination rests on the very sensible claim that there are deeply entrenched social practices that reproduce group-structured inequality even in the absence of intentional discrimination. In the face of such practices, difference-blind policies reproduce systemic inequality along group lines. Critics mistake the effect for the cause when they argue that group-conscious policies generate group divisions in society. Group-based policies do not generate group-structured inequality; they are designed to combat already-existing differences. The second species of the critique of group-based policies focuses on the perceived dangers of 'balkanization'. Its proponents argue that the very diversity and number of groups that might make claims based on past discrimination is likely to strain government's capacity to cope with the competing demands (see for example Glazer, 1981: 22).

'Balkanization' arguments shift moral responsibility for political stability onto the shoulders of the marginalized groups who wish to make justice claims: if destabilizing political conflict ensues from their claims, they ought not to make those claims. The only public good this argument recognizes is the good of stability; it leaves the good of justice out of the picture altogether. In doing so it fails to discriminate just from unjust group-based claims for recognition, and tars them all with the same brush. Consequently, arguments about 'balkanization' close off inquiry into the normative merits of group claims before it has even begun.

In any event I believe that the fear of 'balkanization' as a product of positive action is often misplaced. If we take seriously the criteria for identifying the groups that should benefit from positive action policies, then it is simply not the case that the number of such groups is limitless. We can make judgements about the relative strength of different groups' claims to recognition, as indeed I believe we do all the time. Implicit in the 'balkanization' argument is the fear that recognizing any group's claims as valid will convey the message that marginalized groups' interpretations of the causes of inequality would somehow be privileged. But arguments about the existence of structural inequalities must be made to, and accepted by others, based on evidence they could reasonably accept. Although members of marginalized groups have a strong claim to be heard and taken seriously in the public sphere, this does not mean that their voices are the final authority on what justice requires – any more than the self-proclaimed victim of 'reverse discrimination' can claim the authoritative interpretation of the requirements of justice.

Positive Action Stigmatizes the Groups it Intends to Benefit

A third argument against positive action is that, by requiring lower standards of women or minorities (which, as we have seen above, it does not necessarily do), it reinforces negative group stereotypes and lowers self-esteem within targeted groups (Carter, 1991; Steele, 1994: 41; Loury, 1995: 117–32). These arguments, however, are speculative; they are not grounded in empirical study. Indeed, some empirical studies that have examined the consequences of affirmative action for perceptions of group members' capacities have found that these perceptions are not more negative in institutions that pursue policies of affirmative action (Winkelman, Crosby and Cohen, 1994). Moreover, cultural stigma is one of the contributing causes of systemic inequality; it is not sensible to assume that it will disappear if we abandon affirmative action (Lawrence and Matsuda, 1997: 127). Too often, I believe, North American opponents of affirmative action use it as a post hoc explanation for already-existing group stigmas.

Conclusion

To assess positive action in a clear-eyed manner, we need answers to many empirical questions. At one level, I agree with critics that if positive action policies truly did benefit only the already-well-off members of disadvantaged groups; if it did not yield positions for individuals who are economically as well as culturally disadvantaged, at least in the long run; if it did not help to overcome and redefine cultural expectations about marginalized group members' capacities – then it has no place among the tools of social justice. But existing social science evidence does not support these claims. To the contrary, it sustains the conviction that positive action policies really do increase the number of women and minorities in spheres of education and employment from which they were all but absent thirty or forty years ago; that their presence has helped to change cultural beliefs about the capacities of these groups; that there is little or no empirical evidence to sustain the claim that positive action increases group stigma or diminishes group members' self-esteem; and that, as it has been practised, positive action seldom entails overriding merit criteria.[9]

Notes

1. I am grateful for the research assistance of Benjamin Moerman and the comments and suggestions of Rainer Bauböck, Eugene Sensenig, and Frank Cunningham. None of them, of course, should be held responsible for any flaws in what I have written here. Portions of this chapter are drawn from earlier work (see especially Williams, 1998 and Carens and Williams, 1996).
2. Throughout this chapter, I use the term 'positive action' to designate policies aimed at overcoming the underrepresentation of disadvantaged groups in employment. I use the term 'affirmative action' to designate North American programmes aimed at overcoming the underrepresentation of such groups in the spheres of both employment and education.
3. I am grateful to Benjamin Moerman for prodding me to consider this point.
4. SOPEMI's 1996 Annual Report indicates that the flow of 'third country' nationals into Europe under guest worker programmes has virtually ceased; most such immigration now stems from family reunification policies. Moreover, the movement of 'third country' immigrant populations between European countries also seems to be slowing (SOPEMI, 1997: 13).
5. Antonin Scalia's opinion in *City of Richmond v. J.A. Croson Co.* (1989), is a model of the second of these rhetorical strategies.
6. For a more detailed discussion of these and related arguments, see Gutmann and Thompson, 1996: 319–22.
7. On the distinction between marginal and global equality, see Rae, 1981.
8. I discuss this point at some length in Williams, 1998: 19–22.
9. See, for example, Bowen and Bok, 1998; Plous, 1996; Lawrence and Matsuda, 1997: 152; Montgomery, 1996; Herring and Collins, 1995; Winkelman, et al., 1994.

–5–

Affirmative Action in the US:
the Legal Dimension
Luisa Antoniolli Deflorian

The long series of civil rights statutes in the last century and a quarter are about one thing: as Justice Marshall would say, they are not about charity; they are about opening doors. (R.D. Rotunda).

Introduction

All Western countries have experienced, although with different timing, the recognition of minorities' and women's rights as part of the implementation of a general principle of equality, and all of them have gradually moved from a conception of formal equality to one of substantive equality. This means that while law initially strove to eliminate all rules that treated differently people belonging to various groups, lawyers later developed the idea that in order to provide real equality for all there was a need to devise different legal standards.

The former kind of action posed major difficulties from a political and social point of view, because it implied the removal of deeply rooted social practices that also had significant economic consequences. However, it did not raise severe legal problems: once equality had been established, it followed automatically that all rules discriminating without special justification were unlawful and had therefore to be eliminated. The shift to a substantive idea of equality was much more problematic from a legal point of view: it required a step to be taken beyond formal equality, and the recognition of the existing imbalance in order to devise legal solutions that would redress it. Law thus had to analyse and estimate such extra-legal factors as social practice, economic conditions, diversity, and many more, in order to provide legal solutions able to take all of these factors into account and be fair and balanced. Not only was this technically more difficult, it was also much more controversial, as there may be widely diverging evaluations of the existing situations and therefore of the remedies needed. Nevertheless, no matter how difficult the implementation of substantive equality may be, it is nowadays widely recognized that formal equality is not sufficient to attain fairness.

The constitutional rights to equality are formed by two different kinds of rights: the first is the 'right to equal treatment', 'which is the right to an equal distribution of some opportunity or resource or burden' (Dworkin, 1987: 227); the second is the 'right to treatment as an equal', which is

> the right not to receive the same distribution of some burden or benefit, but to be treated with the same respect and concern as anyone else. . . . In some circumstances the right to treatment as an equal will entail a right to equal treatment, but not, by any means, in all circumstances (Dworkin, 1987: 227).

Of course, the application of this second kind of right to equality is more complex and controversial, because it goes beyond mere formal criteria, trying to reach substantial equality.

The Origin of Affirmative Action in the US

Affirmative action first appeared on the American scene in the 1960s and 1970s, and it was initially devised in order to tackle 'race' discrimination (Farber, 1994).

To outline a story that would need, because of its complexity and importance, much deeper analysis: the turning point was marked by the desegregation policy pursued from the 1950s onwards by both the federal government and the federal courts, which finally recognized that, in spite of the letter of the Constitution, the black population was severely discriminated against in numerous fields, like education, housing and job recruitment (Glazer, 1987). This change of political and legal attitude engendered a widespread review of existing legislation in the light of the principle of equality, and led to the elimination of doctrines such as the 'separate but equal' principle that discriminated among citizens on no other ground than 'race'. Involved at this stage, therefore, was the application of the equality principle in its formal sense and the most controversial and sensitive aspects were not legal, but mainly political, social, and economic. This is the environment where the famous desegregation cases were decided, like *Brown v. Board of Education* (1954),[1] which not only had an enormous impact on the social patterns of the country (Mattei, 1992), but also marked a watershed in the attitude of government towards discrimination that led to very important developments (Dworkin, 1986), like the Civil Rights Act 1964.

As in other forms of centuries-long segregation, which have slowly become part of the lifestyles and culture of the people, restoration of formal equality was not enough to ensure a just and fair share in social life for previously discriminated groups. Although a black could not be officially excluded because of the colour of his/her skin, there were few blacks who managed to build successful careers, or to gain admission to prestigious universities. The long history of segregation had created social conditions that hindered integration even when legal obstacles were removed. The historical context where affirmative actions were introduced is one of persistent racial segregation, where the black minority, and other ethnic groups as well (such as native Americans, Hispanics and Asians), were systematically excluded from an active and rich society.

The situation of crisis and social unrest that arose in the 1960s convinced the ruling class that something more was required in order to avoid the threat of racial violence, new solutions that would positively enhance the chances of minorities achieving equal results. Affirmative action started in this period, when the federal government introduced plans designed to increase the participation by minorities in traditionally segregated sectors, like in the Philadelphia Plan 1967, which aimed at remedying to the widespread discriminating behaviours in the construction industry. This instrument caused strong dissent and resistance, so much that in the end it was dropped by the Johnson administration. The plan was resurrected by the Republican Nixon administration against strong internal dissent; this choice is probably due both to the fear of increasing social disorders and to political tactics (the move led to a split between the white and the black electorate, pushing some of the white liberals towards the Republican party). The mechanism spread to state and local agencies as well, and to a variety of new fields (such as job recruitment, promotion and training). Nevertheless, the idea of affirmative action has been controversial since its first appearance on the legal scene, and there has always been controversy over its constitutionality and its capacity to generate significant social improvements (Abram, 1986; Kennedy, 1986). Today, after more than three decades, the debate is as fierce as ever (Bowen and Bok, 1998), and there are signs that a revision may eventually lead to a severe limitation, if not to the elimination, of the admissibility of affirmative action (Symposium, 1995). It is extremely hard to separate the purely political aspects of this struggle from the legal standards, because the two appear to be closely intertwined. If there is a lesson to be drawn from the American experience, with all its complexity, it seems to be that even when discrimination is openly acknowledged, it is extremely hard to find consensus on the course of action to be taken, and on the standards and principles that should guide it.[2]

The Institutional Framework

Affirmative action is based in the US system mainly on six legal instruments: the constitutional provisions concerning due process and equal protection (fifth and fourteenth amendments); section 1981 of the Civil Rights Act 1886; Title VII of the Civil Rights Act 1964 and the amendments made to it by the Civil Rights Act 1991; Executive Order 11246 (1965).

Fifth and Fourteenth Amendments of the US Constitution

The fifth and fourteenth amendments of the American Constitution establish the fundamental right to due process and equal protection (Cohen and Varat, 1997: 607ff.); this refers to a complex concept, which points not only to procedural regularity, but also to the conformity to general principles of law (Mattei, 1996: 75–7). The fifth amendment concerns federal action, providing that 'No person shall . . . be deprived of life, liberty, or property, without due process of law.' The fourteenth amendment, introduced in the aftermath of the Civil War,[3] concerns state action, and it is formulated in a slightly different way: 'No State shall . . . deprive any person of life, liberty, or property, without due process of the law; nor deny any person within its jurisdiction of the equal protection of the laws'. The addition of the 'equal protection of the law' clause has led the judges to consider for a long time that the standards of control were different for federal and state action, the latter being more stringent. Starting from the 1950s the courts have changed their position, and for reasons of coherence and legal certainty have used common standards for federal and state action, both being expressions of the same principle.[4]

Section 1981 of the Civil Rights Act 1886

Following the abolition of slavery after the Civil War, Congress enacted legislation in order to ensure basic rights to the new American citizens, like the right to own property and to make contracts. Section 1981 provides that all persons have 'the same right . . . to make and enforce contracts . . . as is enjoyed by white citizens'. The US Supreme Court has interpreted this provision as prohibiting all kinds of race discrimination in the employment contract, as well as in other contracts, both in the private and in the public sector.

According to the Court, section 1981 provides independent protection from race discrimination from Title VII of the Civil Rights Act 1964, and their procedures and remedies are therefore autonomous.

Title VII of the Civil Rights Act 1964

The Civil Rights Act 1964 is the result of different bills proposed to Congress the year before,[5] and it is composed of several titles covering widely different areas such as voting rights, access to public facilities and accommodation, education, discrimination in federally assisted programmes.[6]

The enforcement of the statute is assigned to the Equal Employment Opportunity Commission (EEOC). The EEOC is an independent commission composed by five people appointed by the President, and it works through several district offices. It also enforces the Americans with Disabilities Act 1990, which protects disabled people from discrimination in work and other aspects of daily life; the Age Discrimination in Employment Act 1967, which, mirroring the language of Title VII, protects the workers over the age of forty from discrimination in all conditions of employment, and the Equal Pay Act 1963. A General Counsel represents the EEOC in litigation. The commission adopts rules for processing complaints, interpretative guidelines (which are published in the Code of Federal Regulations – CFR), policy statements, statistical reporting and record-keeping requirements. An aggrieved worker can file a charge alleging discrimination to one of its district offices, which will conduct an investigation and undertake, if it finds discriminatory behaviour, the conciliation of the parties. If this fails, the EEOC can file a suit in the courts, but it is not compelled to do so (and in this case the aggrieved party can decide to file a private suit). In the case of federal employers the EEOC works as appellate tribunal for the decisions taken by the federal agencies themselves (Player, Shoben and Lieberwitz, 1995: 47–8).

Section 703 (a) of the 1964 Act prohibits any kind of discrimination in the workplace based on race, colour, religion, sex,[7] national origin by employers, labour organizations and employment agencies.[8] Discrimination is banned in all aspects of the employment relationship, like hiring, discharging, or compensation (Player, Shoben and Lieberwitz, 1995: 23).

Section 703 (j) states that the law does not require any preferential treatment based on these elements. This rule might be read to imply a ban on affirmative action, but the Supreme Court has generally read it as permitting, rather than as imposing, such action.[9] This reading is based on a historical and contextual construction of the statute, which was passed expressly to remedy deep-rooted discrimination against some racial minorities, especially the black: it seems illogical to exclude a priori the actions that aim at remedying exactly the same problem targeted by the statute.

Section 706 (g) grants to the district courts the power to fashion 'equitable relief as the courts deems appropriate', and this provision is interpreted to mean that the courts can also force an affirmative action plan on a discriminating employer.

Civil Rights Act 1991

The amendments to the Civil Rights Act passed in 1991 (Rotunda, 1993; Blumrosen, 1993) are the legislative response to a series of Supreme Court decisions of the late 1980s that interpreted employment discrimination statutes in a very narrow way, together with some changes to provisions that showed various shortcomings.[10]

Section 106 states that it is illegal to alter the scores or to otherwise alter the results in the selection on candidates for hiring or promotion according to race, colour, religion, sex, or national origin. Such a rule makes it harder to create and implement job-related affirmative action plans, since those are often based on a different evaluation of minority candidates that would be eliminated by a formally neutral selection.

Section 107 further declares the illegality of hiring motivated by factors connected to race, colour, religion, sex or national origin, even if they are combined with other elements of selection. The reach of this provision is even wider, because it also strikes down those affirmative action plans that balance 'discriminating' factors with 'meritocratic' elements. Nevertheless, there remains one leeway: the section opens with 'If not otherwise provided by this title', and section 116 expressly provides that the amendments introduced by the 1991 Act to the original Civil Rights Act must not be interpreted in a way that may interfere with judicial remedies, affirmative action, or consent decrees that are in accordance with the law. Clearly, there are some inconsistencies in the statute and these are reflected in uncertainties and difficulties in their interpretation.

Other provisions limit the use of affirmative action: section 101 (b) expressly applies section 1981 (which prohibits discrimination in contracts) to all aspects concerning the employment relationship. Section 102 introduces the jury and punitive damages in Title VII litigation, and this is a drifting mine, because it poses an element of uncertainty and risk that is likely to increase litigation, thereby discouraging the use of affirmative action.[11] Section 108 counterbalances these changes by limiting the types of actions that may be brought against measures implementing judicial consent decrees; particularly, if a class action ends with a consent decree, this cannot be appealed by individuals who had notice of the content of the decree, or by those who were sufficiently represented in other action taken against it.

The recent amendments to the Civil Rights Act have a substantial impact on the use and the content of affirmative action. It is therefore surprising that during parliamentary debates there was no special discussion on the bearing of the new rules on affirmative action; on the contrary, it was said that they would not impinge on them (Rotunda, 1993: 952). This is probably due to the use of an extremely narrow concept of affirmative action, limited to rigid plans fixing quotas and divided selecting criteria (Nager, 1993; Rotunda, 1993: 1057–60, 1089–94). It seems clear, though, that the reach of the statute is much wider, pointing to a general trend that limits the admissibility of affirmative action.

This restrictive trend has been confirmed by the approval in California in the November 1996 ballot (together with the Presidential election) of an initiative, the so-called Proposition 209, amending the Californian Constitution in order to abolish public affirmative action programmes – any programme by the state, cities, counties, public University system, school districts and any other political or governmental subdivision concerning public employment, public education and public contracting.[12] This extremely controversial issue is on the floor also at the federal level, where a Bill named the Civil Rights Restoration Act 1999 is pending before Congress; its aim is to make preferential treatment an unlawful employment practice.[13]

Executive Order 11246

Executive Order 11246 is the only general statutory provision that expressly provides for the use of affirmative action: all the provisions that we have analysed, in fact, are concerned primarily with equality, and they therefore might also be read as banning any kind of discrimination, even benign discrimination.[14]

The first version of the order dates back to 1964, when the Johnson administration pushed for a global plan in order to guarantee the participation to social and economic life of citizens belonging to minority groups. Executive Order 11246 (which was later amended by Executive Order 11375) requires employers who are public contractors or subcontractors not to discriminate, and to undertake affirmative action plans in order that ensure that the selection and the working conditions are not influenced by race, colour, religion, sex, or national origin.

The implementation and enforcement of the executive order is delegated to the Office of Federal Contract Compliance Plans (OFCCP), which is part of the Labor Department. The OFCCP has issued regulations, which define affirmative action plans and establish the procedures for their creation and application. These instruments are the affirmative action plans (AAP), laying down the goals for hiring and promotions, a timetable with intermediate annual goals (which can also fix express hiring ratios) and the criteria for the evaluation of the progress made. They must be adopted after a workforce analysis; if this signals the underutilization of women or minorities as compared to their availability in the area job market, a written plan must be submitted. The plan does not establish a legal obligation for the employer to reach the results, but it imposes a bona fide obligation on him to pursue them. Individuals do not have a private right of judicial action based on EO 11246, because the affirmative action obligations arise from the contract between the employer and the federal government. Workers can obtain redress against violations only by invoking internal administrative proceedings by the Department of Labor, which may cancel the agreement or bar the employer from future contracts with the federal government.

Following the 1995 decision of the US Supreme Court in *Adarand*, which has mandated very strict standards for affirmative action, the Clinton administration has reviewed all affirmative action programmes, in order to ensure that they comply with the new rule, following the strategy 'mend it, don't end it'.[15] This review has led to numerous important modifications in several federal departments, but has nevertheless kept the basic structure of the instrument (Leadership Conference on Civil Rights Online Center, July 1997), in contrast to some Bills pending in Congress that seek to eliminate it.

The Judicial Input

In the US courts and the federal Supreme Court in particular play an extremely important role, being one of the leading formants that shape the existing legal system (Mattei, 1996: 66–9; Sacco, 1991). This is also true in the field of affirmative action, and we therefore need to analyse its case law, as well as some cases decided by the US Courts of Appeals, in order to verify its evolution and impact (Antoniolli Deflorian, 1997).

Education

One of the first relevant cases decided by the US Supreme Court in the field of affirmative action, *Regents of California v. Bakke* (1978), concerned an affirmative action plan for university admission (Dworkin, 1986; Nicolodi, 1994).[16]

Right from these initial cases the Supreme Court has adopted diverging criteria for evaluation, and this divergence remains even today. In fact, the *Bakke* decision contains three different rules: according to the first, the affirmative action plan was contrary to Title VII of the Civil Rights Act, and therefore there was no need to analyse the constitutional aspects.

For the second one, affirmative action is constitutionally legitimate if it remedies previous discrimination and pursues socially useful purposes; the validity of affirmative action is scrutinized through an intermediate standard, which requires an important and articulated benign purpose.

Finally, the third one, proposed by Justice Powell, states that, being discriminatory, it is constitutionally permissible only if it remedies a specific discrimination by the defendant; the fourteenth amendment protects individuals, not groups, therefore the evaluation of affirmative action must concern the position of the plaintiff and the defendant of every single case; besides, affirmative action must correspond to a compelling governmental or state interest. These stringent requirements are known as strict scrutiny test. In spite of these narrow criteria, in the specific case of University admission Justice Powell thought that the aim of guaranteeing an ethnically diverse student population justifies such measures, provided that they do not fix rigid quotas, but evaluate the 'race' element together with all other relevant elements.[17]

The decision has a hybrid nature, because on one hand it holds affirmative action theoretically constitutional under certain conditions, but these conditions are not univocal; on the other hand, the programme under scrutiny is rejected, because Powell's negative position cumulates with the opinions of those Justices who consider affirmative action contrary to the Civil Rights Act. The decision therefore contains diverging views that will later reappear, thereby seriously weakening the legitimacy of affirmative action (Posner, 1979); in fact, *Bakke* will later be used both in support and against them, by using the different opinions of the Justices.

The *Bakke* ruling has been called into question by a recent decision of the US Court of Appeals for the fifth circuit (*Hopwood*), which has invoked the use of the strict scrutiny to affirmative action programmes connected to university admission, and has rejected the aim of a diverse student population as a legitimate ground for action (Dworkin, 1998: 56 ff.).[18]

Another controversial aspect concerns the distinction between 'equality of opportunity' and 'equality of results'. In order to decide whether the programme was lawful, the Supreme Court had to analyse its goals. But is admission to a prestigious university an opportunity or a result? As regards the chances of building a career, it is merely an opportunity:

entering a good university enhances one's chances of finding a good job. On the other hand, as regards education, entering a prestigious university is a result, which presupposes a difficult process leading up to it. If the decision depends on the classification of university admission as an opportunity or as a result, then the result turns simply on how you look at it, as a starting point, or as a point of arrival. This hardly seems a suitable criterion, since it provides little guidance for the interpreter, and generates greater uncertainty, rather than clarifying the object of the analysis.

The point is illustrated by the landmark decision by the Supreme Court, *Brown v. Board of Education* (1954). In the case, the first in which racial segregation was declared unconstitutional, the Court expressly viewed education as an essential opportunity for every American citizen:

> Today, education is perhaps the most important function of state and local governments . . . . It is a principal instrument in awakening the child to cultural values preparing him for later professional training . . . . In these days it is doubtful that any child may reasonably be expected to succeed in life if he is denied the opportunity of an education (Brown decision, 1954: 493).

The reasoning is equally forceful if applied to university education, but one could take the argument even further, and use it in professional training, or even in job recruiting.

In *Hopwood et al. v. State of Texas et al.* (1996) the Court of Appeals has declared the *Bakke* decision no longer valid law, and has struck down a special admission programme of the University of Texas Law School, which until 1992 sought to ensure the presence of racial minorities (particularly students of black and Hispanic origin) in its student population. The rule is not yet finally settled, since the Supreme Court has refused to grant certiorari; nevertheless, this is a clear sign that affirmative action is currently under fire not only in the sector of job recruitment and promotion, but even in a sector in which it has been traditionally (even if conditionally) considered lawful, namely university admission programmes.

The Court of Appeals has considered this programme contrary to the equal protection clause of the fourteenth amendment and to Title VII of the Civil Rights Act 1964: the aim of guaranteeing the presence of minority students in the Texas education system, and through it a diverse student population, is not a compelling public interest. According to it, universities can use several elements in their selection processes, including 'race', but they cannot give general preference to a whole ethnic group, because this amounts to a discriminatory behaviour. Besides, the aim of the action could not be defined as a remedy for past discrimination against those groups: the Court thought that actual discrimination by the acting entity be proved, and this proof was lacking in the case.[19]

This decision is particularly important, because it could be read as an anticipatory overruling of the Supreme Court decision in *Bakke*. It has been severely criticized by many, and in an opinion of April 4, 1996, sixteen of the seventeen justices working in the fifth circuit of the US Court of Appeals have autonomously considered if it was necessary to review the case *en banc*;[20] finally they decided not to, but it is clear that they considered the point as extremely controversial and problematic.

The decision was later appealed by the Texas Attorney General to the US Supreme Court, which has denied certiorari; it seems that the Supreme Court has used one of the doctrines of justiciability, mootness (Cohen and Varat, 1997: 106–12; Mattei, 1992: 206–10), in order to avoid deciding a case that it considered too 'hot' from a political point of view.[21]

Bakke still remains the leading case of the highest American court concerning affirmative action in university admission procedures, but clearly the legal context surrounding it has changed significantly: by now it stands as an isolated stronghold for affirmative action, with an uncertain destiny: the effect of the *Hopwood* decision has been that many universities have eliminated affirmative action plans for student admission, and consequently the number of minority students has dramatically decreased in the last years. 'It will be not only ironic but sad if the Court reverses its own longstanding ruling now, because dramatic evidence of the value of affirmative action in elite higher education has just become available', Dworkin states, referring to the pathbreaking work by Bowen and Bok (1998), full of statistical data that demonstrate the remarkable success of affirmative action in selective higher education (Dworkin, 1998: 56).

Employment

In 1979, one year after *Bakke*, the Supreme Court decided its first case on affirmative action in the field of labour. *United Steelworkers v. Weber* (1979) concerned the compatibility with Title VII of the Civil Rights Act 1964 of a plan instituted thorough collective agreement by a private employer and a local trade union in order to remedy a situation of serious discrimination against black workers.[22] The majority opinion, written by Justice Brennan, held that the aim of the plan was identical to that of the Civil Rights Act, since both aimed at eliminating racial segregation. The primary criterion for evaluation of the legitimacy of affirmative action consists in checking if they provide for equal opportunities and eliminate a situation of disparity. According to the Court, proof of a specific discriminatory behaviour by the person or the entity who sets up the programme would be too complex and rigid, and the risk of increased litigation might frustrate the use of the instrument.

Thereafter the Supreme Court had to scrutinize an affirmative action programme that was set up by Congress. In *Fullilove v. Klutznick* (1980) the decision turned on the compatibility of the Public Works Employment Act 1977[23] with the fifth amendment. The Court held the Act to be constitutional, because its cost-benefit analysis was positive: the white-owned enterprises have worse chances, but this burden is relatively light if confronted with the general positive effects that the plan has for minority enterprises and, through them, for the whole American society.

It must be noted that this analysis, although it solves favourably the case at hand, creates a new standard for the evaluation of the legitimacy of affirmative action: it implies that if so-called 'reverse discrimination' has serious effects on non-minority individuals it may be unconstitutional. As we shall see, the balancing criterion will be used in the first cases where the Supreme Court will invalidate affirmative action programmes. *Fullilove*, nevertheless, merely proposes this standard, without clarifying what kind of sacrifices and benefits will pass scrutiny.[24]

The presence of serious and persistent voluntary discrimination seems to be the deciding element of an important decision of the Supreme Court in *Local 28, Sheet Metal Workers' Intern. Ass'n v. Equal Employment Opportunity Commission* (1986). The case concerned the denial by a local workers' union in the metal and mechanical industry to accept black and Hispanic workers as members. This denial had serious consequences, because the union organized for its members training courses that were necessary in order to get qualified jobs in the area, and in that way minorities were substantially excluded from the local work market. The case was taken repeatedly to court, but the union stubbornly refused to abide by the decision, and was twice condemned for contempt of court. When it finally reached the Supreme Court, it recognized affirmative action as an instrument necessary to remedy continuous and wilful discrimination, as mere removal of the obstacles would not be sufficient to provide equal opportunities for all 'racial' groups. In this case the decisive element is the seriousness and wilfulness of the discriminatory behaviour, and the consequent remedial character of the affirmative action plan.

Among the various kinds of behaviour that are combated by affirmative action, particularly important are the limitations of career opportunities of minority workers. In *Vanguards* (*Local No. 93, International Association of Firefighters v. City of Cleveland* (1986)) the Court has considered compatible with Title VII of the Civil Rights Act a consent decree that imposed that for a limited period of time, part of the promotions should be reserved for minority workers, in order to remedy past discriminatory behaviour by the employer (the municipal fire brigade of Cleveland). The decision is in favour of the plan, even though it is clear that in this case the beneficiaries were not directly affected by past discrimination, i.e. even if the plan was not strictly compensatory.

The same pattern was followed by the Supreme Court in another case, *United States v. Paradise* (1987),[25] where the compatibility of an affirmative action plan in promotions for minority workers with the fourteenth amendment was established even if the beneficiaries were selected on the basis of their racial origin, and not because they were recognized as direct victims of past discrimination.[26]

Affirmative Action and Women

Although the instrument of affirmative action was first developed in the US in order to remedy racial discrimination, by providing better opportunities for blacks and other ethnic groups, when the feminist movement started during the 1970s it appeared that this mechanism could be fruitfully used to enhance the position and chances of women, too.[27] The extension of its use to this new sector was controversial, but the first, and hitherto only, case to come before the Supreme Court dates back to 1986: in *Johnson v. Transportation Agency, Santa Clara County* (1987), the Court had to decide on the lawfulness of a voluntarily adopted affirmative action plan for hiring and promoting minorities and women. When a vacancy was announced, several people applied. The board decided to promote a female applicant, even though her score was slightly lower than that of a male applicant, expressly stating that sex was one among several criteria taken into account. On review, the Court decided that the selection was lawful on several grounds: first, the plan took a moderate, flexible, case-by-case approach in order to improve women's representation in the work force; secondly, the plan did not fix rigid quotas reserved for women, merely setting goals that should be achieved with flexibility, and therefore the encroachment on the legitimate expectations of other employees was limited and acceptable.[28]

The majority opinion does not mark any structural difference between racial and sex discrimination, because both are concerned with unlawful marginalization, and therefore they should be submitted to the same kind of scrutiny (Rosenfeld, 1991: 198–204).

It is important to note that in deciding this case the Supreme Court relied on a precedent, *Weber*, where the standards for judging the admissibility of affirmative action plans was the existence of a conspicuous imbalance in traditionally segregated areas. Other important decisions by the Court, starting with Justice Powell's opinion in *Bakke*, make use of the much tighter standard of the strict scrutiny test, under which affirmative actions are justified only if they redress an actual prior discriminatory practice in favour of people actually discriminated against (i.e. if they are strictly compensatory), if they correspond to a compelling public interest, and if the remedy is narrowly tailored to furtherance of that interest. In recent times the Court has moved back to the use of a strict scrutiny standard, rendering proof of a legitimate use of affirmative action much harder to provide.

If we compare the *Johnson* decision to a case concerning the same issue by the European Court of Justice (*Kalauke* in 1995) the most striking difference seems to derive from the standards used to evaluate the lawfulness of affirmative action. Both systems recognize that affirmative action constitutes a departure from the fundamental principle of formal equality, and therefore both require some further justifying elements, but Community law has devoted less attention to the characteristics of discrimination that requires the use of affirmative action. This might partly be due to the fact that tackling discrimination against several racial groups, with widely different problems and needs, requires greater sophistication and complexity of analysis than when dealing with just one 'minority', as in the case of women. However, this is an ambiguous answer: since women are only improperly called a minority, not just because they form an extremely relevant part of the population, but even more because they are dispersed throughout all other social groups (economic, social, religious, ethnic, and so on), the use of sophisticated techniques for evaluating the degree of discrimination, and consequently the type of action required, is as useful as it is in the American legal system; in fact, Community law has developed similar techniques in a crucial field of discrimination law, that of indirect discrimination. Oddly, these methods have not been applied in the field of affirmative action. The outcome is that whereas the Supreme Court in *Johnson* considered as lawful a decision that promoted a woman that was less qualified than her male counterpart, since preference due to sex was counterbalanced by several other elements (like flexibility, temporal limits, etc.), the European Court of Justice has rejected as unlawful the choice of an equally qualified woman because this amounted to imposing equal results and infringing the principle of formal equality.

Layoffs

The problem of balancing conflicting interests is extremely acute in the cases where the courts adjudicated affirmative action plans set up by public bodies in order to regulate layoffs, a particularly difficult issue, because it affects legal entitlements, not mere expectations or chances. Traditionally, layoffs due to severe economic crisis follow a reverse seniority order – the workers employed later are dismissed first. This practice is very negative for affirmative action plans that have been implemented for a short time, because they eliminate from the work force precisely those individuals that were targeted by the plan. In order to eliminate those effects, some plans provided for an exception to the reverse seniority criterion.

In *Firefighters Local Union No. 1784 v. Stotts* (1984) such a device was inserted in a judicial consent decree. The Supreme Court held that the plan had a severely negative impact on white workers, who were dismissed even if they had greater seniority, and therefore it violated Title VII of the Civil Rights Act. The fact that the entire plan aimed at remedying past discrimination was not sufficient, because this fact concerned only the employer. Proof that the workers protected by the plan were actually victims of it was not given, therefore it was illegitimate to place the burden on innocent white workers.

It seems in this case that the Court has used a tortious liability model: in order to be admissible, affirmative action must be provided by subjects that kept discriminatory behaviour in the past, and must advantage individuals that were victims of past discrimination. This passage is crucial: the Court shifts the focus of the analysis from the groups (the discriminating majority as opposed to the discriminated minority) to the individuals. In this way, the Court moves to a firmer ground, where rules and principles are clearer. Nevertheless, the cost of this shift is high: the focus on individual rights loses sight of the very reason of affirmative action, which is based on a group analysis; the tension between group and individual is solved by eliminating the first factor.

Another case, *Wygant v. Jackson Board of Education* (1986), concerns a similar situation: the limitation to the reverse seniority order in layoffs was introduced by a collective agreement related to a first agreement concerning the recruitment of minority teachers in public schools.[29] The plurality opinion, written by Justice Powell, makes use of the strict scrutiny standard, but modifies it significantly. According to the original criterion, a situation of past discrimination affecting a group of people is not sufficient justification for affirmative action, specific proof on both the active and passive side being required.[30] Nevertheless, in this case Justice Powell states that it is sufficient to prove discriminatory behaviour by the subject that sets up the plans, which therefore can also benefit individuals that were not directly affected by its past action. Because the plan does not provide that proof, it violates the fourteenth amendment. The decision seems to turn mainly on the lack of proof of past discrimination, rather than on the object of the plan.

The dissenting opinions in the case[31] underline that it is very difficult to logically differentiate the legal rules according to the degree of the consequences, i.e. according to the fact that they concern layoff or hiring and promotion: first of all, it is not always true that the impossibility of entering the labour market is less damaging than being temporarily excluded from it because of dismissal; but even more, it seems extremely difficult to reconcile the legitimacy of an affirmative action that aims at racial balance with the illegitimacy of a corresponding action that aims at preserving that result. Once more it is clear that there is a tension between the concept of group and that of individual, and it seems that privileges accorded to minorities are only permissible if they do not infringe individual rights considered to be fundamental.

The same reasoning runs through an important case decided in 1996 by the Court of Appeals for the third circuit, which has reinforced the restrictive trend towards affirmative action of the 1990s. *Taxman v. Board of Education of the Township of Piscataway* (1996) concerned a Title VII action challenging a school board's affirmative action plan preferring minority teachers over non-minority teachers in layoff decisions where teachers were equally qualified.[32]

According to the Court of Appeals, the purpose of the plan did not mirror the aim of Title VII, and was therefore inadmissible: it was not remedial, because there was no record of prior discrimination, nor were black teachers underrepresented or underutilized; in fact, its sole purpose was to promote racial diversity of teachers, rather than remedy past discrimination. The Court rested primarily on the authority of *Weber*, and its two-tier test, according to which affirmative action plans are permissible if their purposes mirror those of the statute and they do not unnecessarily trammel the interests of the non-minority individuals. The School Board has filed a petition for certiorari to the Supreme Court, which was dismissed in December 1997.[33]

The Turning Point against Affirmative Action in the 1990s

At the end of the 1980s, the coming to the bench of the conservative Justices nominated by President Reagan interrupts the series of decisions favouring affirmative action in the field of employment (Dworkin, 1996: 147ff.; O'Brien, 1997).[34] The turning point is marked by *City of Richmond v. J.A. Croson* (1989), where the Supreme Court moves back to the strict scrutiny standard and to a narrow view of the legitimacy of affirmative action.[35] In this case, it considered contrary to the fourteenth amendment a plan by the administration of Richmond (Virginia) which reserved for a five years period a share of the building contracts to minority business.[36] The decision is in sharp contrast with *Fullilove*, where a similar plan had been considered constitutional. The court distinguishes it on the basis that *Fullilove* concerned a plan created by a federal statute, whereas in *Croson* it was established by a local administration, and consequently the standards for evaluating them differ. This distinction is rather suspect, and in fact the Court has not hesitated later to declare that the standards are common, this time in the sense of always using strict scrutiny. In spite of the clear revision of the Court's policy, there is no unanimity in defining which elements are necessary in order to pass the strict scrutiny test: factors like a compelling public interest, a remedial aim and narrow tailoring between discrimination and remedy are common to all analysis, but there is no agreement on what factual situation comply with them. Strict scrutiny, therefore, more than establishing some undisputed criterion, signals a restrictive and distrustful attitude.[37]

After Justices Brennan and Marshall retired, the pendulum has swung even more strongly against affirmative action. Recent developments in the field of affirmative action in the US point to a revisionary trend that will probably severely limit the use of this legal mechanism in the coming years (O'Brien, 1997). In a case decided in June 1995, *Adarand Constructors v. Pena* (1995), the US Supreme Court confirmed the restricting trend of the *Croson* case; in considering the compatibility with the fifth amendment due process clause of a federal agency's contract that contained a subcontractor compensation clause, which gave a prime contractor a financial incentive to hire subcontractors certified as small businesses controlled by socially and economically disadvantaged individuals,[38] the Court made use of the strict scrutiny standard. It reasoned that every preference based on racial or ethnic criteria must be justified by a compelling governmental interest and be narrowly tailored to furtherance of that interest, since it is prima facie against constitutional provisions establishing the principle of equality, and the proof of so-called 'benign' discrimination must be carefully evaluated by courts.[39]

The Supreme Court focuses on the definition of the standards concerning racial classifications deriving from the constitutional principles of the fifth and fourteenth amendments. In the majority opinion, Justice

O'Connor reviews the differences between the two constitutional provisions: up to the 1940s, the Supreme Court thought that the lack in the fifth amendment of the 'equal protection of the laws clause', which was instead inserted in the fourteenth amendment, implied that there was an individual right against discriminatory state action, but not against corresponding federal action. During the 1950s the Court started challenging the possibility of diverging standards, and in the following decades continued along these lines.

The convergence between the two constitutional provisions being established, the Court has now to define the content of this common scrutiny standard. According to the Court, it cannot but be the strict scrutiny; even if it recognizes the presence of different case-law trends, it affirms that any action, federal or state, that is based on 'race' can be legal only if it aims at a compelling governmental interest, implicitly rejecting the intermediate scrutiny, according to which if an action is classified as benign, it can be valid even if it is not strictly remedial. The mere usefulness of such action, or its link with legitimate but not fundamental interests, are not sufficient to make it constitutional, because it clashes with the principle of equality and with due process. Besides, the action must be narrowly tailored to the interest, i.e. it must be strictly proportional to it.

The standard that derives from these criteria is extremely stringent and demanding:[40] by emphasizing the need for strict judicial scrutiny, the court limits the use of affirmative action, because fear of inability to satisfy the heavy burden of proof and of liability for heavy damages in case of failure will probably restrain both public and private employers from using this legal device. As many scholars have pointed out, if the entire area of affirmative action should be submitted to strict scrutiny, the use of this instrument would become so difficult that it would discourage most agents (especially private actors) from undertaking them, limiting them probably only to consent decrees: 'strict scrutiny is "strict" in theory and "fatal" in fact'.[41]

It seems that the Supreme Court of the 1990s is firm in holding affirmative action, if not plainly unconstitutional, at least highly suspect. Justice Scalia's warning is illuminating: 'In the eyes of government, we are just one race here. It is American.'

Nevertheless, many scholars do not agree with the present case law. According to Dworkin:

> The equal protection clause is violated, not whenever some group has lost important decision on the merits of the case or through politics, but when its loss results from its special vulnerability to prejudice or hostility or stereotype

and its consequent diminished standing – its second-class citizenship – in the political community. . . . But the Fourteenth Amendment therefore poses a special difficulty for the courts that must enforce it. It requires them to judge not merely the consequences of legislation for different groups, but the motive behind that legislation (Dworkin, 1998: 56).

This task has been performed by the Supreme Court by scrutinizing legislation in order to 'smoke out' improper motives: if any legal rule imposes serious disadvantages to a group of people through a suspect classification, then such classification must be subject to the strict scrutiny test, i.e. it can be maintained only if it serves some compelling governmental interest.[42] Dworkin nevertheless thinks that the 'level-of-scrutiny strategy' is inappropriate for the issue of affirmative action, both in its strict and intermediate version:

> Judges should inspect such plans, when they are challenged in litigation, on a more case-by-case basis: they should use . . . a 'sliding-scale' approach in order to decide whether there is any convincing evidence that the racial classification actually does not reflect prejudice or hostility of the kind forbidden by the equal protection clause (Dworkin, 1998: 57).

He admits that this approach would imply less predictable results, but this drawback would be more than compensated by the flexibility and the accuracy of the judgement.

Other scholars think that the recent case law of the Supreme Court on affirmative action has moved away from the 'smoking out' standard and has applied a cost–benefit test instead (Rubenfeld, 1997: 428). According to Rubenfeld, this position is indefensible,[43] because all equal protection jurisprudence is based on the analysis of whether a law embodies an invidious or otherwise constitutionally impermissible purpose, and in this case it cannot be saved because its benefits outweigh its cost to discriminated individuals:

> There is something deeply wrong with the cost-benefit picture of strict scrutiny. Economizing equal protection is unacceptable. . . . Offsetting state benefits cannot 'justify' a law violating an individual's equal protection rights. That is what it means to have an equal protection right: the right is not subject to any ordinary cost-benefit calculus (Rubenfeld, 1997: 440–1).

Affirmative action may well be more controversial than other policies for political reasons, but it must be treated in the same way from a constitutional point of view.

Is there a Future for Affirmative Action?

The analysis of the evolution of affirmative action in the US shows different phases: in the late 1960s–70s affirmative action was considered a necessary means to achieve equality for all citizens, an instrument that would go beyond the formal legal dimension and ensure a factual equality of opportunities. Subsequently, the concrete use of this mechanism has forced legal scholars to try to develop a better theoretical definition of its characteristics and limitations, which proved essential after the first wave of affirmative action plans, when it became clear that the use of this instrument might cause hardship for other individuals, and that it was urgently necessary to devise criteria in order to balance the conflicting interests. The solution was anything but straightforward, partly because the characteristics of affirmative action plans varied greatly according to the concrete circumstances to which they were applied, but most of all because there was more profound disagreement on the objectives to be pursued, and even more on the means to those ends. The Supreme Court has fixed some boundaries, spelling out cases where the equal opportunity principle may justify an affirmative action plan (for example, job promotion), and cases where the contrasting legal values must prevail (for example, layoffs), but these have not been unanimous and have changed over time (Rosenfeld, 1991).

> By now, the framing of a distinctly constitutional inquiry into affirmative action should have become quite sophisticated. Surprisingly, it hasn't. Indeed, many of the most important arguments on which current doctrine rests are not constitutional arguments at all (Rubenfeld, 1997: 445).

Political ideologies have undoubtedly played a major role in shaping public opinion on affirmative action: under pressure by powerful movements like the civil rights movement in the 1960s and 1970s, it became widely accepted that formal equality was not enough, and that what was required were equal chances for all. But when the tide changed, and this political ideal gave way to more moderate positions, and sometimes even to political agnosticism, it became clear that the legal system moved in a rather different direction. It provided mechanisms to satisfy these exigencies, but it failed to provide a strong theoretical basis for them. Therefore, once the political impetus had petered out, the legal framework was unable to cope with attacks directed against affirmative action as a workable and admissible legal tool. The line of cases recently decided shows that the dispute ultimately turns on questions of distributive justice, and that it is at this level that the 'match' is decided (Cahn, 1995). The legal form of the solution is a consequence of it, not its basis. This may be an inevitable risk for all problems with a strong 'equity' connotation, and which therefore involve meta-legal questions of resources distribution. Nevertheless, one cannot fail to conclude that the legal framework is extremely weak, and that its contribution to the solution of this problem seems almost entirely limited to giving a (not always) suitable form to a primarily political decision.

It must be underlined that the situation in the US, although highly significant for every Western country, seems to be peculiar, in the sense that the main characteristics of affirmative action are influenced by the fact that they were (and still are) mainly aimed at and shaped by the need to overcome discrimination against the Afro-American population:

> In fact, the true, core objective of race-based affirmative action is nothing other than helping blacks. Friend of affirmative action, if there any left, should acknowledge this objective, and they should embrace it (Rubenfeld, 1997: 472).

Consequently, not all conclusions that can be drawn from the American experience can be directly transplanted across the ocean to Europe. More generally, it must be stressed that any kind of affirmative action is highly dependant on its specific context, and that any action or intervention must be strictly connected and tailored to it (Bowen and Bok, 1998: chapter 10). This means that it is extremely hard to reach general and final conclusions on the usefulness and effectiveness of affirmative action, each judgement being closely tied to the main elements of every case. The US experience shows an astonishing variety of views and ideas, ranging from enthusiastic approval to rejection. None of these contrasting positions seems to be able to be predominant; in this chaotic picture, there is a great need for empirical studies capable of providing reliable and extensive data instead of preconceptions, conjectures and anecdotes,[44] that may be a suitable basis for a judgement that is intrinsically dependent on values.

Yet, the question is not only whether these measures are effective in achieving the result of real equality; it is a much more fundamental one: is there any legal basis for discriminating against someone because someone else has been discriminated against before?

There is apparently a widespread belief that real equality requires not only the elimination of formal barriers, but also positive intervention, in order to ensure that equal results can be effectively achieved. Still, there is some embarrassment when it comes to providing a theoretical framework: at the end of the day, awareness that this result can be achieved only by infringing individual rights undermines the validity of the mechanism. Western legal culture is deeply rooted in individual rights: centuries of evolution culminating in the French Revolution have firmly established a legal paradigm in which rights attach naturally to the individual (Berman, 1983).

The current evolution of Western societies shows an increasing diversity within their populations: differences of economic and social condition, of culture, of 'race'; at the same time, in spite of the severe economic crises suffered by most welfare states, there is a growing tendency of the state to intervene in all aspects of social life in order to implement its objectives (Mattei, 1994). There is, I think, nothing revolutionary in the assertion that the legal framework that was consolidated 200 years ago is an instrument that should be updated in order to regulate changed conditions. It is much more difficult to determine the direction in which new developments should move. Emphasis on individual rights as the bulwark of citizenship is probably the greatest achievement of Western legal civilization, as many examples of tyrannies in our history prove, and this precious heritage must be protected against any attack. But it is clear that lawyers must increasingly take notice of and work on the fact that individuals live and act in groups, and that modern societies increasingly require new means in order to co-ordinate all these interests, which may coincide, but more often clash. This is an enormous challenge for legal science, but past experience shows that law, under strong and sometimes violent pressure, can be an amazingly flexible instrument, capable of keeping pace with change. It seems that new categories of rights and entitlements are needed, capable of giving more accurate definition to the relationship between the individual and the group, in order to limit the elements of arbitrariness in the choice on which of them should prevail (Antoniolli Deflorian, 1996). As a possible example, a first step in the new direction might be to recognize openly that, since we admit that substantive equality cannot be achieved without taking into account the existence of groups in which individuals act, it does not make sense to conceive affirmative action as a limited exception to a constitutional right to formal equality. This should imply the abandonment of the strictly remedial and individual perspective that has been often used: 'Affirmative action is a forward-looking, not a backward-looking enterprise' (Dworkin, 1998: 60).

The history of Western legal tradition shows that law possesses an array of concepts and solutions that, although they cannot solve distributive problems on their own, may help to rationalize their handling and render it more effective (Dworkin, 1986, 1987). Moreover, it also shows that every time that law has sought to avoid social problems that were considered too controversial, this choice has led to disastrous consequences (Mattei, 1992: 10–2).

We are in a world of second best, and the existence of affirmative action demonstrates that there are fields where law has intrinsic limits as a means of resolution of social disputes, and that the abandonment of neutrality is a dangerous path that may lead to the loss of legitimacy of law. Yet, although striking a balance between the right to equality and neutrality is a difficult enterprise, there is no other choice for lawyers but try it. After all, there may be something more to say about law and affirmative action.

Notes

1. The decision has overruled *Plessy v. Ferguson* (1896), affirming the 'separate but equal doctrine', which considered the separation between whites and blacks as constitutional, as long as the services provided were formally equal; in fact, this amounted to an apartheid system.
2. Affirmative action seems to have a cyclical pattern in the world: it started in the US in the 1960s in order to remedy serious phenomena of racial discrimination, and moved to Europe in the 1980s, at a time when they were submitted to severe criticism and revision in their home country.
3. The fourteenth amendment was enacted in 1868, while the fifth dates back to 1791.
4. See *Adarand Constructors v. Pena* (1995).
5. Surprisingly, there are no Senate Committee reports that determine the intent of Congress in this act. The insertion of sex as one of the banned discriminatory factors was initially due to an attempt to defeat the Bill, but it was accepted instead with little debate. The insertion of age, on the contrary, was rejected.
6. Most of the states have fair employment statutes banning various kinds of discrimination, enforced through state agencies. Often these laws are similar to the federal ones, and state courts routinely refer to federal case law.

7. The Pregnancy Discrimination Amendments 1978 (§ 701 (k)) provide that sex includes pregnancy, childbirth or related medical conditions, thereby overruling some judicial decisions holding that pregnancy distinction were 'physical' and not sex distinctions, and therefore valid under Title VII. Sexual practices or preferences are not considered to be covered by the statute.
8. The Equal Employment Opportunity Act 1972, which extensively amended the 1964 Act, reduced the number of employees necessary for the application of Title VII, which is now fifteen. Besides, it extended it to state and local governments and most federal agencies; it also extended the time for filing charges and suits, and gave the EEOC the power to file suit in its own name, along with private action.
9. See *United Steelworkers v. Weber* (1979).
10. President Bush vetoed the act in 1990 and Congress failed to override the veto; the text that was finally approved bore close similarity to the first version, but also some relevant compromises.
11. In the field of disparate impact sec. 105 (a) provides that, once the worker plaintiff has established a disparate impact, the onus of proof shifts to the employer, who must prove that his/her action was due to objective working needs.
12. The amended version of section 31 of the California Constitution states that 'The State shall not discriminate against, or grant preferential treatment to any individual or group on the basis of race, sex, color, ethnicity, or national origin in the operation of public employment, public education, or public contracting'. Soon after the passing of the amendment, it was challenged by a class action on the ground that it violates the US Constitution. Nineteen state legislatures had considered limiting or abolishing state affirmative action; seven tried to place the issue on the November ballot, but finally only California succeeded in collecting the required number of signatures; in the ballot 55 per cent of the voters were in favour of the measure, i.e. more or less the same percentage in favour of Clinton's reelection (which demonstrates that affirmative action is also opposed by liberal voters).
13. Civil Rights Restoration Act 1999, SL6 PCS. (106th Congress).
14. Case law considers affirmative action programmes based on EO 11246 legal if they remedy past patterns of societal discrimination: see *Contractors Ass'n of Eastern Penn. v. Secretary of Labor* (1971) and *Fullilove* (1980).
15. In June 1997 Clinton announced an initiative on 'race', called 'One America in the 21st Century', aimed at a national effort to deal openly

and honestly with racial diversity (http://www. whitehouse.gov/ Initiatives/OneAmerica/about.html).

16. The plaintiff argued that the special admission programme for applicants belonging to racial minorities at the Davis Medical School of the University of California violated the equal protection clause of the fourteenth amendment because the school discriminated on the basis of 'race'. The programme set standards that were less strict than ordinary admission criteria in order to ensure that part of the student population would consist of members of racial minorities, even if their scores and curricula were lower than those of white applicants.

17. Powell J. cites the Harvard admission system as an example of a constitutionally permissible plan, by creating a dichotomy that thereafter will often be used, that between quotas and goals; the first provide for a rigid numerical target and are illegal, while the second, being flexible, are admissible. Such a distinction may be theoretically clear, but is very difficult to apply in practice.

18. A case decided unanimously by the Court of Appeals for the Fourth Circuit, *Podberesky v. Kirwan* (1994), has stated that university scholarship programmes reserved for high-achieving minority students (in this case, African-American) violate the equal protection clause of the fourteenth amendment. Following this decision, other states re-examined their minority scholarship programmes. In 1995 the federal Supreme Court denied certiorari against the decision (see Civil Rights Monitor, http://www.civilrights.org/lcef/monitor/81-2.htm).

19. According to the court, it would have been necessary to prove the actual effects of past discrimination and tailor on them the advantages for the discriminated students. This evaluation should have been limited to the Law School, rather than to the entire University of Texas. It must be noted that the court recognized the existence of past discrimination, but it considered that its effects were already eliminated: see *Podberesky v. Kirwan* (1994).

20. The opinion explicitly states in a footnote that until the Supreme Court explicitly overrules *Bakke*, diversity of the student population is a compelling public interest for the sake of strict scrutiny.

21. The doctrine of mootness implies that a case will not be taken by the Supreme Court if the decision would come too late, and therefore be useless; the leading case is *De Funis v. Odegaard* (1974).

22. The plan provided that half of the positions for training required for qualified jobs would be reserved to black workers, until they reached the percentage of the black labour-force of the area. Black workers

represented less than 2 per cent, against 39 per cent of the local work force. The employer of the case had been charged several times for violating federal statutes banning racial discrimination.

23. The federal statute funded public work by state and local governments and provided that 10 per cent of them had to be given to minority business enterprises (MBE). These funds should be allotted to those enterprises even though their bids were not the cheaper, if the surplus was the effect of past discrimination.

24. According to Chief Justice Burger, the fact that the plan may disrupt non-minority businesses' expectations is constitutionally irrelevant, because it is 'limited and properly tailored' to remedy past discrimination, and therefore the 'sharing of the burden' is permissible (p.484).

25. The case concerned serious discriminatory behaviour by the Alabama Public Safety Department, which led to judicial action. The federal district court found no black worker employed, and ordered that one black worker had to be recruited for every white one until they reached 25 per cent of the workforce. The Department repeatedly refused to comply with the court decisions, and the case came finally to the Supreme Court.

26. Justice Brennan, who wrote the plurality opinion, stated that the programme was compatible with the strict scrutiny test. The opinion also underlined the fact that the plan was temporary, and it did not trammel excessively white workers' rights.

27. A decisive change in the more conservative views on women has taken place in the 1960s, when Congress enacted a series of statutes that explicitly banned discriminatory behaviours against women, as in the Equal Pay Act 1963, which requires equal pay for work of equal value that men and women workers perform in a particular establishment, and the Civil Rights Act 1964. In 1972 the Equal Rights amendment, which prohibited all kind of sexual discrimination, was presented; Congress approved the statute, but it was not ratified by three-quarters of the states, and it finally was dropped. Most of the serious discriminations were later eliminated by sectorial statutes, but the failure of the Equal Rights amendment has meant a defeat for the women's right movement.

28. In a strong dissent to the majority opinion (written by Justice Brennan), Justice Scalia points out that women's underrepresentation in certain jobs stems from reasons completely different from those that determine underrepresentation of ethnic and racial minorities: while in the latter case it may easily be related to discriminatory practices, in the former social attitudes may be the most important

reason, and in this case affirmative action is not justified: 'It is absurd to think that the nation-wide failure of road maintenance crews, for example, to achieve the Agency's ambition of 36.4 per cent female representation is attributable primarily, even if substantially, to systematic exclusion of women eager to shoulder pick and shovel. It is a "traditionally segregated job category" not in the *Weber* sense, but in the sense that, because of longstanding social attitudes it has not been regarded by women themselves as desirable work' (p.688). Although it must be recognized that social practice may sometimes be more pernicious than open discrimination in segregating groups from certain activities, and it therefore forcefully requires contrasting action, there is a strong argument for being suspicious of any kind of paternalistic legal intervention that aims at imposing on people what is best for them, even if they do not want it.

29. The collective agreement provided that the percentage of minority teachers laid off could not be higher than that of employed minority teachers fixed by the original collective agreement.

30. Justice Powell underlines that the purpose of building a model for minority pupils, explicitly stated in the plan, is not an interest that may be pursued through affirmative action, because it does not remedy past discrimination, being instead forward-looking. It seems difficult to reconcile a common ratio with *Bakke*, where Justice Powell had considered that the aim of a diverse university student population justifies the use of affirmative action.

31. Marshall, Brennan, Blackmun JJ. Justice Stevens has written another dissenting opinion, in which he explains that affirmative action plans may be constitutional even if they are merely forward-looking, and do not remedy past discrimination. He distinguishes between inclusive and exclusive affirmative action: the first aims at integrating minorities that are excluded, and is legitimate; the second aims at excluding minorities from certain benefits, and is therefore impermissible.

32. The Board of Education of Piscataway had developed an affirmative action plan in response to a regulation by the New Jersey State Board of Education, whose purpose was to provide 'equal educational opportunity for students and equal employment opportunity for employees' and 'make a concentrated effort to attract . . . minority personnel for all positions'. According to this plan, only if two candidates were equally qualified, the one meeting the affirmative action plan was selected; in case of higher qualification, the non-minority candidate would prevail. Several years after, the Board had to reduce the teaching staff by one; of the two teachers having equal

seniority, one was black (the only one in the Business Department), the other white. New Jersey law regulates layoffs, but it does not provide for the case of more candidates having the same seniority. Generally, in this case the selection is made by a random process, but the Board decided instead to rely on its affirmative action plan, and chose to keep the black teacher, since this would serve the purpose of having a culturally diverse staff.

33. Civil Rights Monitor, http://www.civilrights.org/lcef/monitor/81-2.htm.

34. Particularly, a conservative turn in the Supreme Court was made with the appointment of Justice Kennedy in 1988 in the position of Justice Powell. In the previous years Justices Brennan, Marshall and Blackmun had generally endorsed the policy of affirmative action, while Justices Rehnquist and White were generally against it.

35. Nevertheless, of a majority of six judges, only five based their decision on strict scrutiny, while Justice Stevens used intermediate scrutiny instead; besides, there was no agreement on the requirements, because only Justice Scalia deemed that proof of past discrimination by the employer is not sufficient, it being necessary also to show that the beneficiaries were victims of that past discrimination.

36. The plan reserved 30 per cent of the funds for this purpose, while the percentage of the non-white population was 50 per cent. Richmond has been for long a symbol of racial segregation and discrimination.

37. The decision has caused much worry among American legal actors because of the uncertainty that it created concerning the legality of affirmative action. Some of the most famous American constitutional scholars (Calabresi, Choper, Ely, Michelman, Sunstein, and others) have published in the *Yale Law Journal* a joint statement, where they underlined the constitutionality of affirmative action and proposed some guidelines for its future use; they emphasized the fact that requiring detailed proof of discriminatory past behaviour may not only be hard to be given, but it may also cause racial tensions; finally, they invoked a stand-still period during which local governments could re-examine their affirmative action programmes without being held liable (Joint Statement, 1989; Fried, 1989).

38. Certification is given by a federal agency, the *Small Business Administration*. For people belonging to the black, Hispanic, Asian, native American minorities, there is a rebuttable presumption that they belong to the category of socially disadvantaged individuals.

39. Justice Scalia agrees with the majority opinion that a strict scrutiny standard is required in evaluating affirmative action, but he believes

that government can never have a compelling interest in discriminating on the basis of race. He therefore adheres to a strictly formal meaning of the principle of equality.

40. The decision sets three principal criteria for evaluation: 'scepticism', which analyses every public action that treats a person differently because of his/her 'race' or ethnical origin as inherently suspect (*McLaughlin*, 379 US 184 (1964): 192); 'coherence', because the standard according to the equal protection clause does not depend on the race of those who are benefited or damaged by the classification (*Croson*, (1989): 494); 'congruence', the analysis of equal protection being the same for the fifth and the fourteenth amendments.

41. Gunther, cited in Dworkin, 1998: 57.

42. According to Dworkin, there are two versions of the strict scrutiny test: according to one, defined as the 'overriding necessity version', any racial classification is automatically against the equal protection clause, unless it is mandated by the danger of some dramatic urgency, amounting to an imminent danger to life and limb; this is the version adopted by Justices Scalia, Rehnquist and Thomas. According to the other, called the 'rebuttal version', a racial classification violates the equal protection clause only if it is based on prejudice or stereotype. This softer version is recognized by Justices O'Connor, Souter, Ginsburg and Breyer. Dworkin thinks that only the latter version is compatible with the text of the US Constitution.

    If the classification is not suspect, then a lower standard (so-called intermediate scrutiny) is employed; in the case of 'race', almost invariably considered as a suspect classification, it is very easy for any lawyer to justify the use of strict scrutiny.

43. But see Alexander (1997) for a contrary position.

44. Simms (1995), on the economic cost of discrimination and of affirmative action, particularly in employment opportunities; Bowen and Bok (1998) on selective higher education.

6

Using Historical and Sociological Evidence to Defend Anti-Discrimination Policies

Melinda Chateauvert

Introduction

In this chapter, I consider the historical and sociological justifications for adopting anti-discrimination policies in the US and the use of historical evidence to defend affirmative action policies in the courts. Women of the dominant racial group have benefited the most from affirmative action policies. To a more limited extent, some Asian Americans and some Hispanics have also gained substantially from anti-discrimination measures. However, because racism against black people is the paradigm for American racism, African Americans are the focus of this chapter. Deeply ingrained prejudice against people of the African Diaspora, the result of a contested discourse of 'race' has perpetuated 350 years of systematic discrimination against African Americans. This racial discourse explains the vociferousness of the US debate on affirmative action. A paradigm shift is necessary to eradicate this time-worn process, otherwise the problem of the colour line will continue to hamper our ability to achieve social justice in the twenty-first century.

The US has always been a nation of immigrants, some voluntary and some involuntary, such as indentured servants, prisoners, and slaves. The Declaration of Independence, which contains the famous phrase, 'All men are created equal,' is not a legally binding document. The Constitution of the United States, which is supreme law, declared African Americans 'three-fifths' a person for purposes of enumeration and thus, Congressional representation. The Constitution did not guarantee 'equality' to women, minors, or American Indians, among others.[1] As a dynamic document, the interpretation of equality for African Americans, based largely on the thirteenth, fourteenth and fifteenth amendments, has changed since ratification over a century ago.[2] Historically the nation's economic matters and political affairs have been dominated by a minority of white men.

In the late nineteenth century, recent European immigrants were rewarded with the benefits of 'whiteness' as de jure racial segregation became law under *Plessy v. Ferguson* (1896). Under the exclusion acts of the 1880s, Congress explicitly denied Chinese immigrants citizenship. In the 1950s when the Supreme Court recognized the equality of African Americans in the *Brown v. Board of Education* decision (1954), Asian Americans and lighter-skinned Hispanic Americans were granted a privileged status as 'honorary' whites. One key test for the integration of immigrant groups has been the adoption of racial prejudices against African Americans as some scholars analyse (Roediger, 1991; Ignatiev, 1996). By learning racism and distancing themselves from blacks, immigrants like Irish, Italians, Eastern Europeans, and other groups have been successful in overcoming prejudice against them (Berry, 1997: 68). More recently, some Latinos and Asian Americans have internalized colour prejudices by affirming their 'whiteness' as the key to success in America.

Thus, the vociferousness of the affirmative action debate is not the result of a generalized criticism against all of those who benefit from affirmative action. The attack targets African Americans specifically. Opponents rarely assert that white women are the undeserving beneficiaries of 'preferential treatment.' By playing the 'race card' opponents of affirmative action reinforce divisions along colour and ethnic lines. All persons of colour in the US face discrimination in a variety of sometimes virulent and often subtle forms. However, charges against Hispanics and Asian Americans emphasize their alien status or 'foreignness' and usually target other policy areas.[3] Middle- and upper-class white women share a commonality of experiences and relationships with white men of their class who dominate public power and share the educational characteristics needed to meet traditional standards for higher education. Thus, the attacks against white women have been limited largely to the religious Christian right, who complain that affirmative action undermines traditional gender roles.

The Affirmative Action Dispute

Affirmative action refers to a set of measures that seek to provide improved opportunities for underrepresented minorities and women in higher education, employment, and as entrepreneurs in government contracting (Appelt, 1998: 21). Specific anti-discrimination measures can be divided into 'soft' and 'hard' affirmative action.[4] Soft measures basically seek to advertise available job opportunities or places at educational institutions to a larger section of the public than previous practice allowed. These actions, often undertaken voluntarily by employers and educational institutions, may also be referred to as equal opportunity measures (Bell, 1998: 35–7; Wrench, 1997). 'Hard' affirmative action, which may be judicially mandated, seeks to remedy the present effects of past discrimination and may involve 'quotas'. However, contrary to opponents' propaganda, we have to underline that quotas do not specifically require hiring a 'less qualified' person of a specific racial, ethnic, or gender group over a meritorious white male. In almost all cases, quotas are simply 'goals' that encourage employers to interview members of a targeted group for the job.

This division between soft and hard affirmative action confuses the public debate in the US. Most opponents tolerate 'soft' but not 'hard' affirmative action. Critics such as Nathan Glazer argue that employers and educational institutions can conduct extensive, targeted outreach to underrepresented populations, but should not adopt goals or quotas to redress historic imbalances. Conservative opponents argue that the government should not consider societal discrimination that has benefited white men inter-generationally. Their propaganda redefines the terms, calling 'preferential treatment' illegal when a qualified person of colour is hired over an equally qualified white person. In this same perverse logic, 'fair treatment' occurs when a white person is hired over a person of any colour. This propaganda has strongly influenced public opinion and in turn, has had a considerable impact in judicial opinion (Cooper, 1998: 62–6; Edley, 1996; Greenhouse, 1998).[5]

Implementation and Backlash of Affirmative Action

Affirmative action has been under attack since its implementation in 1965. The civil rights movement demanded electoral democracy and equal opportunity for African Americans. Urban unrest, including race riots in Harlem (New York) and Watts (Los Angeles) raised tensions considerably. Dr. Martin Luther King, Jr, a vigorous proponent of affirmative action, called for a colour-blind society in the ringing words of his March on Washington 'Bounced Check' speech (known as 'I Have a Dream'): 'Not by the colour of their skin, but by the content of their character.' In his book, *Why We Can't Wait* (1964), Reverend King called on the US to 'radically readjust its attitude toward the Negro' and to 'incorporate in its planning some compensatory consideration for the handicaps he has inherited from the past':

> Whenever this issue of compensatory or preferential treatment for the Negro is raised, some of our friends recoil in horror. The Negro should be granted equality, they agree; but he should ask nothing more. On the surface, this appears reasonable, but it is not realistic. For it is obvious that if a man is entered at the starting line in a race three hundred years after another man, he would have to perform some impossible feat in order to catch up with his fellow runner (King, 1964: 134).

In 1965, President Lyndon B. Johnson affirmed King's call in issuing Executive Order 11246.[6] Much of the early success of affirmative action can be credited to a strong black protest movement. African Americans reaped the greatest benefits in the late 1960s and early 1970s, while enforcement and public interest supported racial integration. Many employers, colleges and universities caught up in the civil rights movement, voluntarily recruited white women as well as African Americans. Others did so under the prodding of federal enforcement officials as well as under the protests by African Americans.

At the end of the 1970s, backlash began, heralded by *Bakke v. Regents* (1978). During the 1980s, civil rights stagnated under President Reagan's policy of adverse neglect, federal enforcement of anti-discrimination law came to a virtual halt, and American public opinion had shifted against affirmative action.[7] In these years, conservative politicians deliberately appointed opponents of affirmative action to federal jobs designed to protect civil rights. Moreover, the budgets and personnel of federal agencies designated to review affirmative action compliance were systematically cut, thereby severely constraining the ability of government officials to enforce the law.[8] Clarence Thomas, now an Associate Justice on the Supreme Court, began his public career undoing decades of progress in the Civil Rights Division (CRD) of the Department of Education. He then became chair of the Equal Employment Opportunity Commission (EEOC) where he allowed the agency to sink into a mire of backlogged cases.[9]

The Clinton administration has had mixed results.[10] Enforcement of anti-discrimination measures has declined as the African American civil rights movement petered out. While President Clinton enjoys broad support from African Americans, his Administration's civil rights enforcement agencies have not recovered the ground loss during the Reagan-Bush years. For example, despite thirty years of affirmative action, the federal government has never denied a contract to any company or educational institution as a result of its failure to implement affirmative action guidelines. Nor has the Secretary of Labor, who possesses the authority to publish the names of offenders, made the names of these corporations public, even though civil rights groups have repeatedly called for disclosure.

This brief history affirms that democracy is required for affirmative action to work.[11] Political leaders, must act in concert with business leaders and federal judges for anti-discrimination measures to be effective. Enforcement, through litigation and the careful government oversight, is essential. Yet fundamental changes in racial attitudes will be necessary to eliminate more subtle forms of prejudice. However, the US experience shows that leaders will not challenge the racial status quo without political pressure (Skrentny, 1996: 8). Protest movements and race riots forced presidents to take action. Unless exceptional or extra-ordinary provisions are made for their meaningful participation, riots sometimes appear to be the only recourse that racial and immigrant minorities have to assert political power.

Unfortunately, the reverse is also true: once riots and mass demonstrations cease to threaten the country, a Thermidorean reaction sets in, as conservatives seek to revoke anti-discrimination laws and other progressive social and economic policies. This is what occurred in the 1980s, as opponents devised a counter-discourse to deny the validity of 'race' discrimination and thus the need for legal remedies.

The construction of 'race' (and 'sex') in US history is the combined result of judicial, legislative, economic, and social imperatives. To decide cases judges have traditionally examined the judicial and legislative records of disputed laws and court decisions. However, with the acceptance of sociological evidence in the 'Brandeis' brief, the types of scholarly research allowed to enter in the evidentiary record has expanded. Thus, for *Brown*, John Hope Franklin and other scholars provided a history of the school segregation and legislative intent in the equal protection clause of the fourteenth amendment (Franklin, 1989: 287; 1959: 225–35). In *Croson v. Richmond* (1989) as well as in other, earlier cases, the Supreme Court announced that government officials must show a local history of racial discrimination in order to justify affirmative action.

Not only 'race' but also 'merit' and 'individualism' can be considered as constructed discourses. In the conservative counter-discourse, opponents argue that affirmative action is contrary to merit and individualism, two cherished principles of American uniqueness. Until affirmative action, only white men have historically competed against each other for privileged positions under the banner of 'meritocracy'. As a group, certain white men have systematically benefited from their 'race' and gender. Both arguments have been used by conservative federal judges to deny the continued use of 'hard' anti-discrimination remedies. These myths, of meritocracy and of individualism, can be refuted using historical and sociological evidence.

Alone, such arguments may not change public opinion, but when presented contextually, historical and sociological evidence developed by scholars can provide the necessary proofs for lawmakers and for attorneys to defend civil rights in the courts. The US Supreme Court accepted sociological evidence in the 'Brandeis' brief used in *Mueller v. Oregon* (1923). That document detailed the deleterious effects of long working hours on women's health. John Hope Franklin, Kenneth J. Clark, and other African American scholars prepared historical and social science research for *Brown v. Board of Education of Topeka, Kansas* (1954). Of course, not everything produced by scholars favours the advancement of civil rights. The work of Nathan Glazer was used in *Bakke v. Regents* to justify the end of affirmative action. Writing and researching on current social problems draws on the work done by legal scholars in critical legal studies, critical 'race', and feminist studies. As Derrick Bell (1992), Kimberley Crenshaw (1992), Patricia J. Williams (1995) and others have shown, all legal cases rely on narratives. Every participant has a story. Historians, sociologists and other scholars can help attorneys to elaborate the stories of those who have not traditionally participated in the legal process (Bell, 1992; Crenshaw, 1992; Williams, 1995: 139; Berry, 1999). The anti-affirmative action decisions issued by the Rehnquist Court require the production of a history of discrimination. This historical evidence must be specifically tailored for the court to justify 'race'-based remedies (Glazer, 1964; Glazer, 1987; Glazer, 1998; Traub, 1998).

Addressing the perpetuation of racial discrimination in the courts has been made more difficult for the delineation of separate evidentiary standards for 'race'- and sex-based affirmative action. In the 1995 *Adarand* decision, the US Supreme Court severely constrained affirmative action remedies for 'race' and ethnic discrimination, interpreting the fourteenth amendment of the US Constitution to restrict remedies targeted at blacks and Hispanics as pernicious and subject to strict scrutiny. Such remedies must be narrowly tailored to meet documented discrimination directed specifically at individuals and must be of short duration. No such requirements constrain remedies for discrimination based on sex or gender. This legal differentiation is not required. The law has been interpreted in the past to permit the same remedies for racial exclusion that are now prohibited. The difference is accounted for by policy preferences of the judges.[12] Chief Justice Rehnquist and Associate Justices Scalia, Thomas, O'Connor and Kennedy have joined repeatedly to deny persons of colour the employment and educational opportunities provided by affirmative action.[13]

However, the conservative counter-discourse and judicial constraints on affirmative action can be challenged using historical and sociological evidence to defend anti-discrimination policies. In the remainder of this chapter, I will show how the historical record and more specialized investigations conducted on behalf of civil rights litigants can be used to illustrate the perpetuation of past discrimination (Schnapper, 1983: 828–64).

As noted earlier, 'merit' has historically benefited white men, and as currently applied, continues to protect the job and educational interests of certain white men as well as some white women. At the same time, nepotism is not explicitly prohibited in many job-hiring situations, and in university admissions, athletes and 'legacies', the children of alumni, are often given preferential treatment (Rosenfeld, 1991: 1–2). The privileging of white men is not limited to those with advantageous family connections. Former members of the US armed services receive extra points in government civil service examinations, the ultimate 'merit' test. Special welfare programmes, particularly the GI Bill, adopted at the conclusion of the Second World War, conferred upon veterans specific preferences in the workplace, education, and housing market, coupled with financial programmes that allowed them to take full advantage of those programmes.

Evidence of Racial Discrimination

During the nineteenth century, the US federal government created two of the largest 'contracting' programmes ever. The Homestead Act, established at the end of the US Civil War (1865), allowed whites to claim land at no cost in the western territories of the country; African Americans, native Americans, and Hispanics were not allowed to participate in one of the nation's biggest giveaways. By far the largest programme created the infamously wealthy railroad barons that gave millions of acres of land for the development of an intercontinental, monopolistic, transportation system (Porter forthcoming, cited in Smallwood, unpublished: 10–12).

The question of who is allowed to participate in the construction of the transportation infrastructure is at the heart of the debate over minority contracting programmes. Under current US guidelines issued by the Department of Transportation, this multi-billion dollar industry is supposed to set-aside a small percentage of its annual contracts to minority and woman owned firms. The US Supreme Court's decision in *Richmond v.*

Croson severely limited the scope of this programme. The new guidelines, issued to comply with *Croson*, were recently challenged by a conservative legal foundation in the state of Maryland. As an historian for this case, I examined how the state and local jurisdictions had awarded construction contracts prior to the adoption of minority contracting in order to demonstrate persistent racial discrimination against African American entrepreneurs.[14]

The state already had several studies conducted by various economists establishing the justification for minority contracting. My study looked at the contractors who dominated the state's construction industry historically, particularly roads and bridges, but also other infrastructure such as public buildings and school construction. Using public documents and basic archival materials, I identified the top engineering and building contractors who controlled the construction of a majority of the state's infrastructure development since the 1930s. These contractors formed an interlocking buddy system of 'old (white) boys' who shared in the spoils of public money: as builders, suppliers, subcontractors, insurance sellers, and as civil service employees in the state's engineering department (ministry). These men attended the same racially segregated schools. Many belonged to ethnic clubs open exclusively to Irish (Protestant and Catholic) Americans or to German (Christian) Americans. Their (male) children took over their businesses, and intermarriages among them created powerful banking, insurance, manufacturing, construction, transportation and political dynasties that are still influential in the state's economy. In addition, during a century-and-a-half of public contracting, there were numerous famous scandals involving these contractors and public officials in graft, payoffs, and other forms of political corruption.[15]

African American participation was almost non-existent, even in public building projects where prime contractors were required to make special outreach efforts to attract minority entrepreneurs ('soft' affirmative action measures), except for one: a company that began and has remained in trucking and hauling, a type of economic enterprise that African Americans have historically been allowed to do. (All over the world it seems that 'coloured' folks are the garbage collectors.) A few of the white women (typically wives, a few daughters) of this group have in recent years benefited from minority contracting programmes, in part because they could command access and assistance from their families and other members of the elite. The historical evidence clearly showed the many obstacles minority business owners faced in trying to obtain government contracts.

The fact that German Americans and Irish Americans yielded extensive political power in this state, helps to explain the exclusion of African Americans in government contracting. Ethnic politicians have historically garnered patronage contracts and given government jobs to members of their communities. This type of 'discriminatory' behaviour or 'preferential treatment' is rarely mentioned in considering the necessity for affirmative action and minority contracting programmes. Moreover, while opponents in the US may argue that their forebears never owned slaves, or that they themselves are recent immigrants to the US, they nonetheless enjoy common civilities and a quality of life based on the preferential treatment of white people that is often routinely denied to people of colour. Thus, the 'individuals' in the colour-blind society are neither gender neutral nor 'race' neutral (Pateman, 1988; Wing, 1997; Wildman et al., 1996).

In documenting the contemporary, substantive and historical differences in the treatment of various groups by public institutions, private corporations, and by governments, it is necessary to show concretely how members of certain groups received benefits routinely denied members of other groups. A statistical inference of inequality is one way of measuring these disparities.[16] More persuasively, as required under *Croson*, direct evidence of 'discrimination' and 'preferential treatment' provides the necessary justification for affirmative action remedies.

In *Podberesky v. Kirwan* (1993), historical evidence also proved critical in defending, at the trial level, a minority scholarship programme that sought to increase the number of African American students at the university of Maryland, the state's primary research campus. In this case, the university established these scholarships as part of its affirmative action plan under the order of federal officials in the Department of Education. By recruiting the best and the brightest of the state's black high-school graduates with four-year merit based scholarships, which covered all undergraduate expenses, the University of Maryland sought to develop an elite corps of students to represent the school, help recruit new students, and combat the stereotypes held by faculty, staff and students, that black students admitted under affirmative action guidelines were less qualified than white students. In addition, university's reputation among prospective African American students in the state would improve, as would its faculty and staff recruitment efforts.

With financing from a right-wing, conservative legal foundation, the plaintiff, Podberesky (identified as Hispanic; his father is a third generation Polish immigrant) sued the university. He charged that he had been unfairly denied a Banneker scholarship because of his 'race' and that the programme's racial exclusivity violated the equal protection clause of the fourteenth amendment. The historical research for this case was more straightforward. Following the rules established under *Croson*, we sought to show that the scholarship programme was permitted because it was narrowly tailored to redress proven historical (and statistical) discrimination. The historical brief reviewed the history of slavery in Maryland and the legacy of de jure and de facto racial discrimination. More specifically, it examined the dual education system that segregated African Americans from whites (including Hispanics) beginning in kindergarten through graduate school. That history makes racial integration of its traditionally white and historically black colleges and universities difficult. The historical record showed a clear pattern of underfunding and downright neglect to the state's public schools for African Americans, while the University of Maryland campuses and other white schools received the vast majority of financial resources and other benefits. The state's segregated educational institutions, by the way, had already been defendants in five of the precedent-setting cases leading up the original *Brown v. Board of Education* decision. The third part of the brief drew on university archives and state records, and established the institutional reaction to racial integration. It uncovered explicit, smoking-gun evidence of racial prejudice from administrators, staff and faculty. The evidence was critical to winning at the trial level, although the university lost, on other grounds, in the Court of Appeals.

Historical evidence, developed using wage rates and statistical analysis provided proof of discrimination in *UAW v. State of Michigan* (1987). In this case, female civil service workers contended that they were the victims of deliberate, long-standing sex-based wage discrimination. Statistical evidence taken from reports published by the state's civil service system since its implementation in 1923, tracked the wage rates of selected predominantly or exclusively female jobs (i.e. Clerk-Typist I) and male jobs (i.e. Janitor I) through 1980. Jobs were ranked according to the education, experience, skills and responsibilities necessary to perform them, without explicit acknowledgement of the gender of the workers. Pay was determined by job grade class; thus, clerk-typists were paid the same rates as janitors; nurses the same rates as electricians, and other skilled craftsmen. But over time, female workers began to earn less than men, even when working in jobs of the same grade. By 1985, there was almost 30 per cent difference in pay scales for these same jobs. In short, the civil service system appeared to have started on an egalitarian principle, but became gender discriminatory.[17] This established quantitative evidence for the plaintiffs. Additionally, archival research revealed that the original designers of the classification system had deliberately lumped almost all female civil servants in lower level job grades.

Further historical research into the private firm that designed the job classification system found direct evidence of gender discrimination. Although the firm did not leave extensive records, letters exchanged with members of the Civil Service Commission included written statements that the firm had purposefully placed female jobs in the lower job grades. All women were therefore confined to grades one through twelve while men, particularly in the professions and supervisors in the trades, could be ranked as high as grade sixteen. Although the issue in this case was wage discrimination, this same research methodology could be used to defend affirmative action policies.

Conclusion

As Erna Appelt notes, 'Affirmative Action . . . mean(s) the termination of unjustified preference' (Appelt, 1998: 51). One can also assert, as Appelt does, that 'male, white professional beginners (are) . . . under certain circumstances even disadvantaged' by affirmative action policies, because they now face greater competition or even reduced opportunities for choice managerial posts.[18] As the historical evidence in the cases discussed here shows, this group of workers has enjoyed greater privileges than other groups in the US. It is, however, essential to keep in mind that affirmative action is supposed to work 'downward' too. Secretarial positions, for decades denominated as 'women's jobs' are now available to men, as is work with children, in the household, and certain types of manufacturing operatives. Similarly, traditional 'Negro jobs' in the US are now open to men and women of all 'races' and ethnic identities.

In the long term, opening of these jobs to white men may, in fact, lead to positive changes in the working conditions traditionally associated with these types of jobs. Wages may increase; unionization of these workers may be looked upon more favourably; advancement opportunities may be made more available; and the conditions of work, including working hours, management supervision, implementation of new technologies, health and safety concerns, may also improve. More importantly, diversification of such jobs will help to eliminate 'race' and sex stereotyping that also affects social and cultural spheres.[19] Evidence for these positive changes can be drawn by reversing this scenario. For example, in the US banking industry, bank tellers were traditionally an apprentice route to bank management prior to the feminization of this job class. As more women became tellers, bank management ceased to offer career opportunity ladders to their predominantly female workforce. The 'masculinization' of some jobs may help to eliminate gender discriminatory practices. The same could also be true for people of colour.

Affirmative action is an important means for addressing invidious 'race' discrimination. For civil rights laws to work, enforcement by both the judiciary and the administration is essential. President Clinton's 'mend it, don't end it' policy announced in July 1995 has kept affirmative action in place but barely, as the current Supreme Court systematically undermines its force and scope. However long affirmative action and other anti-discrimination measures last, combating 'race' and sex discrimination requires using all of the tools available to government and the public. Historical scholarship provides one useful tool to advance civil rights. In a democratic system of government, the other tool appears to be a powerful political movement led by people of colour.

Notes

1. Amended to grant suffrage to women in 1921, and to those 18 years and older in 1972, the US Constitution does not grant equal citizenship (suffrage and other rights) to Native Americans living on reservations, to convicted felons (even those having served their sentences), to prisoners, or to certain other groups. Naturalized citizens cannot hold some elected offices (see Kovig, 1996: 168ff).
2. For example, multi- and transnational corporations are granted 'equality' as 'persons' under the fourteenth amendment (Horwitz, 1992: 66–70).
3. For example, more vigorous border enforcement, tightening of immigration and asylum laws, the elimination of multicultural and multilingual school curricula, and the enactment of social welfare reforms that deny aid to both legal and undocumented immigrants.
4. See Glazer in this volume.
5. See arguments of D'Souza (1996) to *Adarand Constructors Inc. v. Pena* (1995).
6. President Johnson announced the 'war on poverty' and the 'great society program' in June (which led to massive anti-poverty efforts) and signed the Voting Rights Act in September of that year. Note, however, that President Johnson refused to accept the Kerner Commission Report (1968), although he adopted several of its recommendations (Johnson, 1967; Patterson, 1996).

7. *Regents v. Bakke* (1978). In the 1970s, young black college graduates were as likely as whites to gain employment in managerial and professional occupations. By the late 1980s, they were 13 per cent less likely than whites to gain such jobs. After the 1990–1 recession, according to EEOC data, blacks were the only racial group posting a net loss of jobs; whites and other minorities recouped jobs losses with an upswing in the economy. In higher education, African Americans lost ground through assaults on affirmative action, major changes in the college student aid programmes that shifted money toward the middle class, and the eradication of minority scholarships. So severe was the crisis that higher education officials in the 1980s held national conferences on 'black males: an endangered species in higher education?' By the mid-1990s, African American men 18 to 25 years of age were more likely to be in jail than in college (*Wall Street Journal*, 14 September 1993).

8. The Equal Employment Opportunity Commission (EEOC); the Office of Federal Contract Compliance (Department of Labor) (OFCC); the United States Commission on Civil Rights (CCR); the Civil Rights Division of the Department of Justice; and the Office of Civil Rights in the Department of Education.

9. When Clarence Thomas took the Office of Civil Rights post in the Department of Education, the black college-going rate was on par with the white rate. During his tenure, proportionately fewer and fewer African Americans attended college as the federal government made massive cutbacks in student aid programmes, and from lax enforcement of civil rights laws designed to provide equal opportunity in higher education, such as Title VI and Title IX of the Civil Rights Act of 1964. Similarly, African American progress in employment equity ended during the Reagan administration. During the 1960s, the gaps between blacks and whites in the labour market began to close, with the most rapid progress occurring in the 1970s. In the 1980s, the EEOC and the Department of Justice Civil Rights Division refused to pursue class action 'race' and sex discrimination cases, and submitted 'amicus curia' briefs to the Supreme Court opposing affirmative action and civil rights laws. Not surprisingly, the integration of African Americans in the labour force slowed while the racial wage gap stagnated (Mayer and Abramson, 1994: 76–9, 118–44).

10. In 1997, the unemployment rate for black men 20 years and older was 8.4 per cent, its lowest annual average since 1974. The white male rate also at a 20-year low, was 3.6 per cent (Economic Report of the President, 1998).

11. See Cunningham in this volume.
12. In Western Europe, broad remedies for 'race' and sex discrimination appear equally permitted. On 17 October 1995, the European Court of Justice (ECJ) held in *Kalanke v. Freie Hansestadt* that a German state law guaranteeing women automatic priority over men in the labour market was contrary to the European Equal Treatment Directive that prohibits sex-based discrimination. For this decision and the following *Marschall* decision see Schiek in this volume.
13. From the US, it appears that Western European law is more favourable toward affirmative action based on 'race' and sex. However, the European Advocate General has constrained affirmative action as a remedy for sex discrimination in the *Kalanke* (1995) case. In issuing his opinion, the Advocate General drew upon recent American case law regarding the compatibility of affirmative action with the equal protection provisions of the fourteenth amendment of the US Constitution (Moens, 1997; *Kalanke:* opinion of the Advocate General: 182 n.10; see Antoniolli in this volume).
14. Because this litigation is not yet resolved, rules regarding confidentiality prohibit the release of specific data at this time.
15. Indeed, the resignation of a US Vice President, two governors and prison terms for many others, all resulted from public contracting scandals in this state.
16. Schnapper (1983) describes the basis for such historical research. Schnapper argues that discriminatory systems, established and institutionalized in earlier periods when racism was common and legal continue to adversely affect people of colour. Such evidentiary proofs need not condemn a generalized systemic problem (structural inequities), but specific policies that create unfair disadvantages or preferences for certain groups.
17. Note, too, that in 1923, the women's suffrage and women's trade union movements had reached their pinnacle in the US, suggesting once more the importance of political power in achieving civil rights in a democratic system.
18. Several universities in the US recently acknowledged that the growing gender imbalance of women to men in matriculation rates has forced them to lower admission standards for white men (see Lewin, 1998: A1).
19. See Schiek in this volume.

7

Racial Discrimination and Affirmative Action: Canada's Experience with Anti-Discrimination Legislation

Caterina Ventura

Introduction

This chapter focuses on the judicial and institutional conditions for affirmative action in Canada. In order to understand where Canada is now concerning affirmative action, it is necessary to recognize the historical progression from prohibiting discrimination to promoting equality.

As with other countries, notably the US, the inception of human rights statutes in Canada[1] was based on prohibiting 'race' discrimination. Various statutes emerged in the mid 1940s prohibiting discrimination. These early statutes left the burden of enforcing equality squarely on the victim of discrimination. Discrimination was viewed as a rare and isolated intentional act, and the individual who was personally harmed was responsible for defending his or her rights. These laws failed to achieve their objectives because they reflected a narrow understanding of equality and provided no practical means for the individual to achieve it (Pentney, 1985: 2–3).

I will start with a discussion of non-discrimination or human rights' statutes. These statutes prohibit discrimination and require the individual victim of a discriminatory practice take action for human rights to be ameliorated. There is no obligation on employers or service providers to ensure equality; they need only respond in the event of a complaint. Stronger protection is provided by the equality provisions of the Canadian Charter of Rights and Freedoms, which recognize an individual's right to equality but do not impose a positive obligation on the government; now, as before, the individual victim bears the burden for bringing court challenges to government discriminatory legislation or practices. The onus for eliminating discrimination finally shifts with the Employment Equity

Act, which requires employers to take positive measures to eliminate barriers to attain a representative workforce.

Human Rights Legislation

Human rights legislation[2] has evolved over the past few decades. Today all provinces and one of the territories have human rights Acts. Human rights legislation empowers human rights commissions to investigate, mediate and determine human rights complaints. These commissions were created to administer human right statutes and to provide practical assistance to victims of discrimination. They assign investigators to analyze the complaints. The commission will then determine whether the complaint should be dismissed, referred to conciliation (attempted settlement), or referred to a tribunal (quasi-judicial body that determines if the legislation has been infringed). Furthermore, human rights Acts in Canada empower tribunals or boards of inquiry to order the rectification of an act of discrimination.

Over the past thirty years human rights codes, and human rights commissions have had to adapt to keep up with the changes in society. The number of grounds of discrimination covered has expanded, and the Supreme Court has interpreted the statutes broadly, as is required of statutes that are viewed as quasi-constitutional in nature. The statutes, however, are limited. They are based on the premise of prohibiting discrimination and speak generally of 'freedom from discrimination'.

In the course of time, the general intentional discrimination rule was expanded to include the notion of unintentional or adverse effect discrimination, recognizing that discrimination is not just the result of isolated incidents, that a mixture of direct, intentional, and adverse effect discrimination can result in certain groups being denied equality. This systemic discrimination requires systemic remedies.

Since it was recognized that barriers to equality exist in society, the equality discourse began to shift the burden from the disadvantaged to the responsibility of the general public. The responsibility for the elimination of discrimination is shared by all Canadians, not only through government funding of human rights commissions, but through the application of human rights standards to the public and private sector alike.

Thus, human rights legislation has advanced from prohibiting the intentional isolated discriminatory act to prohibiting systemic discrimination. The advantage to those concerned with equality rights is more than theoretical: by prohibiting systemic discrimination, human rights law moved from remedying an individual problem to requiring a change to a discriminatory policy or practice. However, although a systemic remedy has a much wider impact, the onus still remains with the individual to affect change.

Affirmative Action Programmes

The next stage in the evolution of human rights theory was the realization that positive policies to overcome the effect of discriminatory employment practices on certain groups with unchangeable characteristics – whether those practices were intentional or not – could not be considered as discrimination against those who did not share those characteristics. The method used to assist the disadvantaged is by way of special programmes or affirmative action programmes. Affirmative action provisions, which exist in all Canadian human rights statutes, allow organizations to implement positive policies or practices to ameliorate disadvantage. These provisions are not mandatory but rather permissive.

There are few cases dealing with the affirmative action provisions of human rights legislation. This is, in part, due to the effective screening out by human rights commissions of complaints filed by members of non-disadvantaged groups alleging that special programmes that exclude them are discriminatory. As affirmative action is endorsed as necessary for achieving equality and is legislatively protected, human rights commissions have refused to proceed on these types of complaints. The limited jurisprudence does nonetheless provide a basis for outlining some basic principles that can be used to assist in the interpretation of special programmes.

The first case to reach the Supreme Court of Canada that resulted in a special programme was brought pursuant to the systemic discrimination provision, section 10 of the Canadian Human Rights Act. The complaint was brought by an advocacy group concerning a railway company's hiring practices. The inclusion of systemic discrimination allowed advocacy groups to share the burden with complainants in challenging policies that adversely effected targeted groups. Although it is still the disadvantaged challenging the practice, the burden is spread among individuals and groups and the remedies have a greater impact. In *Action Travail des Femmes v. Canadian National Railway Co.* (1987), the Court approved a quota ordered by a human rights tribunal that one of every four new employees hired be a woman until 13 per cent of the blue collar (labourer) jobs on the railway were filled by women. The tribunal order also stipulated numerous modifications to the manner in which the respondent tested for entry-level positions, to job requirements, and to the dissemination of employment information and hiring practices. The Supreme Court upheld the tribunal decision. Chief Justice Brian Dickson elucidated on how employment equity is designed to break a continuing cycle of systemic discrimination. The Court stated:

> The goal is not to compensate past victims or even to provide new opportunities for specific individuals who have been unfairly refused jobs or promotion in the past, although some such individuals may be beneficiaries of an employment equity scheme. Rather, an employment equity program is an attempt to ensure that future applicants and workers from the affected group will not face the same insidious barriers that blocked their forbears (*Action Travail des Femmes* p. 1143).

The only other case resulting in the order of corrective measures was the Canadian Human Rights Tribunal decision in *NCARR v. Health Canada* (1997). The decision (which has not been appealed) concerned a systemic discrimination complaint filed by a racial minority advocacy group (*NCARR*) against Health Canada (a government department) alleging that Health Canada had discriminatory practices that deprived 'visible minorities' of employment opportunities in management positions.

The tribunal reviewed statistical evidence of the underrepresentation of 'visible minorities' in management positions. It ordered detailed permanent and temporary measures including training for all managers and human resource professionals on bias-free selection; appointment goals of double availability for five years for permanent appointments into management positions; review mechanisms to ensure the remedy is implemented and quarterly reports to the Canadian Human Rights Commission on implementation.

This decision is very significant for its analysis of systemic discrimination and the remedy ordered. This case is an example of how developing the law in the area of systemic discrimination provides the groundwork for the subsequent, more progressive piece of legislation, the Employment Equity Act. The features of the decision that are useful for employment equity purposes are as follows. The decision found:

- statistics serve as an indicator of a problem and are useful in designing the remedy;
- specific aspects of the employment systems which pose barriers must be identified and characterized;
- stories from individuals bring life to the data and demonstrate the bias;

- a comprehensive remedy is needed in order to break the cycle of discrimination and to reach a critical mass of the underrepresented group in a reasonable time.

Having considered the cases where affirmative action programmes have been ordered to remedy discriminatory practices, we need to examine one of the first cases to reach the Supreme Court of Canada challenging a special programme. In *Re Athabasca Tribal Council v. Amoco Canada Petroleum Company Ltd.* (1981), the Supreme Court[3] found that a special programme to improve the lot of native people was not a breach of the Alberta human rights legislation. It is noteworthy that the human rights statute did not contain a special programme provision at the time the complaint was initiated. The Court could not see how a programme that is designed to enable Indians to compete on equal terms with other members of the community, i.e. to obtain employment without regard to the handicaps which their 'race' has inherited, could be construed as discriminating against other inhabitants.

However, the lower courts did on occasion steer away from the path set by the Supreme Court. Some judges took a restrictive view of special programmes provisions and interpreted the section as an exception to the general provision of equality in section 15(1) rather than a complement to it. There are many problems with this approach. Primarily, it derogates affirmative action programmes to a lower level of equality right, which is interpreted in a narrow manner. This is based on the general principle in human rights law that human rights guarantees are to be given a large and liberal interpretation and any exceptions to those guarantees are to be interpreted narrowly. It also leads to the conclusion that one is not achieving equality by implementing an affirmative action programme but rather permitting an exception to it (Day, 1990: 1; Vizkelety, 1990: 299).

The Supreme Court of Canada decisions in *Athabasca Tribal Council* and *Action Travail des Femmes (ATF)* exemplify the Court's purposive approach to human rights law and recognition of affirmative action as a remedy to overcome systemic discrimination. In *ATF*, the tribunal, affirmed by the Supreme Court, recognized that imposing a quota alone would not remedy the systemic discrimination. Rather, along with the quota, the tribunal ordered a review of the systems that created the discrimination. This reasoning was followed in *NCARR*. These decisions resulted from convincing evidence of the underrepresentation of the groups in question.

It is now recognized that differentiation in treatment is sometimes necessary to achieve equality, which leads to the conclusion that special programmes are an aid to achieving equality rather than an exception to it.

What has been discussed so far is still based on the original model, that of a prohibiting discrimination model. The special programme provisions are voluntary. Employers are not required to develop and implement them under human rights statutes except when ordered by a tribunal in exceptional cases such as the *ATF* and *NCARR* complaints.

Although the individual from a disadvantaged group has the right to be free from discrimination, this may not be enough to address the variety of barriers, exclusions or impediments that prevent that individual from learning about the job opening or obtaining the training to qualify. Even if the individual is prepared to launch a multitude of complaints and expend the energy, time and effort needed to see each through to the end, the fact is that by the time these are redressed (even with an efficient complaints system) the job will be gone. The process may assist future applicants and may develop a point of law, but it remains that the onus is on the individual to challenge the discriminatory practice.

The Canadian Charter of Rights and Freedoms

Before discussing employment equity legislation, which shifts the onus of eliminating discrimination to employers, a focus on the expansion of equality theory resulting from the inception of the Canadian Charter of Rights and Freedoms is warranted.

The Canadian Charter of Rights and Freedoms (referred to as the Charter) is part of the Canadian Constitution and therefore the supreme law of the land. The equality rights provisions in the Charter include a general equality rights section (section 15) and two declaratory sections that provide for Canada's multicultural heritage and equality based on sex. The Charter applies to government or state action, including the state as an employer, but not to private action. The equality rights section includes a general right to equality provision as well as a special programme's provision.

The landmark case that provided guidance on the interpretation of the equality rights provision, section 15, was the Supreme Court of Canada decision in *Andrews v. Law Society of British Columbia* (1989). Mr. Andrews, a British citizen, successfully challenged the citizenship requirement for entry into the legal profession contained in the Barristers and Solicitors Act (British Columbia) on the grounds that it violated his right to equality.

The general principle that guided the court in *Andrews* was the view that laws should not have an adverse effect on disadvantaged groups. Therefore, in considering section 15 applications, the main concern must be the impact of the law on the individual or group concerned. The equality guarantee takes its meaning from the context in which it operates.

The Court rejected the concept that similarly situated people must be similarly treated and differently situated people must be treated differently. The promotion of equality has a more specific goal than the mere elimination of distinctions. Achieving equality may well require differentiation in treatment. This is commonly referred to as the substantive equality theory.

This theory formed the basis for the Supreme Court's rejection of Charter challenges by male prison inmates alleging that surveillance and routine frisk searches by female guards contravened their privacy and equality rights, as female prisoners were not subject to the same searches by male guards. The Court determined that the difference in treatment was reasonably necessary to the success of the affirmative action programme for women guards. The Justices were not sympathetic to the male applicants as they are members of a group that has no historical pattern of group-based discrimination (*Weatherall v. Canada* 1993) and recognized that differences in treatment and special programmes may be required to achieve equality.

The courts appear more willing to read the equality rights section as a whole, the general equality provision along with the affirmative action provision, that embraces one consistent concept of equality. The Ontario Court of Appeal in *Lovelace v. Ontario* (1997 – under appeal to the Supreme Court of Canada), upheld a government affirmative action programme that shared revenues of a casino built on a First Nations Reserve with the Ontario Aboriginal Bands. The Court found the impugned affirmative action provision recognizes that achieving equality may require positive action by government to improve the conditions of historically and socially disadvantaged groups.

The Supreme Court's interpretation of the equality protection as provided in section 15 of the Charter is pragmatic. It recognizes that differences in treatment are sometimes necessary to allow individuals to compete on an equal footing. The Court has stated that the purpose of the guarantee provided in the Charter, in this case, the pursuit of equality requires a generous rather than legalistic interpretation. The equality right must be placed in context so that protection is afforded to members of traditionally disadvantaged groups. These groups may require accommodation to achieve equality. Affirmative action programmes therefore must be seen as an aid to equality, not an exception to it. Applications under the Charter by groups that have not been historically disadvantaged to strike down programmes that assist disadvantaged groups will most likely be rejected by the Court.

Although the Charter refers to a right to equality rather than freedom from discrimination, it does not impose a positive obligation on the government to reduce discrimination. The onus remains with the disadvantaged individual or advocacy group. The Charter's strength lies in the breadth of its impact, where it strikes down discriminatory legislation that may have a large impact.

Employment Equity Act

A right to equality implies more than a right to be free from isolated incidents of discrimination, whether intended or not. It implies a right to equal access to the benefits of society, and a corresponding obligation on those with the power to take the steps needed. This approach forms the basis of the 1996 Federal Employment Equity Act (EEA). The current law was built on the foundation of the original 1986 statute, although its reach has broadened. This legislation now covers all large employers within federal jurisdiction, including government departments. The purpose clause of the EEA is a concrete expression of the right to equality:

> The purpose of this Act is to achieve equality in the workplace so that no person shall be denied employment opportunities or benefits for reasons unrelated to ability and, in the fulfilment of that goal, to correct the conditions of disadvantage in employment experienced by women, aboriginal peoples, persons with disabilities and members of 'visible minorities' by giving effect to the principle that employment equity means more than treating persons in the same way but also requires special measures and the accommodation of differences.

In order to achieve this purpose, the Act requires employers to take systematic steps towards the achievement of equality, including a survey of the workplace to determine who works where in comparison with the qualified local available workforce, and a systems review to examine whether artificial or unnecessary barriers to equality exist. Where a comparison of the workforce with the local qualified labour force indicates that one or more of the groups are substantially underrepresented, or where the employer discovers artificial barriers, a plan is to be developed with concrete goals and specific measures to address these situations.

The employers are asked to shoulder this responsibility, because ultimately only they can remedy the problem by undertaking special measures, by accommodating differences, and by eliminating barriers. They must implement employment equity within a consultative and collaborative framework involving employee representatives and union bargaining agents. Employers are required, as with the 1986 legislation, to submit annual reports to (the federal administering department) Human Resources Development Canada, on the status of the four designated groups in their workforce. They must cooperate with compliance officers from the Canadian Human Rights Commission who will audit their performance. In order to ensure that substantial progress is made, the employers can seek technical assistance from Human Resources Development. Employment equity requires organizations of a certain size to develop employment equity plans, goals and timetables to eliminate barriers to employment for disadvantaged groups (women, disabled, 'visible minorities' and aboriginals) and thereby increase their representation in employment. The Canadian Human Rights Commission will be conducting audits of all federal employers under this law over the course of the next five years.

The Canadian Human Rights Commission's enforcement role is defined in the Act as emphasizing negotiation and persuasion to resolve cases of non-compliance. If the audit indicates that employers are not in full compliance with statutory requirements, compliance review officers will negotiate undertakings that will be reviewed in a follow-up audit within a reasonable period of time. Should this process fail, or should employers not cooperate with the audit, the Act permits the Commission to issue directions and references to tribunal, but clearly this is seen as a last resort.

The new Act was designed to resolve long-standing weaknesses with the 1986 Act. The major shortcomings of the 1986 Act were:

- the Act covered a small portion of the Canadian workforce;
- the government was imposing the legislation on some employers but not on itself (the public service was not included);
- there was no enforcement mechanism for not complying with the Act;
- there was no clear indication of the agency responsible for the implementation, monitoring and enforcement of the Act.

The new Employment Equity Act was strengthened in the following areas:

- the coverage was extended to include the federal public service;
- the Act gave the Canadian Human Rights Commission the authority to conduct on-site audits to verify and gain compliance;

- the Act ensures that the requirements of the Federal Contractors Programme (employers doing business with the government of Canada), with regard to implementation of employment equity, will be equivalent to those of employers under the Act.

The new Act specifically prohibits a tribunal from requiring or ordering quotas. It defines quotas as 'a requirement to hire or promote a fixed and arbitrary number of persons during a given period'. The Act specifies that seniority rights related to layoffs are not considered barriers, and that no direction or order can require that these rights be changed. Employers are required to examine the implications of seniority for the designated groups and to work voluntarily with their unions to find ways of reducing any adverse impact. Employers are not expected to put in place measures that would create undue hardship for the organization, nor can they be required to hire and promote unqualified persons, to set aside the merit principle, or to create new positions in order to achieve representation.

Conclusion

The Canadian experience regarding anti-discrimination statutes illustrates that equality is not a static concept and therefore methods to achieve it cannot remain unchanging. Each institutional or judicial advancement has been based on earlier experience and an expansion of our understanding of what is required to provide Canadians with equality. We have progressed from the most basic level of protecting human rights dealing with the intentional, isolated incident where the complete onus for redress was on the victim, to the creation of human rights commissions that responded to individual complaints, to the development of the theory of systemic discrimination; to the perception of the Charter and the substantive equality theory – all of which still lay the onus of ameliorating the situation on the individual or advocacy groups; to employment equity – where we recognize it is more effective if the onus is passed on to the employers who have the ability to make the changes to avoid discrimination. Canada has been fortunate to have a pragmatic Supreme Court bench that has interpreted equality provisions in a generous rather than a legalistic manner, always keeping in mind the purpose of the equality guarantee. The judiciary's pronouncement that differences in treatment are sometimes necessary to allow individuals to compete on an equal footing, provides the basis for the implementation of affirmative action programmes. In order to achieve equality, accommodation of disadvantaged groups through affirmative action programmes is necessary. Affirmative action programmes are therefore a complement to the equality guarantee rather than an exception to it.

There are still great challenges ahead of us in the attempt to reach the elusive goal of equality, but I am confident that we will ultimately meet that goal if we continue to adapt our processes and keep firmly in mind that equality is not an abstract concept for those who are denied it.

Notes

1. Canada was colonized by the British and French; non-Europeans, particularly non-white immigrants, were regarded as foreigners and were subject to differential treatment based on their 'race', colour, origin and citizenship.
2. Canada is a federation of ten provinces and two territories. Powers are distributed between the provinces and the federal government pursuant to the Canadian constitution. The provincial governments have authority to pass human rights legislation dealing with infringements that fall within matters delegated under the Constitution as being provincial. Examples of provincially regulated employers include manufacturers and the service industry. Matters falling within federal jurisdiction include railways and banks.
3. All members of the Court were in agreement with the final result that the board attempting to require the affirmative action programme did not have the jurisdiction to do so. However, five members of the Court found it unnecessary to specifically deal with the question of whether the affirmative action programme was discriminatory because the Human Rights Act in question had been amended to include provisions for affirmative action prior to the case reaching the Supreme Court. The other four members who determined the issue concluded that the programme was not discriminatory.

8

Affirmative Action and 'Race' Relations: 'Affirmative Action' as a Model for Europe

Nathan Glazer

In my contribution I will discuss the question of what Europe can learn from the thirty-year experience of the US with affirmative action. Further, what has been the effect of affirmative action on 'race' relations in the US? Has it been overall a positive or a negative influence? In trying to answer these questions, Americans will also be interested in what they can learn from the European experience with its equivalent of our affirmative action, which is generally called positive action. Both America and Europe are committed to shaping societies with a greater degree of equality between the older, established elements of the population and the newer groups, often of different religion and 'race', that have now become a permanent part of these societies. We are also interested in shaping societies with a greater degree of harmony between established and marginalized groups. So we must consider not only whether and how affirmative action can help achieve a greater degree of equal opportunity and achievement for these new groups but also how we can move toward a society in which racial discrimination and racial discord are sharply reduced. It is to these questions that those of us from the US who have studied and lived with the policies and the problems we sum up under the term 'affirmative action' can make a contribution.

These are, of course, not simple questions. The literature on affirmative action in the US is enormous. The Harvard University library lists 563 items under affirmative action programmes, and although there is some duplication in this list, and some items refer to developments in Canada, Australia, New Zealand, and some European countries, that is by no means all the literature on the subject. The programmes, public and private, that engage in some form of affirmative action in the US, are without number. Just what we mean when we say 'affirmative action' is also not at all clear. Different ways of sampling public opinion on affirmative action get very different results, because people do not know just what is included in affirmative action. We know that if we ask a question about 'racial preference' in jobs or admissions to universities, a large majority will disapprove, but if we ask the same question about 'affirmative action' without specifying just what is involved, the numbers disapproving will drop sharply.[1] This was demonstrated clearly in a vote on affirmative action programmes in the city of Houston, Texas. The opponents of affirmative action had put on the ballot a referendum on whether the voters wanted to continue programmes giving 'preference' to minorities. The defenders of these programmes, the mayor of the city and its business leaders, managed to get the wording of the referendum changed to ask whether the voters wished to continue 'affirmative action programmes'. They did manage to change the wording, and the referendum failed: affirmative action has a positive aura about it; racial preference does not. Successful referenda in the states of California and Washington to eliminate state affirmative action programmes did not use the term 'affirmative action', but instead asserted that there should be no discrimination on grounds of 'race' or national origin by state agencies in giving employment, in admission to public colleges and universities, and in the granting of contracts.

Affirmative action policies have a variety of objectives, and they are not necessarily consistent with each other. Policies that advance the interests of racial minorities, which open up jobs for them, which increase their numbers in colleges and universities, can at the same time exacerbate racial and group conflict. Such policies might simultaneously advance the interests of members of minority groups and increase the antagonism and resentment against them. We see some evidence of this in the US, and we would find disagreement among informed observers over whether the improvement in the economic and social position of minorities outweighs and makes worthwhile the tensions and conflicts that have been created by affirmative action policies (Sniderman and Piazza, 1993; Sniderman and Carmines, 1997).[2]

Indeed, there is also disagreement about whether these policies have actually improved the condition of minority groups, or whether this improvement, which is, real has not alternatively been the result of the growth of the economy and the decline of discriminatory and prejudiced attitudes, independent of policies of affirmative action (Thernstrom and Thernstrom, 1997).

In this paper, I select only a few themes that are important for this assignment. I will first lay out some distinctive characteristics of affirmative action policies in the US. It is not necessarily the case that policies designed for similar ends in other countries will be similar to those that have developed in the US. Nevertheless, to examine the experience of the US, the country with probably the widest and deepest experience of affirmative action, will be helpful in understanding the limits of affirmative action and the possible negative consequences that can flow from such policies, whatever their good intentions.

Second, I will emphasize some distinctive characteristics of the US that inevitably shape the policies it has created, and suggest that positive action, as it is called in Europe, will have to be somewhat different from affirmative action in the US because of these characteristics. I know the term 'Europe' covers many countries with rather different political systems, histories, and social characteristics, and it is all too easy to construct an ideal type that corresponds to no country in particular, yet the special American characteristics I will discuss that have led to the creation of our type of affirmative action do indeed distinguish the US from all Western European countries. I will also consider the impact of affirmative action on 'race' relations in the US.

Third, I will make some very tentative comments on whether affirmative action policies of the type we have in the US, even if possible, would be desirable in Europe.

What is American Affirmative Action?

What are we speaking of when we speak of affirmative action? Affirmative action describes policies that aim to improve the position of minority racial and ethnic groups that have suffered from racial and group discrimination. But its distinctive characteristic is that it goes beyond neutrality in the treatment it advocates for members of minority groups to call for some degree of special concern or preference. In the US, women have been added as a group protected by affirmative action, even though there are many differences between the kinds of disabilities racial and ethnic and religious minorities face, and the kinds of disabilities that women face. We will not discuss in this paper the issue of women in affirmative action, although it plays a large role in discussions of affirmative action in the US.

It is necessary to emphasize the difference between policies that aim to eliminate discrimination and policies that go beyond this to advocate or demand a degree of special concern or preference, although there are indeed close connections between these two kinds of policies. There is little controversy in the US concerning policies that target discrimination on racial or ethnic or religious grounds. The laws that have made discrimination on grounds of 'race', religion, and national origin, in employment and in many other key areas of life, illegal, are solidly established, and are disputed only by a few. The distinctive characteristic of affirmative action, however, is that it goes beyond non-discrimination. It therefore must be distinguished from policies that aim to prevent and punish and eliminate direct discrimination.

In the US, different agencies have been created for these two objectives: to prevent discrimination we have most prominently the Federal Equal Employment Opportunity Commission, created by the great Civil Rights Act of 1965, which has as its central mission responding to individual complaints of discrimination. Beyond that, and more important, it seeks out and attempts to eliminate discrimination by employers, and practices it considers discriminatory. To promote affirmative action we have most prominently the Office of Federal Contract Compliance Programmes, which has as its central mission the overseeing of programmes of affirmative action by employers who have contracts with the federal government, a category that includes almost every large business, every college and university, every hospital, because all of these receive funds from the federal government, directly or indirectly (for example, student loans and grants).

The key characteristic of affirmative action, in its original conception and today, is that it is intended to reach beyond non-discrimination. A non-discriminatory employment policy, aiming at the employment of persons with certain levels of skill, or a non-discriminatory admission policy by a university aiming at admitting students with certain qualifications, may be truly 'colour-blind', but may result in a situation in which very few persons of a minority group will get the job in question or be admitted to the university programme in question. When this happens, and it was clear this was happening in the US of the 1960s in the wake of the powerful and sweeping Civil Rights law of 1965, the question comes up 'should we not go further, and ask employers and colleges and universities to reach out, to seek out the qualified of the underrepresented groups, to inform them they are welcome and that the employer or university is eager to employ or admit them?'

This was the original conception of affirmative action. We can call it 'soft' affirmative action. It is not controversial. Much affirmative action is of this type. Colleges and universities will send out students who are from minority groups to their former high schools to tell prospective students that they are welcome in the institution they attend, and to give a public demonstration by their presence of the fact. Employers will add to their advertisements that they are 'affirmative action employers' by which they mean to inform applicants that they welcome persons from minority groups and women. Employers may set up special programmes for persons from the underrepresented groups to prepare them for higher skilled jobs. Colleges and universities may do the same. There are many policies of this sort that might best be labelled 'soft' affirmative action, the sort of affirmative action that eschews the attempt to reach a specific numerical goal.

Very early in the effort to root out discrimination in the 1960s, government agencies whose task was to enforce anti-discrimination laws came across the problem of underrepresentation of minorities and women among employers who insisted they were acting without discrimination, and in whose practices no cases of direct discrimination on grounds of 'race' or sex could be found. What was to be done to increase the numbers of minorities and women in jobs in the absence of evidence of discrimination? What was done was that the federal government began to require of employers that they set targets or goals for minority or female employees that they expected to reach using the soft means of advertising, training, assisting. But once one sets a target, a goal, a number so and so many blacks, Hispanics, or women by such and such a date one has what we might call 'hard' affirmative action.[3]

'Hard' and 'soft' are not terms in law or administration: I use them to separate out the policies of reaching out, advertising, training and preparing, from the policies that aim at achieving certain numerical goals. Because it was not easy for anti-discrimination agencies to find and litigate successfully cases of actual discrimination, the hard goals were added on to the soft policies in the effort to advance the interests of minorities and women. This is the essential factor that makes affirmative action so controversial: numbers instead of general effort, statistical measures instead of examination of specific cases. These numerical goals, it is generally believed, lead to the selection of one person instead of another on the grounds of 'race' or sex.

Once set on this course many things unintended in the original civil rights law or by civil rights advocates followed. How was one to set a goal? How was one to monitor its achievement? In order to do so, one had to have numbers on how many minorities and women were employed in each firm, and how many one might have expected would have been employed in the absence of discrimination. Employers were therefore required to keep records of how many persons of certain minority groups and women they had employed, and in what positions, universities were required to keep records by 'race' and sex of the students they admitted. While civil rights law prohibits all discrimination on grounds of 'race', national origin, religion, sex, four specific racial and ethnic groups were chosen for which employers would have to keep and report these statistics: blacks, for whom the most accepted name today is African American; Hispanic Americans, that is, persons from the Spanish speaking countries of the American continents, now commonly called Latinos; Orientals, for whom the preferred name is now Asians; and American Indians, now called Native Americans.

Just how these four specific categories were chosen in the 1960s as those on which employers and universities had to report to government agencies, and as the groups whose protection became the special concern of government in monitoring affirmative action programmes, has never been completely clear, despite the effort that has gone into research on the origins of affirmative action. Clearly, only one of these four groups was central in the civil rights revolution, as both its proponents and its subjects: American blacks or African Americans. But it is the nature of government and bureaucracy to generalize, and one assumes that it was decided that all non-white 'races' should be covered by the reporting form, as well as that group that is quasi racial in the American mind, Latin Americans. Such a decision was facilitated by the fact that the US records the numbers in all these groups, either because they are labelled specific 'races', or listed separately as 'Hispanic'. The anomalies in selecting these groups have been pointed out often, particularly by critics of affirmative action (Glazer, 1987).[4] For example, by the late 1960s, Japanese Americans and Chinese Americans, the only two groups of Asians found then in substantial numbers in the US, had already achieved levels of income and education equivalent to the European white population. Did they need 'affirmative action'? The Hispanic category included Cubans, then almost entirely white and middle class, who had arrived as refugees from Castro's Cuba, and who benefited from generous refugee aid programmes. Did they need affirmative action in addition? Native Americans, or American Indians, have many special programmes designed to improve their condition, and one can ask the same question about them. Since the time when these four groups were set as special beneficiaries of affirmative action, two of them, Asian Americans and Latinos, have doubled and redoubled in number as a result of immigration. No one intended, when affirmative action began, that some of its major beneficiaries would be immigrants.

Once set, it has proved impossible to change the reporting categories. Indeed, there has been no effort to do so, despite their irrationality. The minority group beneficiaries of government affirmative action programmes have remained unchanged since, even while their numbers have increased greatly through immigration and they now include groups, such as Asian Indians, which were hardly visible in the US of the Civil Rights Act, but which are among the most prosperous in the US today.

In order to set affirmative action goals for these four groups and for women, it was necessary to determine what numbers of each group and what numbers of women might have been employed in the absence of discrimination. The basic assumption that governed the construction of these figures, the assumption that there is an 'expected' employment figure for each ethnic or racial group in the absence of discrimination, would not be accepted by most sociologists, since it ignores such factors as historical experience, varied interests, the role of niche opportunities, etc. Even in the absence of significant discrimination, ethnic groups in the US have very different occupational distributions. But regardless of these difficulties, such figures and such unrealistic assumptions were necessary if one was to set a goal. Goals were determined for each employer on the basis of the number of those who were considered qualified to fill the position. The employer was then to attempt through 'affirmative action' to reach that goal.

Words and their meanings have played an enormous role in the controversies over affirmative action. The proponents of affirmative action government agencies, civil rights groups insisted these numbers were simply 'goals'. The employer was to try to reach that goal. A 'good faith effort' to reach the goal that failed would incur no penalties, the defenders of affirmative action insisted. The opponents of affirmative action insisted that the goals were 'quotas', a harder and tougher term. Failure to reach a goal might be considered innocent, the result of a well-intentioned effort that simply fell short. Alternatively, failure to reach a goal might trigger punitive government action – withdrawal of contracts, for example. 'Goal' has a positive connotation – it reflects honest effort; 'quota' has a negative connotation – it suggests tough requirements and tough penalties. The opponents of affirmative action insisted that when government was the decider of whether there had truly been a 'good faith' effort to reach the goal, and could punish the employer who had not reached the goal, we were dealing not with a goal but a quota.

In the American situation, 'quota' also carried another important negative connotation. Until the 1960s, major American colleges and universities, and in particular law and medical schools, limited the number of Jewish students. Much anti-discrimination law, passed in the late 1940s and 1950s at the state level, was directed specifically against this discrimination against Jews, against the 'quotas' imposed by colleges and universities and medical and law schools. These laws were passed through the efforts of coalitions of Jews and blacks, with Jews playing the leading role. 'Quota' thus represented to the public mind, and particularly to Jews and Jewish organizations, the ceilings that had limited their opportunities to enter good colleges and universities and good professional schools, rather than the 'goals' hoped for to improve the condition of blacks. One way to attack affirmative action was to label their 'goals', which might on their face seem unexceptionable, 'quotas'.

This brief description of affirmative action must be supplemented by some consideration of the areas within which affirmative action operates, and the kinds of authority under which it operates. Affirmative action affects employment, by private and public employers; the granting of contracts by public authorities; the granting of licenses in areas under public authority, such as licenses to run radio and TV stations. There are policies that attempt to reach or maintain certain proportions of 'races' and ethnic group in public and semi-public housing that can be called 'affirmative action', although that term is not used in housing. One of the most controversial policies in 'race' relations in the US is school desegregation, which is clearly a 'numbers-driven' policy, aiming at certain percentages of black students in majority white schools, or white students in majority black schools. This is an area in which 'quotas' are set, in particular to limit the number of white or Asian students in higher status public schools, schools that one can enter only on the basis of a selective examination, in order to make room for African American or Hispanic students who do not score as high in competitive examinations. But for these policies, despite their similarities to certain affirmative action policies, we do not use the term 'affirmative action'.

Finally, in this overall description of affirmative action in the US, it is necessary to say something about the authority under which affirmative action is pursued. All levels of government are involved – federal, state, county, city – but the most important forms of affirmative action have been instituted and maintained by the federal government, and specifically the executive branch of government, the office of the President, under its authority as a 'contractor'. In its role as a contractor with employers, private and non-profit and public, the federal government requires affirmative action plans, with targets and goals, for the four minority groups and for women. It pursues this objective with varying intensity, less under Republican administrations, more under Democratic.

The legislative branch of government – the Congress – sometimes sets its own affirmative action goals, the most important of which are in appropriation bills for the building or repair of roads, which require a certain proportion of the contracts to go to minority and women contractors.

But on the whole Congress has been much less supportive of affirmative action than the executive branch of government.

The judiciary, the federal courts, play a major role in affirmative action. Requirements that local police and fire departments, for example, hire certain proportions of minorities are instituted as a result of federal action in the courts to overcome presumed discrimination. These are some of the most controversial types of affirmative action, because they require the revision or the setting aside of the results of civil service examinations, and upset the expectations of candidates who have scored high but are not of the favoured groups. The legal basis for such policies of quota hiring is a demonstration of discrimination in past practices. One controversial but common way of demonstrating there has been discrimination in government employment is to argue that the tests for these jobs are discriminatory, and one proves they are discriminatory by showing that applicants from minority groups perform poorly on them. It is up to the judges, on the basis of expert testimony and lawyers' arguments, to determine whether the tests are biased. Litigation of this sort, which is generally instituted against states and cities by the federal government, will commonly lead to a decision or to a 'consent decree' (a technical legal term describing an agreement by the defendant to fulfil certain conditions), in which the city or state agrees to hire certain numbers of percentages of minorities. This is not technically 'affirmative action', which does not require any demonstration of previous discrimination, but in the popular mind a quota set by a judge is considered affirmative action, and is considered no different from a goal set by a federal agency for a contractor under affirmative action requirements. Both may lead to resentment among majority group persons who believe a job or promotion they should have received has been given to a less-qualified person.

States and counties and cities generally have their own affirmative action programmes, both for contracting and for employment.

Finally, independent of any public action, employers, private and non-profit, may have their own voluntary programmes. These may have been initiated originally under government pressure, or under pressure from civil rights groups. Today they are maintained even in the absence of any governmental requirement. They may exist because of political pressures from customers and employees, or because the employer honestly believes in them, and considers 'diversity' in his work force very important, as a way of reaching customers, or appealing to public opinion.[5]

The area of affirmative action that has recently become most controversial, college and university admissions, for the most part consists of voluntary programmes, not required by government, and adopted by the institutions themselves. These programmes are distinctively American, and are only possible because admission to leading American colleges and universities, in particular the private institutions that form a large part of the college and university system, is not determined exclusively by tests or academic achievement. It is hardly likely that we will see any equivalent to such programmes in Europe.

In discussing affirmative action in the US, one must be aware of the large role played by voluntary action, independent of legal requirement, by employers and by colleges and universities.

The reach of affirmative action in the US is thus wide and deep, affecting many areas of life, under various kinds of authority. Some of these forms of affirmative action may be surprising to Europeans. For example, the major foundations, which are so important in maintaining scientific research in the US, are among the chief supporters of affirmative action. Scholars applying for grants for research projects will often be asked to add minorities and women to their research team by the foundation to which they are applying, and may well take this into consideration in making up their research team even before they are asked.

In the last few years, we have seen some significant successful attacks on affirmative action. This is surprising because affirmative action has been maintained and extended over thirty years without major successful attack, and persisted even under the national administrations of Presidents Ronald Reagan and George Bush, who were opposed to affirmative action. Nor is there any evidence that public opinion on affirmative action has changed in any marked degree. Public opinion has always been against affirmative action, but the negative percentage varies depending on the form of the question, and the opposition to affirmative action has never been at the top of the public's agenda in urgency. As with so many other public issues, those for affirmative action support it with a passion and commitment that politically has outweighed the lukewarm majority that is against it. The success of recent referenda banning state affirmative action in California and Washington suggests that there has been a change in the politics of affirmative action. Independently, there has been over the past few years a shift in the position of Supreme Court on some aspects of affirmative action. It has restricted affirmative action in the granting of contracts by public agencies. The federal courts may be moving to a more critical view of the legitimacy of affirmative action under the Constitution and civil rights laws. A federal appeals court has ruled that the affirmative action programme of the University of Texas Law School is unconstitutional because of its preference for black and Hispanic applicants, and that 'race' must not be taken into account in university admissions. This ruling has not been reviewed by the Supreme Court, but it has already led to a radical change in admission procedures in the public universities of Texas.

But the large structure of affirmative action, while damaged, persists. Affirmative action in employment, public and private, has not yet been affected by these changes. Private colleges and universities have not changed their practices. Public colleges and universities outside Texas and California resist changing their practices. Even in Texas and California, new approaches are being developed to keep up the number of black and Hispanic students. In the case of contracting, cities regularly now commission studies to show they did discriminate in the past in order to be able to justify their affirmative action quotas under the requirements of the Supreme Court. Yet undoubtedly affirmative action has been damaged. The attack on affirmative action, fuelled by individuals who feel they have been discriminated against on the ground of their 'race', and by persons and groups committed to the principle that government must never take 'race' into account, and supported by conservative foundations, will continue.

Why the Strength of Affirmative Action in the US?

To the second large question: why have we had this remarkable development of affirmative action? I believe it is essential to recognize three distinctive conditions in the US that have supported and made possible the institution and spread of affirmative action. These three conditions are, first, the existence of a large lower caste throughout American history, whose fate has often been at the centre of American history and politics; second, the existence of an immigrant society, in which the authority and status and power of the founding element has for many years been declining, to be replaced by the ideal of the incorporation of immigrants into American society as equals; and third, the distinctive and continuing role of the founding documents of American society, the Declaration of Independence and the Constitution, and the unquestioned authority and power of the Supreme Court in interpreting them.

The situation of the African Americans has no parallel in any contemporary advanced modern society. They are twelve per cent of the American population. They were present from the beginning of the English colonies out of which the US was created, and formed one fifth of the population of the US at the first census in 1790. Their slave status was the decisive cause of the Civil War, the greatest trauma in American history, and the most important amendments to the American Constitution were passed after the war to free them and make them citizens. They were nevertheless subjected, after the end of slavery to continuing severe prejudice and discrimination, both public and private. In a major section of the country, state and local laws imposed this condition, and in other parts of the country a pattern of prejudice and discrimination was tolerated. This situation was only brought to an end thirty years ago. The civil rights revolution of the 1960s was carried primarily by African Americans and their liberal allies. The point of the civil rights revolution was to raise the condition of blacks, who from the point of view of education, income, occupation, were on the bottom rungs of American society.

There would probably be no affirmative action today for minority groups were it not for the civil rights revolution and the condition of blacks. However, affirmative action as a policy was not limited to blacks. Three other groups, with varying and very different claims on American society, were added by bureaucratic decision to the categories that were to be aided by affirmative action. But it is clear why affirmative action exists in the first place: it is because non-discrimination was not enough to raise the condition of blacks.

This caste characteristic of American blacks still persists. It is evident in the fact that children born of black-white marriages, which are increasing in number, are always considered black. As a comment by a historian puts it: how is it that a white woman can give birth to a black baby, but a black woman can never give birth to a white baby? It is because African Americans, uniquely among American minorities, are still to some extent bound by caste rules created under slavery.[6] This does not prevent blacks from attaining high positions in government: some have been considered for the very highest, or high positions in education and in business. Blacks have headed major universities and colleges and foundations. Yet on average the educational and economic position of blacks is the lowest of any major group in the American population. This is the motor that drives affirmative action.

Other groups, with a much lesser historical claim to redress, benefit from affirmative action too. This is because of the too easy acceptance of the idea that American society is generally racist and discriminates against all non-whites. Yet the degree of discrimination has varied greatly historically, and today scarcely affects some of the groups that are benefited by affirmative action. American racism arose primarily, I believe, from the contacts between whites and blacks, when blacks were in an inferior slave condition, at the very beginnings of English settlement in the New World. Other groups were also affected by American racism and so there was some logic to the original expansion of affirmative action to cover all non-white 'races'. This theory of a general American racism directed against all non-white groups once reflected reality, but groups in the US change their non-white racial status as they become better educated, move into elite occupations, and attain middle class incomes. Under these circumstances, the group 'whitens' in the US: that is to say it is no longer considered different from other Americans, and joins the majority. It is considered 'assimilated' or 'Americanized'. This is what happened to major immigrant groups, as historians have recently pointed out: Irish, Italians, Jews, considered of a different and inferior 'race' at the time of their immigration, in time came to be considered part of the majority (Ignatiev, 1996; Jacobson, 1998). I believe this is happening to the major Asian groups. It has happened to the more prosperous Hispanic groups, for example the Cubans.

The caste condition of a major element in the American population is the primary reason why we have affirmative action. The special role of immigration in the history of the US adds a complication that affirmative action policy in general has not faced. It is interesting and revealing that two of the countries that come closest to the US in affirmative action policies and in policies that privilege minority groups, such as multi-culturalism, are also countries of immigration, Canada and Australia. In all three countries, immigration policies to populate the country have been among the key decisions shaping the nation, and still continue to be an essential part of their politics with great consequences for their future.

The contrast with European nations is striking. In these nations, while immigration became massive in the first two decades after the end of the Second World War and in recent years with the upheavals following the end of communism, it is taken for granted that it is no part of the national interest to regularly add to the population through immigration from abroad. This is a universal consensus among leaders and voters. Immigration in these countries is based on the specific circumstances of the individual such as an individual's desire to bring in family members, or an individual's need for political asylum, or on a specific need for labour in times of prosperity. There is no general immigration policy.

An immigration policy implies some point of view, some policy, as to the relation of immigrants to the existing settled society. This can be a relation of inferiority, and it often is, but in a nation that is itself made up of immigrants, and is guided by the general principles of liberal political society that are now near universal in advanced societies, the new immigrants are expected to become full partners in the society. In the US, this full partnership has often been hampered and delayed by prejudice and discrimination, but in time this full partnership has become the norm for all immigrant groups.

The particular connection between the common American assumptions about immigration and affirmative action is that affirmative action, because its coverage was extended beyond African Americans to other non-white 'races', now in large measure covers immigrants, and quite recent immigrants. This is an anomaly from the point of view of common American attitudes as to what is owed to immigrants. They are owed non-discrimination and opportunity, as the birthright of all Americans, but they are not owed the additional protection given by affirmative action. Immigrants of non-white 'race' are protected from racial discrimination by anti-discrimination laws. Should they be further protected by affirmative action, which in theory and even in reality implies preference for non-white immigrants over other immigrants and the native born who are white?

This is an Achilles' heel of American affirmative action. It is evident, in particular, in affirmative action requirements for contracting, which now give preference to entrepreneurs and businessmen of various Asian groups who are immigrants. But affirmative action was not designed for immigrants. In the American context, they are expected to make progress with no more aid than non-immigrants, and always have. It would seem to be an easy matter to correct this anomaly, but politically it is not. No politician will support removing Asian Americans, for examples, whose education and income are equal to or surpass that of average Americans, from the affirmative action category, because of the fear of the charge of racism, and of punishment from Asian American voters. The US has not fully considered the relationship between immigration and affirmative action. It is in the anomalous position today of trying to control illegal immigration, while illegal immigrants in protected affirmative action categories have in some respects greater privileges than natives or illegals who are white.

Yet a third factor shapes and colours affirmative action in the US: the pre-eminent role of fundamental constitutional principles, their almost sacerdotal character, and the great power and respect of the Supreme Court in its role as interpreter of key constitutional provisions. It serves as a counterbalance to democratic institutions that I think has no equivalent in other democratic countries, although one does see an increasing role for constitutional courts in some of the countries of Europe and in Canada. The role of the Supreme Court was to undertake a revolution in the interpretation and application of these key principles demanding equality before the law in the 1950s, at a time when the Congress would not do so, and to protect the development and expansion of affirmative action in the 1960s and 1970s. It is now playing a key role in the counterrevolution that is hemming in and limiting affirmative action, again at a time when the Congress will not for political reasons do so. It would take us too far afield to try to explain how this undemocratic institution, unelected and unresponsible to the people, nevertheless serves to keep the democratic order on an even keel, yet I do think that is what is happening today. The legislative bodies will not act to limit affirmative action, and the popular will sometimes goes too far in limiting it. In this complex situation, the federal courts and the Supreme Court have a key role to play.

What Effect has Affirmative Action had on the Condition of Minorities in the US?

This is a disputed and difficult question. In the key area of employment, it seems clear that the state of the economy, the decline in racist sentiment, and the major laws banning discrimination on grounds of 'race', religion or national origin have been the key factors in the improvement of the economic condition of black Americans. Indeed, some argue that even the effect of laws banning discrimination was not crucial in determining the economic rise of blacks: the buoyant economy, the migration to the north and west of southern blacks, and the decline of racist sentiment, was sufficient (Thernstrom and Thernstrom, 1997; Sowell, 1981).

The additional effect of affirmative action is hard to estimate or quantify, although there have been many econometric studies that have attempted to do so, with varying results. But as its chief impact is on large employers with government contracts, and on local, state, and federal government, one would be safe to conclude that affirmative action has had an effect in concentrating black employees in those sectors of the economy. It does not seem to have had a similar effect on Hispanic Americans, who are not so concentrated, or on Asian Americans.

The effects of affirmative action are perhaps clearest in the case of college and university admissions, where a recent major work has documented both the degree of preference given to blacks in those institutions that are selective, and the presumed effects of this preference in the lives of those who receive it (Bowen and Bok, 1998).[7] Most American colleges and universities are not particularly selective, and grant admission to all who apply with minimal qualifications. Unfortunately we have no similar major work dealing with employment effects of affirmative action.

What Effect has Affirmative Action had on 'Race' Relations?

This is not an easy question to answer. If affirmative action has raised the social and economic position of minority groups, increased equal status relations between members of minority and majority groups as minority group members attained positions in which they interacted and worked with the majority, if it has increased minority incomes so that they have become more equal to those of the majority, one might conclude that affirmative action has improved 'race' relations. But there are many assumptions that have to be made in concluding that a rise in the social and economic status of a deprived group will improve relations between that group and the majority. Further, as I pointed out above, it is not clear to what degree this economic rise, which has occurred, is owing to affirmative action, as against other significant factors, such as the redistribution of the black population from the south to the north and west, the strength of the American economy, and the effects of anti-discrimination laws and the great change in American attitudes on the issue of 'race'. Looking at all these factors, one may well ask whether affirmative action was necessary for the rise of the black population, and there is no easy answer.

Finally, there is no question that affirmative action has also exacerbated relations to some extent. It divides sharply the white population and the black population. (Other beneficiaries of affirmative action – Hispanics, Asians, women – are more divided on the issue.) This division is evident in public opinion polls, and becomes public and intensely divisive when affirmative action becomes a public issue, as in the case of the conflict over the referendum in California to ban affirmative action. It is one of the costs of affirmative action.

Lessons for Europe?

What lessons follows from all this? Reviewing these distinctive character-istics of American society, I see two lessons:

Europe does not have a lower caste, or anything like it. It has distinctive regions in some European countries, some with distinctive cultural characteristics, and it has immigrants. I do not think positive action in Europe is thought of as playing a role in correcting regional inequalities. General economic policies, and the policies of the European Union, are expected to deal with that. Europe does have immigrant groups, now with large second generations, and these second generations, generally of educational and occupational status below that of the longsettled inhabitants, do raise disturbing policy questions. Are these questions to be answered by positive action? If Europe is to have positive action policies, can they possibly have as much authority as affirmative action has in a society with the distinctive history of a lower caste, long held in subjection, and a society which is now earnestly trying to erase the status and indicia of the lower caste?

Would it do more good or harm to have positive action for these groups in Europe? Certainly protection from discrimination for these groups in employment, education, housing, law, is the first obligation of a liberal political order. But positive action goes further than this and raises the question, how much more than this is necessary or desirable? Is there not a danger in creating what to the non-minority element of the population would appear to be a special privilege, with resultant resentments? This must be carefully considered. In the US, the research of Paul Sniderman and his colleagues suggests strongly that affirmative action to some degree increases resentment and antagonism against blacks, and forms a kind of check to the uniform improvement in white attitudes toward blacks that has been underway for more than half a century. As Sniderman and Piazza (1993) write:

> It is unfortunately . . . true that a number of whites dislike the idea of affirmative action so much and perceive it to be so unfair that they have come to dislike blacks as a consequence . . . . In the very effort to make things better, we have made some things worse . . . . Wishing to close the racial divide in America, we have widened it.[8]

This is not necessarily decisive, whether for affirmative action in the US or positive action in Europe. This perhaps modest negative risk will be more easily accepted in the US, which is trying to resolve a difficult centuries-old problem, than in Europe, which is dealing with a rather more limited problem only a few decades old.

To conclude on my first point: Europe has no major caste problem. It does not therefore need radical solutions. It does have an immigrant problem, and a second generation immigrant problem, but there are different categories of immigrants in each country, and their problems are different. The problem of defining the categories eligible for positive action would be difficult and disruptive. Of course positive action covers a huge range of policies, as is true of affirmative action in the US, and many of these may not be very controversial, and can be defended as part of the general effort that we see in all European countries to raise the skills and qualities of labour. But positive action also suggests the possibility of the hard affirmative action that is so controversial in the US, and that kind of affirmative action would be best avoided.

A second point: where is the authority to define and impose policies that many in the native population will consider harmful to themselves? Here we must consider the structure of authority that has permitted, in the US, the development and maintenance for thirty years of policies most Americans oppose. There is no equivalent in Europe, in its power to shape and impose key decisions in a society, to the American Constitution and the American Supreme Court. Under these circumstances, positive action in Europe would be in large measure a bureaucratic creation – as it is in the US – and would therefore be seen as distant from the popular will. It would not have the sanction that unpopular policies have in the US when they are approved and upheld by the authority of the Supreme Court interpreting the Constitution. Further, if these policies stem from decisions of various organs of the European Community, they are likely to have even less authority in the eyes of those who find them distasteful. Laws need moral authority as well as proper legal status to be effective. I see where the moral authority for affirmative action comes from in the US; I do not see anywhere near equivalent authority for positive action in Europe. Once again, this suggests that Europe should go slow in pushing toward positive action.

Notes

1. For example, a Washington Post ABC poll of 1995 asked opinions about programmes 'that give preference to minorities or women to make up for past discrimination'. Three quarters were in opposition: 47 per cent wanted such programs changed, 28 per cent favoured their outright elimination. A Gallup poll of the same period showed 55 per cent in favour of 'affirmative action' (McWhirter, 1996: 4).
2. Paul Sniderman and various colleagues, through the analysis of national opinion polls and through some ingenious experiments they have devised for use in public opinion polls, have made this argument.
3. On the shift from 'hard' to 'soft' affirmative action in the late 1960s and early 1970s, and in particular the role of bureaucratic considerations in leading to such a change, see Skrentny (1996).
4. In particular the introduction to the 1987 edition.

5. The ramifications of these business programmes may extend far beyond the simple initial aim of increasing the number of minority employees. Consider for example, an advertisement in New York Times of 7 January 1999, paid for by the Mobil Oil Corporation, entitled 'Diversity in business starts in the classroom'. It points to the need for and difficulty of recruiting 'emerging minority talent'. It continues: 'In today's global, diverse, business environment, successful corporations view finding and keeping minority employees a business imperative. But turning to business schools, job offers in hand companies find far too few African Americans, Hispanic Americans, or Native Americans waiting to meet them.' The advertisement points out there are very few faculty members of these groups in business schools, and this may be one reason there are so few students of these groups there. 'That's why in 1994, several corporate executives and academics developed The PhD Project . . . . The PhD Project works to increase the ranks of minority business professors. It reaches outstanding candidates of colour now working in business, encourages them to switch careers and earn a business PhD.'
6. The literature on the distinctive position of African Americans among American minorities is voluminous, but for a summary of some of the key distinguishing characteristics see Glazer (1997: chapter 6).
7. See a review and discussions of this book by Glazer (1999).
8. They write this on the basis of an ingenious experiment in opinion polling which I will not describe here. Their point is not determinative, of course. It merely indicates one possible consequence of positive action that must be taken into account.

Part II
The European Experiences

Positive Action in the United Kingdom
Paul Taylor

Introduction

In the UK lawful positive action measures have been available for over twenty years, however they have not been widely adopted by organizations. This chapter will firstly outline the UK legislative framework that allows positive action to be taken. It will then consider the context within which effective positive action should be taken. Finally, the chapter will consider some examples of positive action that have been taken by organizations within the UK. Throughout the chapter I will consider why positive action has not been more widely used and the ways in which the legislative framework could allow for racial discrimination to be tackled more effectively. Concerning the term 'positive action' the following definition will be used throughout the paper:

> Positive action is a range of measures which employers can lawfully take to encourage and train people from underrepresented (racial and ethnic groups) in order to help them overcome disadvantages in competing with other applicants. However, selection for interviews and jobs must be based on judgements of individuals' ability to carry out the work required.

The Legal Framework

The Race Relations Act 1976 (RRA) makes provisions for employers and training providers to encourage members of particular racial groups to apply for posts where it can be shown that they have been previously underrepresented. The RRA was strongly modelled on the Sex Discrimination Act 1975, which contains a similar provision for positive action to be taken in relation to countering sex discrimination. The RRA makes it lawful for an employer to provide training to members of underrepresented racial groups to equip them to do particular work. The aim of this type of positive action is to allow members of underrepresented racial groups to compete with others on equal terms for available jobs. Positive action may be able to help increase general levels of representation within an organization as well as among more senior and skilled jobs. It can therefore be used at both level of entry to an organization and in relation to internal promotion processes. Selection must, however, be based on merit and assessed using criteria which are relevant to the demands of the job.

Within the UK legislation underrepresentation is a key prerequisite of any lawful positive action measure. Employers are able to implement positive action measures provided that they can show that underrepresentation currently exists according to one or more of the following conditions:

- there are no persons of that racial group employed in that work by the organization;
- that the number of employees engaged in that work who belong to that racial group is small in proportion to:
    (a) their representation as a percentage of the Great Britain workforce;
    (b) their representation amongst the population of the area from which the organization normally recruits either locally or nationally.

The specific lawful positive action measures that can be taken, provided the conditions of underrepresentation are met, are derived from sections 35, 37 and 38 of the RRA. Welsh et al. (1994) distinguish three different types of positive action which are lawful: encouragement measures, pre-entry training and in-service training. Encouragement measures (sections 37 and 38 of the RRA) allow an organization to encourage persons of a particular racial group to take advantage of opportunities for doing particular work in an area of employment where they are currently underrepresented. An example of this might be within job advertisements where an organization includes a statement which encourages applicants from a specific racial group to apply, explaining that currently they are underrepresented. Pre-entry training (section 37 of the RRA) may be provided only to persons of a particular underrepresented racial group in order to equip them with the skills required for the specific area of work. In this situation trainees must not have employee status during the training and must not receive a guarantee of a job at the end of the training. Such training should allow successful participants to compete on equal terms for available job opportunities. They are then judged on merit in the competition for jobs. In-service training (section 38 of the RRA) can be provided by an employer to employees of a particular racial group in order to equip them for work in an area where they are underrepresented, hence assisting possible career progression. Such training may also be provided on the employer's behalf by a training organization. In this case they will have employee status and the training will be focused on promotion prospects. The RRA (section 35) also renders lawful any acts done in order to afford persons of a particular racial group access to facilities or services to meet the special needs of that group in relation to education, training or welfare. An example of this is the provision of English language training where people have another first language. This was a common early form of training provided in the UK, which was not specifically a type of positive action but was instead focusing upon assimilation of recent migrant groups (Wrench and Taylor, 1993: 8–9).

Many other policies and actions are often referred to by employers as positive action. However, the legislation is very specific about what is permissible and largely hinges on the issue of first proving underrepresentation as already outlined. Positive action in the UK allows employers to take steps to assist members of underrepresented racial groups to a position from which they can compete on equal terms with others. The principle of equal treatment then applies, selection and appointment being based on merit. Positive action is often misunderstood or confused with positive discrimination or reverse discrimination. The latter is illegal in the UK and consists of setting illegal quotas (not to be confused with targets) whereby an employer decides that it must increase the proportion of an underrepresented group by a certain percentage and does so by preferential recruitment and promotion. Targets are allowed within the legislation and encouraged within some national campaigns as a way of focusing policy on particular problem areas. Targets provide an aim to try to achieve and therefore can enable effective monitoring of progress.

A stronger form of legislation exists in Northern Ireland under the Fair Employment Act 1989 (FEA). This is acknowledged to be the strongest piece of equality legislation in Western Europe, although it is primarily based on religious groups. It is aimed at the active promotion of fair employment practices by employers and the use of affirmative action to remedy underrepresentation of either the Protestant or Roman Catholic religious community in Northern Ireland. At any time the Fair Employment Commission (FEC) can investigate an employer and instruct it to take mandatory affirmative action (as positive measures are called in Northern Ireland). Affirmative action refers to actions designed to secure fair participation in employment by means of adapting current practices to encourage levels of representation or the modification or abandonment of practices that have restricted participation. Broadly speaking affirmative action in this context equates with positive action in

Great Britain under the RRA. However, the major difference is that whereas employers in Northern Ireland may be encouraged to take affirmative action measures if they do not do so they will be instructed to do so by the FEC. This is unlike the experience in mainland UK where positive action remains voluntary. The role of the Commission for Racial Equality (CRE) in the UK was established alongside the RRA. The CRE's role is largely one of promotion and education surrounding the intent of the legislation. The CRE does have the power to carry out formal investigations of organizations where it has reason to believe discrimination is occurring. However, it does not have the power of its equivalent in Northern Ireland to instruct organizations to take particular policy measures.

The Context for Positive Action

Positive action should be seen as an integral part of an overall initiative aiming to increase equality and levels of representation amongst an organization's workforce. For positive action to be successful it needs to be supported by an organizational framework that is committed to the provision of equality to all potential and existing employees. This organizational framework has three key elements which help to ensure that positive action measures achieve their aims: an effective equal opportunity policy; an analysis of the workforce and an analysis of the organization.

Effective Equal Opportunities Policy

An increasing number of employers in the UK now have an equal opportunity policy or statement. The quality and effectiveness of such policies varies tremendously from a strongly worded, very detailed policy through to a simple statement that outlines no areas of action. The impact of the policy is also determined by the strength of its wording, the support it has and how it is put into practice. Jewson and Mason (1992) distinguished two ends of a spectrum of approaches to equal opportunities as the 'liberal' and the 'radical' approaches. Clearly, as a theoretical model, it is unlikely that practice within organizations neatly fits into either the radical or liberal approach. A radical approach to policy considers fairness as equality in outcomes and may therefore rely on positive discrimination to achieve its objectives. The more common 'liberal' approach draws on theories of classical liberalism and defines the task of equal opportunities as securing free competition by eradicating unfair discrimination. The liberal approach will intervene in the free competition for employment using positive action where it is necessary to overcome disadvantage that hinders access to competition on equal terms.

Positive action should ideally occur within the context of an equal opportunities policy as suggested by the UK's Employment Department (Employment Department, 1993). However, the equal opportunity policy itself should be an effective working policy. In order to be effective an equal opportunity policy should be negotiated and supported by both managers and workforce representatives. The policy should then be widely publicized to the current workforce and all potential employees. Areas for action should be identified and prioritized, possibly with targets and a timetable for their achievement outlined. The policy should be supported by ongoing monitoring of the workforce to assess its impact. The results of the monitoring should then be used to revise the policy, and its priorities, as appropriate. Therefore, if positive action takes place within an active policy of this kind it should stand a greater chance of being accepted by the workforce and being effective in tackling underrepresentation.

Also key to effectiveness is the way an equal opportunities policy, and hence positive action, operates alongside other organizational policies. Jewson et al. (1995) distinguish different model types that indicate the way in which an equality policy may be linked to other organizational practices. Policies may be characterized by a formal written statement but a lack of implementation (dissociation model). A preferred type is the integration model where equality practices, including positive action, are 'comprehensive, proactive and focused around an elaborate, ongoing, formal equal opportunities policy' (Jewson et al., 1995). In some organizations, with a long history of commitment to equality, it may be difficult to identify specific equality activities because equality policies and provisions have become part of other organizational practices (assimilation model). Positive action requires a supportive framework in order to be effective but it is also most likely to occur in those organization that have a history of commitment to equality objectives and where organizations are closer to Jewson et al.'s integration or assimilation model types. Unfortunately previous research suggests that equal opportunities policies do not often involve elaborate or ongoing processes and frequently stand in isolation from other organizational policies and decision making processes. This is true in a number of areas of employment and has been well documented for the university sector in a series of surveys of institutional policies (CUCO, 1994).

Analyse the Workforce

The purpose of an equal opportunity policy and positive action should be to encourage change and move towards the genuine provision of equality. It is therefore essential initially to analyse the workforce in order to provide a baseline from which to assess progress. When taking positive action it is even more essential to have this baseline information in order to assess whether underrepresentation, as legally specified, exists, and to what extent, in order to allow lawful policies to be introduced. The initial analysis should be regularly updated with equality monitoring data to help identify key areas requiring change and, at later stages, those areas where further attention is required. The data should, as a minimum, cover ethnicity, gender and disability which are the main areas covered by UK legislation. The ethnicity categories used should enable a comparison with nationally available data and also be specific to the organization and reflect, if necessary, particular local ethnic groups from which recruitment occurs.

An analysis of the workforce is often one of the first barriers that prevents positive action being taken by organizations. A detailed analysis is required in order to show that underrepresentation exists. The workforce analysis therefore needs to be accompanied by an analysis of the potential workforce that may be local or national and may also need to take account of the particular skill area involved. Hence, among some organizations that are keen to overcome apparent underrepresentation the problem of having sufficient data to prove that lawful positive action is necessary can become insurmountable. Internally some organizations may have difficulties collecting ethnicity data on all of their current workforce because such data can only be collected voluntarily and individuals may often be suspicious of what the data will be used for. Externally organizations may have difficulties obtaining precise data about the available workforce within their specified recruitment skill/experience area due to a lack of very detailed data about local populations.

Analyse the Organization

Unless policies relating to equality and positive action are understood at all levels of an organization they are unlikely to be effective. To be successful, as suggested above, such policies need to become integral to the working of the organization and introduce the notion of equality management to the work of all those within the organization. It is therefore necessary to analyse the way the organization operates. This analysis needs to consider basic elements of the organization's operations such as recruitment and advertising procedures, the appropriateness of application forms, as well as any tests and interviews that are used. This should help to reveal particular problem areas, particularly those that may be acting as unnecessary barriers for certain ethnic groups. These barriers should be removed in order to comply with the non-discrimination intention of the RRA. The analysis should also expose recruitment and promotion hurdles that are necessary and justifiable but that disproportionately affect particular ethnic groups. Hence, it can reveal the areas where positive action may be necessary and lawful in order to overcome existing levels of underrepresentation.

In summary the context contributing to successful positive action includes:

- a detailed programme of action that is specific to the organization and identifies clear and realistic objectives;
- the compilation of accurate data about the current and potential workforce to allow realistic goals or targets to be set;
- effective monitoring systems that provide information on progress and levels of success;
- the support of all members of the organization, particularly those with key responsibilities, in order to reduce any potential backlash and resistance.

The Rationale for Taking Positive Action

The reasons for organizations undertaking positive action can be drawn from some of the literature providing case studies of different types of examples that have been implemented by organizations in the UK (for case studies see EOR, 1990, 1991; Pollert and Rees, 1992; Welsh et al., 1994). Some of this literature concentrates upon the legal necessity to address discrimination and the moral obligation to provide equality (Taylor, 1992; EOR, 1987). Other examples discuss the business benefits of providing greater equality and diversity through the use of positive action (CUCO, 1996; EOR, 1994). It is useful briefly to consider the rationale that has been put forward in this literature for introducing positive action as it provides an indication of commitment to such policies as well as the desired organizational outcomes. Many of these arguments have yet to be researched in order to reveal whether or not the anticipated outcomes are actually achieved as a result of adopting certain policies. Until these are actually tested and documented by research it is uncertain what the additional benefits of taking positive action are. Without such information it is difficult to encourage employers to adopt these often controversial measures. This is perhaps particularly the case with the 'business benefits' that some literature argues follow from such actions.

Equality Commitment

The growing number of employers with an equal opportunity policy suggests that there is an increasing awareness of employers' responsibilities towards the provision of social justice and equality. The UK is a multi-ethnic society in which those from minority groups, despite the existence of anti-discriminatory legislative protection for over twenty years, continue to suffer unfair discrimination. One way organizations have further expressed their commitment to tackling some of the existing inequalities has been through the introduction of positive action. These schemes often seek to address past organizational inequalities. They may also have other benefits of improving relationships with minority ethnic groups or organizations within the local community or at a national level. Strengthening such relationships may result in greater and wider support for positive action as well as improving its likelihood of success. Furthermore, positive action schemes that directly address specific areas of individual or organizational behaviour may result in challenging other discriminatory behaviour that may eventually result in changing the attitudes of employees. This is often a desired long-term feature of anti-discrimination training that is carried out as part of equality programmes (Taylor et al., 1997).

Business Benefits

Much of current policy advice in the UK recommends that equality and diversity should be considered within organizations due to the positive effects they can have on business. This is particularly true for ethnicity within the 'Race for Opportunity' national campaign, which uses key employers with a good track record in the area of equality to persuade other organizations to set targets for change in a number of areas of activity (Taylor, 1996). One of the major ways in which organizations are thought to benefit from equality and positive action initiatives is through an improved market image. Introducing a positive action scheme can assist organizations in overcoming preconceptions held by potential employees and thus attract a wider pool of applicants. By increasing the range of applicants organizations may also benefit from recruiting individuals with a greater range of high quality skills. Positive action, by targeting a more diverse range of appropriate potential employees, allows an organization to have a wider recruitment net and thus may limit the impact of future labour shortages. Positive action may also increase the motivation of existing employees due to opening up promotion procedures or opportunities. Ultimately the employment of a more diverse range of employees could also increase the opportunity of winning contracts through an assumed better understanding of different types of communities and by meeting the contract compliance requirements of certain organizations.

Legal Obligations

Whilst UK legislation has been strongly criticized for being too weak it does include the possibility of cases of discrimination being taken against an organization by individuals. Evidence, however, suggests that the outcome of industrial tribunals, where the majority of employment discrimination cases are heard, provides little incentive to ensure employers do not discriminate. The burden of proof is on the individual and the response of tribunals tends to be unsympathetic (Lustgarten and Edwards, 1992: 273). Furthermore the compensation provided to individuals has only recently had no upper limit whereas previous settlements tended to be for relatively small sums. The threat to employers is therefore more likely to be in terms of the bad publicity received rather than the fines imposed where cases taken to tribunal are found to be justified. This is, in a way, the alternative to the positive image that can be generated by developing equality and positive action initiatives. However, no matter how committed an organization is to removing discrimination it is impossible to guarantee that no legal action will be taken against it. Hence, the better an organization can demonstrate that equality policies continue to be developed the more convincing a defence can be presented and the less damaging publicity will be. Thus, some organizations may adopt positive action to help overcome known inequalities that have existed in the hope that it will prevent a legal case being taken.

Examples of Positive Action Programmes

This chapter has so far shown how the supportive context for positive action is crucial to its possible success and the way in which the underlying rationale may affect the type of positive action adopted. Consideration of specific examples of how positive action has been used in three different types of organization helps to illustrate how these principles operate in action. Each of the three examples illustrates how an employing organization, dedicated to the improvement of equality, can use legal positive action to improve the situation for those from minority ethnic groups. Alongside this they also indicate how important the context for positive action is for its implementation.

Media A

Media A is a large media company that has a very high profile and is a prestigious national recruiter. Media A has a long history of tackling discrimination and has a number of equality policies in operation. A number of different positive action policies have been pursued in order to increase the number of employees from minority ethnic groups. The various activities undertaken have included three forms of pre-entry training:

- offering promising minority ethnic freelancers developmental bi-media training and work placements to increase their prospects of securing jobs with Media A;
- offering promising broadcasters from minority ethnic groups short-term contracts to acquire experience, with the objective of increasing their chances of competing for available vacancies;
- the provision of eight Asian and African-Caribbean production traineeships to provide relevant experience to help the successful trainees apply for available vacancies.

Media A clearly has a strong context into which positive action has been introduced. The company has developed over a number of years a series of different policies tackling a range of areas of inequality. This profile of equality policies has probably helped to educate the workforce about the importance of tackling inequality as well as confirming the organization's own approach. This helps to ensure the policy's success, particularly in relation to reducing the likelihood of a backlash from employees. Part of the rationale underlying the policy's introduction is Media A's desire to comply with the legislation, which is given additional incentive due to the organization's high public profile.

Communications B

Communications B is a large communications company that recruits nationally and has many regional offices. In some geographic areas minority ethnic groups are well represented but throughout the organization they are underrepresented at more senior levels. Communications B has adopted positive action to try to counter this by providing some in-service experience. The company finances a network for staff from minority ethnic groups, which has an input to senior management decisions on certain issues. The network consists of representatives from across the company. Communications B also finances 'experience days' hosted by the network where other minority ethnic employees are invited to attend a range of events. The company also held a series of 'open days' in some of its departments in order to encourage existing employees to consider other areas of work. Some of these days, following an idea from the network, were specifically for minority ethnic groups. As a result of these days a number of minority ethnic staff are known to have applied for vacancies in areas they visited and others have registered an expression of interest in other areas should vacancies arise.

Like Media A, Communications B has a long history of introducing different policies aimed at reducing inequalities amongst its workforce. In this example the development of an appropriate and supportive context is illustrated by the company's move towards 'diversity management', which it sees as a development of attempting to both reduce discrimination and provide equality. By pursuing this approach Communications B is trying to ensure that it tackles other areas of inequality other than those covered in the legislation. Again this is indicated by the key role the organization is playing in a national campaign designed to encourage employees to tackle racial discrimination. Alongside the desire to fulfil legal obligations this company sees positive action as enabling it to maximize the use of existing resources, skills and abilities from its existing staff. The sort of internal positive action illustrated here is a prime example of staff development that benefits both the organization and the employee.

University C

University C is a city-based large provider of higher education and has for some time been concerned about the underrepresentation of minority ethnic groups within its academic-related administrative grades. This is against a background of higher unemployment among minority ethnic graduates compared to their white peers. In order to provide such graduates with quality work experience, and at the same time to identify a pool of potential applicants, two one-year placements were established in administrative areas. The trainees received a salary for the year, which involved experience in two different central administrative areas. The placements were designed to help the participants to market themselves as potential university employees. It is hoped that at the end of the placements there will be some vacancies for which the participants will be encouraged to apply.

Like the previous two examples University C has a history of introducing policies to combat inequality and discrimination in relation to both staff and student issues. However, the structure of universities can often reduce the power of central policies due to the autonomy of different departments or sections. Whilst, again, legal obligation was an important aspect of the policies introduction in this example there was particular pressure due to the geographic location of the university and the relatively high local minority ethnic population.

Each of the examples illustrates a number of key points about the limitations of positive action, particularly in the UK, but more generally about the underlying principles of positive action. The examples indicate the importance of the correct context and how this can reduce the potential backlash that may be experienced as a result of introducing positive action (as is currently being experienced in the US in response to affirmative action). The examples also show that the need for positive action arises partially as a result of the current legislation being relatively weak and thus failing really to combat discrimination; effectively. However, positive action cannot actually combat discrimination; it can at best offer a way around, or over, discriminatory barriers for the few that become involved in such programmes. The examples also suggest that positive action may not necessarily involve preferential treatment but it may instead be viewed as appropriate treatment to suit particular circumstances.

Conclusions

Three main types of positive action are lawful under current UK legislation: encouragement measures to attract applicants; pre-entry training to increase the pool of potential applicants; in-service training to increase the potential for career advancement. Taking lawful positive action relies strongly on the principle of firstly proving underrepresentation exists. This can often act as one of the first hurdles employers have to overcome.

The necessary context in which positive action should occur in order to help ensure its success includes the development of an effective equal opportunities policy. Organizations should also carry out an analysis of the current and potential workforce in order to prove underrepresentation and to identify the potential labour/skill pool. An analysis of the organization should also be carried out in order to identify existing unnecessary or discriminatory practice and procedures that positive action can aim to overcome. Without this context, organizations are unlikely to be in a position to design appropriate positive action. Similarly, it is unlikely that any positive action will be accepted by other employees without resistance or that its outcome will be effective.

The motivations for undertaking positive action can vary tremendously and may be a result of a combination of factors. Three main types of motivation may exist.

1. Organizations may have a genuine commitment to equality and the removal of unfair and unlawful discrimination.
2. Employers may undertake positive action for perceived business benefits of increased profitability, improved market image or improved efficiency of recruitment processes.
3. Companies may also introduce positive action in order to reduce the likelihood of legal cases being successfully taken against them.

In general it does not matter what the motivations or rationale for taking positive action are, although this may suggest the degree of dedication given to the policies' success. Whatever the reasons for introducing positive action the most important consideration is that it is designed appropriately and introduced into a supportive context that should ensure its success. It must also be remembered that positive action only offers an alternative route to compensate for previous discrimination. It provides a way of dealing with the consequences of discrimination rather than dealing with the causes.

–10–

Positive Action: the Dutch Experience

Lilian Gonçalves-Ho Kang You and *Louise Mulder*

Introduction

In the Netherlands members of minority groups endure rather unfavourable social and economic conditions and live in disadvantaged circumstances. Above all, the unemployment rate among minorities (between
22 per cent and 25 per cent) is between three and five times higher than
among members of the indigenous majority population. This alarming
situation is caused by lower education levels, insufficient command of
the Dutch language, lack of a social network in the labour market,
replacement by people with better educational qualifications as well as
direct and indirect discrimination. People applying for jobs, as well as
those already in employment, find themselves facing personnel recruitment staffers who tend to prefer white, young, male employees (Tesser
et al., 1996). An Erasmus University research has shown that approxim-
ately one-third of personnel staff in the Netherlands acknowledge that
they discriminate in recruitment and selection procedures (Veenman,
1995). Even where members of ethnic minorities are employed it may
be difficult for them to keep their jobs.

Positive action policies relating to ethnic minorities in the Netherlands
focus mainly on the four principal immigrant groups: the Surinamese
being the largest, numbering around 282,000, followed by Turks (272,000),
Moroccans (225,000), Dutch Antilleans (93,000) and 354,000 members
of further minorities from a non-Western cultural background. Whereas
immigration from Surinam and the Dutch Antilles has been historically
linked to the colonial past more and more immigrants were attracted to
the Netherlands in the decades after the Second World War to meet the
demand for unskilled labour.

Positive action policies and programmes in the Netherlands do not
involve education, such as admission to schools and universities. The
scope of this action is generally limited to the area of employment. Note

that the quota system is not favoured as a model in the Netherlands; the numbers are targets, not quotas.

Policies to Improve Employment for Minorities

Equal Treatment Legislation

The legal basis for positive action in the Netherlands is the national and international principle of equality and non-discrimination. This allows, either implicitly or explicitly, for positive action in favour of women and ethnic minorities. In 1983, the principle of equal treatment was introduced into the Dutch Constitution. According to article 1 of the Constitution all persons in the Netherlands must be treated equally under equal circumstances. The equal treatment principle as embodied in the Constitution has been specified for civil law relations in the Equal Treatment Act (*Algemene wet gelijke behandeling*). This act came into force in September 1994 and established a commission to interpret the law and promote its enforcement.

The Equal Treatment Commission considers complaints and gives rulings on direct and indirect unequal treatment based on religion, personal conviction and views, political orientation, race, gender, nationality, sexual preference or marital status. It is forbidden to treat people differently on any of these grounds in the following situations:

- employment and liberal professions;
- when offering goods or services;
- when providing advice about educational or career opportunities.

Since 1 November 1996, the Commission also considers complaints about unequal treatment relating to the duration of employment.

Above all, the Commission has to consider complaints in individual cases and to give rulings. Beside this, it is also empowered to initiate investigations into cases of persistent discrimination under the relevant laws, either in the public sector or any other sector of society. The Commission can also make recommendations in specific cases to further compliance with the relevant equal treatment regulations. The Commission may also take legal action to obtain a court order.

With regard to employment, article 5 of the Equal Treatment Act prohibits differential treatment in recruitment, selection procedures, commencement or ending of employment, terms and conditions of employment and promotion. The Equal Treatment Act outlines a number of general exceptions on the grounds of race or nationality to the equal treatment rule. These relate to forms of indirect discrimination that are not objectively justified and to the positive action of those belonging to a particular ethnic or cultural minority group. An exception relating to 'race' can be made when a person's racial appearance is a determining factor, as when selecting a candidate for the role of Othello, for example. The law provides for an exception relating to nationality where differential treatment is based on generally binding regulations or on written or unwritten rules of international law and in cases where nationality is a determining factor.

Government Policy on Employment of Minorities

In 1987 the Dutch government initiated a programme promoting proportional employment for minorities in the civil service (*Etnische Minderheden bij de Overheid*, EMO). Although some departments failed to meet the targets, others tended to over-represent minorities, so that the overall result was satisfactory. Nevertheless, the envisaged level of proportional employment had not been attained by the time the programme ended in 1995. Today, the government continues to pursue proportional minority representation through a policy of positive action both at national and municipal level.

This positive action policy is applied to candidates who meet the job requirements. Depending on the degree of ethnic minority underrepresentation in the regional occupational population, applicants are required to have either adequate or equal qualifications.

The government anticipates that general policy measures aimed at the lower strata of the job market will also improve the position of minorities as they are overrepresented in this segment. One of these measures, offering job subsidies for the long-term unemployed, will create up to 40,000 places. Although this project is not specifically designed to improve employment prospects for minorities, the project has already benefited members of minority groups considerably. Participation by minorities reached around 34 per cent in 1997.

Special Measures to Improve Employment for Minorities

The government, unions and industry have been involved in joint efforts to achieve proportional employment for minorities. Trade unions and industry have encouraged these measures to be included in collective labour contracts.

On 1 July 1994, a law to promote proportional employment for minorities (*Bevordering Evenredige Arbeidsdeelname Allochtonen,* BEAA) came into force. Under this law an enterprise with a workforce of thirty-five or more is obliged to register the ethnic origins of its employees. If minorities are underrepresented, the company is required to draw up a plan to improve its ethnic diversity. This proved very unpopular among employers and only 14 per cent have complied fully with the provisions. The government therefore invited unions and industry to devise a new plan to improve the employment situation. This resulted in new legislation to stimulate minority participation (*Stimulering Arbeidsdeelname Minderheden,* SAMEN). This law incorporates ethnic monitoring; the penal sanction has now been replaced by civil law enforcement measures. It also provides for publication of numbers of ethnic minority employees, an annual report with a plan of action and monitoring by job inspectors. This less rigorous legislation seems to fit better to the consultation-based consensus culture of the Netherlands and will hopefully have a more positive impact on the employment situation among ethnic minorities.

The 1997 minority policy report of the government stated that despite evidence of discrimination against ethnic minorities and although proportional employment has not yet been achieved, the results of the Government Employment Agency have improved, and large numbers have succeeded in finding employment. Of those registered as unemployed in 1997, 23 per cent were of ethnic minority origin; of those employed through the Agency, 15 per cent were of ethnic minority origin. This led to a new government action plan aiming a proportional participation among ethnic minorities by 1 January 2000 at the latest.

This plan envisages greater participation by members of minority groups in the employment agency itself and promotion of expertise of its consultants. Moreover, the number of special minority consultants will be raised from the present fifty (Smeets et al., 1997). Finally, the government has installed a special minorities and labour-market task force to stimulate all those involved and to promote best practices.

Positive action often raises new barriers if the situation is not managed with care. This is as true in the Netherlands as elsewhere. The special action programmes outlined in this paper have been created in close consultation between the government, unions and industry to suit Dutch society – the so-called 'polder' model – and are designed to have a more positive impact on the employment situation of ethnic minorities.

Positive Action

Positive action in favour of persons belonging to a particular ethnic or cultural minority is permitted, provided the aim is to eliminate or reduce de facto inequalities, and on condition such regulations are in proportion to that aim.

Positive action is not limited to recruitment and selection procedures or to promotion. It can also apply to conditions of employment, such as the distribution of child care places or educational facilities, if the purpose of these regulations is to stimulate participation by women and/or ethnic minorities.

In Dutch legislation and judicial decisions, positive action is defined as a deviation from the general rule of equal treatment. Positive action is therefore subject to strict legal guidelines. It is only permissible if the following specified conditions apply: it must aim to enhance the position of women and/or ethnic minorities; there must be a substantial difference in the actual position of these and other population groups; the disadvantage must be demonstrated; the nature of the positive action must be in proportion to the extent of the disadvantage and it must be shown that some kind of positive action was applicable in the relevant case.

The disadvantage experienced in the labour market must be demonstrated in figures. The world of statistics can be alien and confusing, however. It can lead to doubts surrounding the frame of reference. One case of positive action, for example, led to the appointment of a woman as head of a secondary school in Amsterdam. This use of positive action caused a major row, not least because a number of parents disapproved of the candidate herself, who at that time was deputy head of the school. As the matter went to court three different legal bodies issued different rulings on the legality of the preferential appointment.

The decisive factor proved to be the frame of reference for the figures relating to the disadvantage of women in comparable positions.

One court examined the overall picture of secondary schools in Amsterdam and found that women suffered no significant disadvantage when it came to the position of head. The second noted that there were no female heads at the two local secondary schools and concluded that positive action was appropriate. The third looked at the figures for headmistresses at secondary schools across the country and discovered the requisite substantial disadvantage. The need for those figures sets a problem relating to positive action on racial grounds. For ethnic minorities and non-Dutch citizens it is mostly impossible to cite employment statistics to legitimate positive action because in most cases there are no specified figures available. Cases therefore have to be based on so-called 'generally known facts' and other fictions.

The example of the Amsterdam school is characteristic of the principle of positive action. People are quick to disagree about the legality, legitimacy and functionality of the instrument. So it is all the more remarkable that the introduction and/or application of positive action has not led to resistance and debate in the Netherlands.

Cases Considered by the Equal Treatment Commission

So far the Commission has considered only a few cases relating to positive action of members of minority groups. In one case a member of an ethnic minority was one of fifteen candidates to apply for a job. Five were invited for an interview, among whom was the petitioner. He was not accepted because the employer preferred a candidate who had already been employed previously in the same position.[1]

In another case a person complained that over the years he had applied five times for a position. The last time he had been turned down on account of his age. The advertisement had stated a preference for candidates under 30, reflecting the age composition of the department. Thirty candidates had applied, only one of whom was a member of an ethnic minority.[2]

There were certain similarities in the work environment in the two cases. Both employers maintained a policy of positive action, so that in the event of equal qualification for the job, a member of an ethnic minority would be selected. Although a policy of positive action had been maintained for many years in recruitment, this had not produced any positive results. Most vacancies had been filled through internal recruitment.

The Commission judged that, under these circumstances, opportunities for ethnic diversity of personnel were limited to positive action in external recruitment. Since there were relatively few vacancies, it was up to the employer to make an extra effort to achieve this goal.

The Commission stated that the principle of positive action involves a duty to find out whether a candidate is equally suitable for the job. In the first case the Commission considered that the mere fact that the successful candidate had been employed in the same position in the past, did not imply that he was more suitable for the job, thereby justifying a deviation from the positive action principle.

In the second case the Commission considered that it was up to the employer to set guidelines for the age-composition of his personnel. However, if positive action was also applied, a certain cohesion should be established in personnel policy to achieve a level of ethnic and age diversity. Age may only prevail above positive action if it is a necessary requirement for a particular job. This was not the case, so the Commission judged that the recruitment procedure had not conformed with the requirements relating to positive action.

Decisions of the European Court of Justice and their Implications

The European Directive on Equal Treatment contains an equal treatment clause relating to equality of opportunity. In this context, positive action is regarded as an exception to the principle of equality.

Recently, two prominent decisions of the Court caused a major upset: the *Kalanke* case and the *Marschall* case.[3] In the *Marschall* case in particular, the Court developed a new approach to the admissibility of positive action for women. The Court stated that positive action should aim to provide equal opportunity and not to achieve equal results, which in the Marschall case was defined as a fifty/fifty male/female balance on the work floor. Moreover, regulations to promote positive action must include a clause to the effect that, in each case, male candidates with equal qualifications will be objectively assessed and that all relevant criteria must be considered. And crucially, if one or more relevant criteria supports a decision in favour of a male candidate this must override the principle of positive action for women.

This emphasis on opportunity means that positive action for women has to be legitimated by existing prejudices, gender images, gendered evaluations of men and women and so on: all the familiar factors that have disadvantaged women in their equal opportunities in the professional development. The disparities in employment figures cannot in themselves be the only legitimation for positive action on a individual basis.

Another interesting aspect of the *Marschall* case ruling is the fact that the Court specifically allowed positive action where male and female candidates were equally qualified. This raises the question of whether other forms of positive action are illegal. If so, the ruling has made it impossible, for instance, to interview only women for a vacancy.

Finally, the Court's rulings have impacted on the legal nature of positive action itself. Before, positive action was seen as a kind of group right to be pigeonholed under the equality principle, designed to correct the unequal divisions in the job market. Now it resembles an individual right to a proper selection procedure and – in the Court's opinion – positive action has been relegated to just another instrument designed to ensure the objectivity of these procedures.

As stated, the rulings of the European Court of Justice relate to gender only because the relevant directive focuses on the equality of men and women. In other words, the legal basis for positive action of minority groups remains unaffected by these rulings and continues to be based on national law. This has its advantages. As said before, the Court appeared to restrict positive action to those cases where a man and a woman are equally qualified. Dutch law stipulates that a degree of proportionality is required between the type of positive action and the actual disadvantage. The disadvantage suffered by ethnic minorities is greater than that suffered by women. This difference between the position of women and ethnic minorities in the job market gives the latter wider legal scope to apply other modalities of positive action than the 'equal qualifications' one.

An interesting matter involves the feasibility of differentiation in positive action programmes on the grounds of 'race' and/or nationality. It may be argued that the legitimation of positive action on gender grounds is not quite the same as the legitimation of positive action on racial grounds. For instance, the causes of disadvantage in the job market are different. For women the main barriers in the job market relate to the traditional caring role of women and the image that this engenders. The problem of ethnic minorities and non-Dutch citizens relates more to discrimination based on certain human characteristics and a social hierarchy based on skin colour.

It is therefore rational to operate different positive action programmes for different population groups.

Positive Action as an Obligation

As mentioned above, positive action is generally seen as an exception to the principle of equality. However, another way of looking at positive action would be to see it as an inherent element of equal treatment itself. In this sense it forms one of the positive obligations that can result from the equality clause.

The concept of positive obligation, of taking positive measures, is linked to the exercise of constitutional rights. It appears mainly in cases concerning conventional rights where non-intervention by the government proves inadequate and intervention is required to obtain implementation.

The relevant government body is, in effect, free to draft its own policies with regard to the appropriate measures. However, the court may decide whether a positive obligation exists in individual cases. In so doing, the Court must bear in mind the need to strike a fair balance between the general interests of the public and the private interests of the individual.

The positive obligation in question may entail the passing of specific laws, the implementation of certain regulations, or the realization of special administrative or financial measures.

It is argued that the concept of positive measures may also be applied to article 14 of the European Convention. This prescribes equal treatment in the exercise of Convention rights. This principle embraces actual as well as formal equality. It obliges governments to take steps to implement Convention rights. This concept may also be brought to bear on other principles of equality.

With regard to the principle of equality, positive measures are not explicitly cited in court judgements. They may nevertheless be implied. It is not argued in these cases that the principle of equality presupposes a right to actual implementation. What the arguments boil down is that the neglect of certain positive measures contravenes the rules of equality on which the case is tried. The American Supreme Court applied a similar approach as early as 1974 in the case of *Lau v. Nichols*. This concerned a collective court action instituted by 1,800 children of Chinese origin who were attending school in San Francisco. None of the children could speak English. The school did not provide special teaching to rectify this situation, nor did it provide standard teaching in a language that the children could understand. The court action was based on the ban on discrimination in the Civil Rights Act of 1964, which prohibited racism in federally funded institutions. In its interpretation of the ban, the Supreme Court unanimously decided that the Chinese-speaking minority enjoyed fewer of the advantages of the respective school system than the English-speaking majority, so that the minority was denied meaningful participation in the educational programme, constituting an act of discrimination against which the provisions in the Act were directed. Despite the fact that the school governors were not responsible for the children's inability to benefit from the teaching, the Court still found that they were responsible for adopting positive action to deal with the actual inequality of the Chinese children in the educational system.

The Dutch Equal Treatment Commission adopted a similar course. The Commission considered the neglect of positive measures to be a breach of the equal treatment principle in several instances. It was, for example, accepted that an employer had a positive obligation to look after employees from minority groups as a consequence of their weak position in the job market.

Conclusion

In the Netherlands the law provides for positive action for ethnic minorities. None the less, there are strict conditions relating to the implementation of these regulations. Despite considerable experience with positive action for women, there are legal and practical reasons for treating positive action on racial grounds differently. Furthermore, it seems reasonable to have different programmes for different population groups. For legal reasons it may also be worth exploring the possibilities of the concept of positive obligation as an aspect of human rights.

It should be emphasized, however, that positive action measures do not in themselves diminish the disadvantaged position of ethnic minorities in the job market in a substantial way. As stated, this disadvantage is caused by many different circumstances, including invisible processes and attitudes. Positive action must therefore be seen in the broader scope as promoting the proper functioning of a multicultural society, which includes the promotion of ethnic diversity on the shop floor.

Equal opportunity and recruitment procedures being free from direct or indirect discrimination is not enough to promote ethnic diversity on the shop floor. This requires greater involvement on the part of management and employees, not just through tolerance, but by accepting and acknowledging cultural differences. That is why positive action for ethnic minorities should include management training in cultural diversity and training of employees to cope with multiculturalism on the shop floor in everyday situations.

That, however, does not mean that we do not acknowledge that legal provisions promoting positive action are in themselves a necessary contribution when it comes to combating inequality.

Notes

1. Equal Treatment Commission ruling 97–11, 29 January 1997.
2. Equal Treatment Commission ruling 96–119, 23 December 1996.
3. *Kalanke* 1995, C 450–93; *Marschall* 1997, C 409–95.
4. Equal Treatment Commission ruling 96–62, 9 July 1996.

Positive Action in Sweden: from Central Solutions to Local Responsibility for Combating Ethnic Discrimination

Maritta Soininen and *Mark Graham*

Introduction

In the 1990s, policies were pursued in the Swedish labour market in order to increase ethnic diversity in the workforce and to counteract ethnic discrimination, but one cannot fully comprehend the nature of these policies and the terms in which they are understood without seeing them in the context of the Swedish institutional framework consisting of the welfare and policy-making model.

The Swedish welfare model's cornerstones have been a Keynesian economic policy, a fair wages policy and an active labour market policy. The social-democratic labour market policy has traditionally been used as a tool to ensure high employment, low inflation, a wage policy designed to promote solidarity within the labour movement, and rapid economic growth (Rothstein, 1986). A large public sector employer has been an integral part of this model.[1] Up until the 1980s, this policy was judged to have been highly successful by international standards in terms of employment levels, moderate income differentials, and economic growth. Labour immigrants have been able to benefit from this policy along with the rest of the population.

Since the beginning of the 1990s, there has been consistent high unemployment which has been tackled by an expanded labour market policy. Increasingly, targeted measures for disadvantaged groups, including immigrants, have been introduced. Some of these can even been seen as positive action measures. By positive action we mean measures intended to help ensure that people compete with one another on equal terms. In a very few cases positive discrimination, in the sense of quotas for ethnic minority members, has been used as a labour market measure in Sweden.[2]

We examine the labour market policies and programmes as expressions of the Swedish institutional context. It is this context that has been ultimately responsible for legislation against ethnic discrimination; and it is the character of this legislation that is clearly reflected in the employer and trade union positive action programmes and policies for promoting a multicultural workforce and tackling ethnic discrimination.

We argue that democratic ideals, which are central to the workings of the Swedish welfare state and labour market organizations, are contradicted by the occurrence of ethnic discrimination and that consequently there has been a reluctance to acknowledge its existence and take effective measures to deal with it. Furthermore, the egalitarian ethos of the Swedish social democratic welfare state has also militated against using the term 'positive action' to describe special labour market measures for immigrants, as such a term can be understood as presupposing a salience of ethnic distinctions that is foreign to the class-based Swedish model.

Finally, we briefly examine the latest proposals for a new law against ethnic discrimination in working life, which are far more radical than previous legislation and represent a shift in how ethnic discrimination is conceived. This shift can be understood as a product of recent institutional changes – organizational and ideological – in Sweden and the growing influence of international factors, including European integration, on policy making.

The Active Labour Market Policy: the Cornerstone of the Swedish Model

The labour market policy pursued by the National Labour Market Board (AMS) has traditionally stressed the creation of measures, such as retraining, education, and the active placement of job seekers in order to hold down unemployment and to strike a balance between the demands of the labour market and the skills of the workforce. This policy has informed relations between immigrants and the labour market authorities.

Providing immigrants with the same treatment in the labour market schemes as native Swedes is in keeping with the Swedish welfare state's emphasis on universal welfare. A primary political goal has been equality between individuals and groups in society to be achieved through conscious efforts to remove the most obvious class inequalities and create equal life chances. Public services were made available for the entire population and characterized by uniformity and standardized solutions (Tilton, 1990; Rothstein, 1994).

Historically, the social democratic idea of equality has been closely associated with the picture of society as a *Folkhem* (people's home), which includes the idea that everybody feels that they have a place in society. This even applies to the immigrant policy (Tilton, 1990), which is a generous one when seen in an international perspective. The difference between immigrant and native Swedes and between citizens and non-citizens in terms of political, social, and civil rights has been kept to an absolute minimum. Of the three goals of Sweden's immigrant policy (or integration policy as it has been called since 1996) – 'equality', 'freedom of choice' and 'partnership' – the first is regarded as of special importance for labour-market policies (Statens offentliga utredningar (SOU), 1996: 55).

The socioeconomic prerequisites for a policy of full employment have deteriorated since the late 1980s with a sharp increase in the number of unemployed. After a degree of recovery during the second half of the 1980s state finances deteriorated dramatically in the beginning of the 1990s (SOU, 1997: 57). Since the 1990s, Sweden has, in practice, been forced to abandon the goal of full employment (Lindbeck, 1997). An expanded public sector is no longer seen as the solution but rather as a problem for the national economy (Premfors, 1996). During recent years the government has increasingly questioned the range of the state's public sector responsibilities (SOU, 1997: 57; Riksrevisionsverket (RRV), 1996: 50). It is within this context that the AMS, which is responsible for the active labour market policy, has to work. The Board's main responsibility is to help maintain full employment. It also has the responsibility to work for labour market efficiency and to safeguard the labour market position of groups that are disadvantaged.

Labour market policy programmes in 1997 included vocational general preparatory courses for the unemployed; job-seeker courses; work experience schemes; and special public sector employment for the long-term. Self-employment is encouraged with the help of start-up grants, and special programmes for the occupationally handicapped, including grants for employers who hire occupationally handicapped persons. Immigrants have the same access to these programmes as the rest of the population.

Those immigrants who came to Sweden in the 1950s and 1960s, in the form of labour immigration from neighbouring Nordic countries and from southern Europe, met an expanding labour market, especially within manufacturing industry. The proportion of immigrants in employment was even higher than for the general population. Since the beginning of the 1990s, the situation has been very different with high unemployment and low workforce rates among people with foreign and especially non-

Nordic backgrounds. During 1996, 30.6 per cent of non-Nordic citizens who were part of the workforce were unemployed whereas for Swedish citizens the figure was 7.3 per cent. During 1997, 33 per cent of non-Nordic citizens were without work (Ura, 1997: 3; Ura, 1998: 1). A person's position in the labour market has an important impact on housing, access to education, health and political and social participation. The situation for immigrants in these spheres of life has worsened since the 1980s (Socialstyrelsen, 1995; Bäck and Soininen, 1998; SOU, 1996: 55).

According to the AMS, the prospects for non-Nordic citizens will continue to be bleak even in the event of improved economic performance and a general fall in unemployment (Ura, 1998: 1). The private and public sector will continue to become more effective and unskilled jobs will continue to disappear. It is perhaps not surprising that the Board's budget proposal for 1995/96 contains the goal of having a higher proportion of non-Nordic citizens in special programmes than is their actual proportion of the unemployed workforce (Ura, 1998: 1, 26). In short, something that strongly resembles a mild form of positive action. The goal was achieved. But even with the help of positive measures, the AMS does not think it possible to get certain categories of non-European immigrants into work.

Explanations for the weak labour market position of immigrants include the replacement of labour immigration by refugee immigration since the 1970s, the dramatic deterioration of the labour market, the impact of structural changes within sectors of Swedish industry that have traditionally offered work to immigrants, new requirements in working life, such as communications skills, and individual factors among immigrants such as language difficulties, and a lack of suitable qualifications (SOU, 1995: 76). The latter is especially relevant in the case of many refugee immigrants.

According to the AMS, much of the high unemployment among non-Nordic citizens is due to insufficient basic education and problems with the Swedish language due to ineffective Swedish language instruction. This is especially true of groups from Africa and Asia, only 50 per cent of whose members have completed primary education. Immigrants from Eastern Europe, especially from the former Yugoslavia, have been more successful. This relative success has been attributed to their better educational backgrounds and greater proficiency in the Swedish language (Ura, 1998: 2).

The part played by ethnic discrimination in determining the labour market position of immigrants has been debated for decades in commissions of inquiry and other bodies (Graham and Soininen, 1998). In 1990,

Sweden's Discrimination Ombudsman (DO) stated clearly that ethnic discrimination is a factor in the Swedish labour market (Diskriminerings Ombudsman, 1990), and the role of ethnic discrimination has increasingly been cited (Soininen and Graham, 1995; SOU, 1996: 55, Appendix 3, 480).

Legal Protection

Legal protection against discrimination consists of general rules in the constitutional law (*Grundlagen*) that guarantee protection against ethnic discrimination, on the basis of the so-called 'ethnic factor': 'race', skin colour, national and ethnic origin, religious faith, or membership of a minority. State employers are bound by the constitutional law to employ someone on the basis of merit. In 1986, a general law against ethnic discrimination was passed and the office of the Discrimination Ombudsman created. A comprehensive law forbidding ethnic discrimination in the Swedish labour market did not however come into effect until 1 July 1994, due, in part, to pressure from abroad (Graham and Soininen, 1998).

The 1994 law was designed not to be too comprehensive and risk provoking displeasure in the majority population that might adversely affect immigrants and ethnic minorities. Protecting a specific immigrant interest — i.e. providing immediate protection against ethnic discrimination in the labour market — was not the primary goal of the government (Graham and Soininen, 1998). The proposal was criticized on this point when the legislation was being drawn up. It was the long-term impact of the 1994 law on public opinion its so called 'signal effect', which was of greatest importance. The signal effect was to be achieved through effectively prosecuting cases of discrimination and drawing public attention to them.

The way in which the law was formulated has been criticized by various bodies, including DO which has the main responsibility for seeing that the law is enforced (Soininen and Graham, 1995; SOU, 1997: 174). For example, the law forbids discrimination that has 'obvious' (*påtaglig*) consequences for the discriminated party. This sends an ambiguous signal to the general public about the law's intentions. Another problem with the law is the fact that it only covers cases where there is an intention to discriminate and where this can be proven to be the case. Unintentional indirect discrimination, which has been identified as the most usual type, is not covered by the law, thereby making it more restrictive in its definition of what is considered unacceptable discrimination than is the case with the legislation against sexual discrimination in Sweden.

The failure of the law's signal effect was brought to public attention when a newspaper report in December 1995 revealed how the state employment services complied with requests from employers not to send them applicants with an immigrant background (*Svenska Dagbladet*, 7 January 1996).

The content of legislation against ethnic discrimination in Sweden must be understood in the context of the Swedish policy-making model. This has traditionally been characterized by an element of corporatism, consensus, low levels of conflict, compromise, and the use of expert testimony and opinion. In keeping with the main tenets of the model, the government left responsibility for solving the problem of ethnic discrimination with labour market partners until 1994. Ethnic discrimination was defined primarily as a question for the labour market organizations rather than the legislature. The content of legislation against ethnic discrimination, particularly its limited scope and the difficulty of applying it, must be understood in the context of this policy-making model, which has been constructed around class-based interests, rather than ethnic needs among society's members (Graham and Soininen, 1998).

Although anti-discrimination legislation has scarcely been the favoured method of the labour market partners and the government to strengthen the position of immigrants in the labour market, they have none the less been covered by the active labour market programmes and some have been tailored specifically for them. Given that illegal immigration scarcely occurs in Sweden, all immigrants are able to participate in labour market measures.

Immigrant Unemployment: a Public Sector Problem and a Market Solution

The extensive labour market measures are not presented as partial solutions to problems caused by discrimination. Indeed, ethnic discrimination occupies a very subordinate place in the AMS's understanding of the situation of immigrants. The traditional method for maintaining high levels of employment has been the use of active labour market measures and schemes. A wide range of specific measures within the more general framework of traditional labour market policy have been directed at immigrants.

The most common kind of measure for non-Nordic citizens has been labour market training in the form of courses. This was true of 60 per cent of those who were in labour market measures in 1994. However, they have found work to a lesser extent after completing the training than Nordic citizens: 19 per cent compared with 29 per cent to be exact.

Non-Nordic citizens have a relatively high share of the labour market education places but a low share of places on Work Experience Scheme – jobs for unemployed persons needing to keep in touch with the labour market – and in Workplace Introduction Schemes. Unlike labour market education these two measures lead directly to temporary contact with a workplace. According to the AMS, 'employers display a weaker interest in offering training places to immigrants compared with Swedish citizens' and this applies to both industry and the public sector (Ura, 1998: 1, 27). Not surprisingly, perhaps, the Immigrant Policy Committee in its final report in 1996 suggested increased use of practical training places to counteract high unemployment (SOU, 1996: 55). Recently, the AMS has demanded significant measures to enable immigrants to establish them-selves in the labour market, but it has also complained that the existing labour market resources available for this are insufficient (Ura, 1998: 1).

There is, however, a measure that has proved to be fairly successful and in which the government has great faith for lowering unemployment, namely starting one's own business. It is with the help of this measure that the largest share of non-Nordic citizens have found work. This is also the measure where the difference between the proportion who are placed in work is least between non-Nordic citizens and others (Ura, 1998: 1). The role of immigrant businesses has also been identified by the Immigrant Policy Committee in its 1995 report (SOU, 1995: 76) as an important part of the solution to immigrant unemployment.

Another solution recently advocated by the AMS has been the creation of work for unskilled job seekers (Ura, 1998:1, 36). The proposal was made in the context of an account of the situation facing immigrants who lack or have never completed primary education. This suggestion marks a radical departure from the traditional Swedish labour market principle of equality and solidarity expressed in the improvement of skills and education for all workers, rather than accepting that certain categories of people will be confined to unskilled, low-status jobs.

However, debates in the 1990s in Sweden have questioned the wisdom of traditional social-democratic legislation that stresses equal outcomes, low wage differentials for all and guaranteed employment as being counter-productive and a brake on economic growth. Acceptance of differential treatment in labour market policy evident in the official acceptance that some categories of immigrants cannot be helped, signals a departure from the egalitarian ideals that have informed the policy for so long.

Several state commissions of inquiry have recently pointed out that there is a clear risk for the emergence of an ethnically and socially segregated labour market and a new form of class society divided along ethnic lines (SOU, 1996: 55; SOU, 1997: 174). The government sees the active labour market policy measures as a means to counteract this and to promote integration. The stress on integration as a political response to the exclusion of immigrants from the labour market is evident in the recent renaming of the Immigration Minister as 'Integration Minister', and immigrant policy to integration policy. However, it is reasonable to ask whether the suggested measures – an ethnic labour market not in competition with Swedes, possibly resulting in a dual labour market (Bonacich, 1972), as well as the acceptance that certain categories of immigrants will remain at the bottom of the labour market hierarchy – are likely to reinforce these tendencies rather than counteract them.

The Labour Market Partner Initiatives

The content of the 1994 legislation has set the tone for the voluntary measures taken by the Swedish labour market partners. In accordance with the Swedish model they have been delegated chief responsibility for labour market issues and consequently also for combating ethnic discrimination in working life. For this reason, their programmes are comparable in importance with government policies. The Swedish Trade Union Confederation (LO), which represents blue-collar workers, has had an immigrant policy programme since 1979. The first version stressed the need for equal treatment regardless of nationality, race and religion. Up until 1995, information had been produced by the partners that condemned racism in general terms, but usually not as it can manifest itself concretely in specific Swedish workplaces and organizations (Soininen and Graham, 1995). Much of the work in Sweden to prevent ethnic discrimination has taken the form of changing attitudes and frames of reference, rather than changing behaviour directly (Soininen and Graham, 1995, 1997). Ethnic discrimination is most often discussed in terms of statistical discrimination in Sweden (SOU, 1995: 76). Since the mid-1990s, the labour market partners have been involved in a number of different initiatives inspired in part by the 1995 Florence Declaration on the Prevention of Racial Discrimination. A Joint Declaration made by LO, The Confederation of Professional Employees (TCO), and the Swedish Employers' Confederation (SAF) in 1995 sets out a range of measures that can make a positive contribution towards preventing racism in the workplace. These policies are designed to facilitate equal treatment in recruitment and selection, work allocation and promotion, training and development, and dismissal and redundancies, as well as dealing with discrimination, and showing respect for cultural and religious differences.

Information

Until the mid-1990s most of the stress in the documents produced by the labour market partners was on the need for equal treatment and mutual understanding in the workplace in order to promote integration. Managing cultural diversity among employees in multiethnic workplaces has been one of the major aims of the measures taken. Greater knowledge of immigrants, immigrant cultures, and one's own assumptions has been understood as necessary to create a well-functioning workplace and labour market.

Recognizing of Discrimination

Attention to discrimination, xenophobia and racism in Swedish workplaces was not addressed in any detail, with the partial exception of LO, prior to the 1990s. During the 1990s, a shift is evident in the discourse employed to argue against discrimination. In the 1991 LO programme, attention was given to harassment and to stopping xenophobic expressions with the help of information, and discussion groups. The programme also recognized the problem of ethnic discrimination, partly under the influence of the attention paid to the issue by the Discrimination Ombudsman, and asked for a law against discrimination in working life. The LO also has a special integration committee that has organized seminars on ethnic discrimination in working life. This is perhaps not surprising given the very large number of its members who have immigrant backgrounds.

For the TCO, ethnic equality in working life has been a policy issue since 1995. In that year, TCO, together with LO and SAF, produced a joint policy document against ethnic discrimination in the private sector and also contributed to an equivalent policy document for the public sector. The TCO's immigrant policy group has produced an organizational policy for immigrant questions, and in 1997 the TCO decided to work actively against ethnic discrimination. One part of this action is to identify foreign members and their union roles and to disseminate information.

Many of the documents produced in order to combat ethnic discrimination address the problem of indirect and/or institutional discrimination particularly in the context of recruitment. The question of ethnic inequality in working life is placed on the agenda by being approached from different perspectives. Sometimes by providing examples of indirect discrimination and its concrete consequences in order to increase personnel staff and union awareness of the problem.

Until 1994, the SAF had no explicit policy on the subject of immigrants in the workforce or on the subject of ethnic discrimination. But since

October 1996, the SAF has worked with the project 'Migration and Multi-cultural Business'. Particular effort has been put into working with informational material focused on entrepreneurial skills and business, xenophobia and racism, and multicultural leadership. The material is recommended for personnel managers and in training.

Representation and Monitoring

The TCO has expressed opposition to the idea of ethnic monitoring in individual workplaces in its policy programme proposal, and this is also true of the policy documents produced together with the labour market partners, the SAF and the LO, although in the joint document some monitoring of which applicants are called to interviews is suggested (Soininen and Graham, 1997). There has also been internal work within the unions intended to increase the number of immigrant union representatives so that it reflects the proportion of immigrants among the membership. A representative union membership and leadership presupposes some form of monitoring and the existence of accurate information in order to be able to assess how representative an organization has become. For example, the TCO has said that the ethnic composition of its own organization ought to be monitored to some extent so that the backgrounds of elected union representatives reflect the ethnic composition of its membership. In this respect, the TCO is somewhat more radical in the demands it places on itself than on the organizations in which its members work. The Sveriges Akademikers Centralorganisation (SACO) has devoted attention to highly educated and skilled immigrants in the Swedish labour market. A survey of the situation of 'international members' and the occurrence of ethnic discrimination is to be conducted. Working to change opinion and attitudes is seen as a means of attaining this goal but monitoring is also an acceptable tool. The SACO also plans a survey of its membership's ethnic affiliation.

Integration through Business

During recent years, there has been a noticeable increase in the attention paid to immigrant businesses and their development in Sweden both by the government and the SAF. In particular, the advantages that can accrue to a company or organization with a multicultural labour force: ethnic diversity is profitable.

The SAF has stressed the importance of immigrants starting their own businesses as one solution to the problem of high immigrant unemployment. In its 1994 prognosis, 'The Way to Growth', the SAF states that: 'The competence of immigrants as fellow workers or entrepreneurs, is to be exploited to the full.' The SAF has paid most attention to the problems facing immigrant entrepreneurs in a number of articles in its member newspaper *SAF Tidningen*. The key to success, it is argued, is a better climate for small businesses in general, including new rules for hiring and dismissing, incentive schemes, lower initial pay, and lower company taxes (SAF, 1995: 13). These suggestions can also be seen as calling into question the Swedish model's traditional favouring of large companies (Lindbeck, 1997).

Numerous articles in national newspapers have also been devoted to the topic of immigrant entrepreneurs. Among other things the debate has centred on the cultural resource that immigrants represent: a resource that not only enables immigrants to start their own businesses, but can also provide Swedish companies with much-needed cultural skills in, for example, contacts with foreign customers (see, for example, *Svenska Dagbladet*, December 1994; *Dagens Nyheter*, 14 December 1996; *Dagens Industri*, 8 March 1997).

Labour Market Policies: the Prospects for their Success

The policies and programmes adopted by the labour market partners share features with anti-discrimination work in a number of other countries (Wrench, 1996). In Sweden, the measures are in line with the 1994 law's stress on long-term attitude changes. These labour market measures are also top-down policies (Sabatier, 1986) which are initiated at national level by the policymakers in the central organizations, to be applied by the affiliated organizations and their personnel at the local level. What, then, are the conditions for success of these initiatives?

Top-down positive action initiatives address gatekeepers as a final target group. How street-level bureaucrats, gatekeepers, recruiters, and local union representatives understand organizational policy determines whether or not the general policy goals eventuate in concrete results (Lipsky, 1980). This means that those who implement the policy have considerable discretion when interpreting its goals and putting them into practice. Positive action programmes are often the result of bargaining and compromise, making them the kind of policies that can have low priority and diffuse goals (Vedung, 1997). This makes it all the more important that gatekeepers have adequate knowledge, resources, and the willingness to implement them. It is well known that these are often in short supply for policies enjoying low priority.

Whether ethnic discrimination takes place has been questioned for decades as has the need for special measures with which to tackle it. Political support in Sweden has been consistently weak. It took almost a quarter of a century to pass the 1994 law and it was in part the result of international pressures. Once introduced, the law was quickly found to be ineffectual. This historical background is not exactly conducive to the successful implementation of labour market partner initiatives. A large change in attitudes is probably required both among the top-level policymakers as well as among members in the workplace.

Positive action initiatives are not alone in having consequences for ethnic discrimination and the promotion of a multicultural workforce. Other programmes can also influence the final results in a specific policy area either by promoting them or blocking them (Vedung, 1997). At worst, they may even result in unintended indirect discrimination. An interview survey among randomly chosen employers presented in a state inquiry revealed that job seekers with limited social networks can be subjected to discrimination because informal avenues play an increasingly central role in job recruitment (SOU, 1997: 174). However, as recently as 1995 the government recommended the increased use of informal channels in order to make the work of employment services more efficient (SOU, 1996: 34). Given the problematic historical background of the anti-discrimination legislation and the programmes, it is hardly surprising that the ways in which other measures may contradict them has not received more attention. It is no coincidence that all government policy proposals in Sweden today are obliged to examine their implications for sexual equality, as this has been on the political agenda for much longer.

Policy success is not only discussed in terms of historical background, but also in terms of the type of policy. Policies that have redistributive consequences in terms of resources or power — regulatory and constituent policies — are often problematic (Lowi, 1972; Hill, 1997) and risk polarizing the situation. Positive action programmes obviously belong to this category, which can create difficulties in their formulation and introduction.

Equal opportunities policies have also been identified as particularly at risk of becoming 'symbolic policies' (Edelman, 1988; Hill, 1997) in which policymakers give the impression of taking action in order to maintain political support, rather than to tackle the problem in hand. At least in theory, labour market positive action initiatives are faced with a number of important obstacles, which they must overcome.

Changing the Focus: the Proposal for a New Law

In the light of the well-publicized shortcomings of the 1994 legislation, the government appointed a new commission of inquiry in 1997 charged with the task of drawing up a new law. The commission of inquiry and the law proposal mark a clear shift in the way that ethnic discrimination has been understood and debated in Sweden (SOU, 1997: 174; Regeringens proposition, 1997/98: 177). The new law came into effect in May 1999.

A starting point is that protection from discrimination is a basic human right. Furthermore, discrimination should not be seen as something that is only characteristic of racists, but as a common daily occurrence in Sweden. According to the commission of inquiry it is misleading to see discrimination as always deliberately intended. It further argues that discrimination can often be expressed through structures that are integral to the way society functions without this being recognized. This is why the part played by ethnic discrimination in the exclusion of immigrants is routinely underestimated whereas other factors such as education, structural changes, and language difficulties are recognized.

The proposal for the new law forbids direct and indirect discrimination whereas the 1994 law only covered cases of direct discrimination. The definition of ethnic discrimination is no longer confined to the existence of an intention to discriminate. The primary goal put forward in the White Paper is to protect the individual. This is a clear departure from the 1994 legislation's main aim of influencing public opinion. In sharp contrast to the 1994 law, the proposal states that changing the behaviour of the majority has to be the primary goal rather than expecting the behaviour of ethnic minorities to change. Whether or not people with unacceptable attitudes change these or not is of less importance.

The proposal thus signals a clear shift in assigning responsibility for combating ethnic discrimination. It demands that employers actively promote ethnic diversity in working life, for example, by ensuring that vacancies are sought by persons with different ethnic backgrounds. These active measures can even extend to positive special treatment or quotas according to the commission. The registration and monitoring of ethnic background is mentioned as a tool in an active process related to the promotion of an ethnically diverse workplace.

Ethnic monitoring has been a highly sensitive issue in Sweden. But the situation of immigrants has been routinely monitored as part of welfare policy, and the Immigrant Policy Committee suggested in its final report that 'a special body be established in the government office to follow and evaluate the development of the multi-cultural society' (SOU, 1996:

55, 389). Part of the AMS's responsibility is the regular gathering of relatively detailed statistics on immigrants in the workforce that show how different categories of immigrants fare during and after participation in labour market measures. It is this type of monitoring which made it possible for the AMS to take measures in 1995/96 as far-reaching as positive discrimination intended to soften the effects of employer reluctance to offer practical training or long-term employment for immigrants.

There is therefore extensive 'monitoring' in official statistics, even if it is not referred to as such and is not meant to translate into a differentiated welfare service. Nor is it meant to have an impact on workplace relations, which are normally the responsibility of the labour market partners. As we have seen, unions like the TCO are opposed to monitoring in the workplace. Opposition to monitoring from private companies can be understood as expressing the more general private sector dislike of external interference in private organizations. The Commission of Inquiry that has examined the need for a new law against ethnic discrimination in working life has pointed out that: 'Since the issue of registration and monitoring can be considered to be sensitive, it is important that an employer's personnel are informed about the purpose.' Ethnic monitoring is seen as being in conflict with the regnant principle of identical treatment for all regardless of ethnic background. There is, then, a degree of conflict between the egalitarian ethos of the universal welfare state and the targeted measures seen as necessary to guarantee welfare for vulnerable and disadvantaged groups. Furthermore, a policy of ethnic monitoring in the workplace would also require different institutional arrangements within the labour market.

The Changing Institutional Framework

The content of the new law is, then, more radical than its predecessor the 1994 law and earlier voluntary positive action measures adopted by the labour market partners and other organizations. It reflects recent changes in the institutional framework of the Swedish welfare state and policy making. The previous virtues of compromise and consensus are not felt to be as vital as in the past.

The controversial aspects of the new law reflect what seems to be a greater tolerance for disunity and differences of opinion over legislation within Swedish politics than was the case in the past. The Commission of Inquiry predicted a critical reception for some of its proposals and several of the Inquiry's members did indeed express reservations about some of the measures suggested in the White Paper. The demand for active measures by employers has also resulted in a great deal of mass media debate (*Svenska Dagbladet*, 8 May 1998; 12 May 1998; 26 May 1998; 31 July 1998), but although the proposal went further than had previously been the case in Swedish anti-discrimination legislation, the Commission of Inquiry argued that in several respects it simply incorporates into Swedish legislation what is already part of European law. The law proposal took its lead from expert international opinion rather than domestic expertise as in the past. The proposal makes an explicit comparison with legislation and other measures used in various countries to come to terms with ethnic discrimination. Great Britain, the Netherlands, Canada and the US are mentioned as countries with effective laws and other measures that are intended to provide protection against ethnic discrimination in individual cases as well as promoting ethnic diversity in general. International influence was instrumental in getting the 1994 law onto the statute book and is also evident in the content of the proposal for new legislation. Such influence also helped to initiate measures against ethnic discrimination that appeared in the mid-1990s among the labour market partners.

Historically, the labour market partners were responsible for tackling ethnic discrimination, but the 1997 legislative proposal charges individual employers with this responsibility to a much greater extent than previously. The large corporate actors seem to have lost some of their traditional influence. This can also be seen as part of a trend beginning in the 1980s of questioning strong faith in political solutions to social problems and in central planning (SOU, 1997: 57, 45; Rothstein, 1998: 25). The belief in the benefits of social engineering coincided with a period of strong economic growth. However, severe economic and financial problems have forced the government to reconsider the cornerstones of the Swedish model. Among other things it carried out the most comprehensive policy of financial savings in any industrialized country since the war (Riksrevisionsverket (RRV), 1996: 50, 72). The collapse of full employment removed one of the prerequisites for the traditional active labour market policy (Lindbeck, 1997: 84). More generally, since the late 1980s a political desire to hand over public services to the market has been in evidence (SOU, 1997: 57, 47). The reduction in the power of central organizations extends to the labour market partners and their influence. This development reflects a more general ideological shift in a neoliberal direction in which the market, its actors, and the individual occupy a more central position in society (Rothstein, 1998: 25–6).[3] We have seen specific evidence of the above changes in the government's faith in small businesses as a solution to immigrant unemployment rather than in traditional labour market measures, the acceptance of low-wage jobs for certain categories of immigrants, and a greater acceptance of social inequality and widening income differentials in society in general in response to market demands (see Lindbeck, 1997: 82).

The decentralization of responsibility for combating ethnic discrimination from a few organizational actors at the central level to a large number of local employers and workplaces is part of this more general process. The market's main actors, the employers, are charged with responsibility for finding a solution rather than the actors within the public sector. The law aims to mobilize local level actors, including individual employers and recruitment personnel; it encourages identification with the measures adopted, and greater flexibility in tackling the problem. Actors in the workplace may solve the problem of discrimination through individual initiatives, whereas individual immigrant workers may have greater opportunity to influence decisions at their own places of work. They no longer need to appeal to the union or employer for support, but can appeal directly to the provisions of the law and its demands for active measures. In accordance with neo-liberal tendencies, the status of the active individual, whether employer or employee, is promoted as is the emphasis on individual rights in contradistinction to the more traditional emphasis on collective values. This is evident in the new law proposal's emphasis on the rights of the individual to protection from ethnic discrimination.

Concluding Remarks

It can seem paradoxical that a country like Sweden, which strives after fairness and equality, has had difficulty recognizing and acknowledging the impact of ethnic discrimination on society's members. Yet, if one assumes that ethnic discrimination is often embedded in how society routinely operates, then an absence of effective anti-discrimination policies amounts to the presence of positive action on behalf of the ethnic majority population.

An explanation for this paradoxical situation might be that in a society that understands itself in terms of the ideals of social and economic equality, organizations imbued with egalitarian ideals experience great difficulty recognizing and acknowledging discrimination on their own doorsteps. Moreover, egalitarian ideals in Sweden are class based. Class inequalities attract attention and the class-based corporate policy-making model attempts to find means to remove their worst expressions. Other types of inequality do not provoke the same kind of attention. This has tended to exclude questions of ethnic inequality including ethnic discrimination from the labour market agenda (Graham and Soininen, 1998).

We have seen how this neglect of discrimination is reflected in the 1994 law's main focus on changing public opinion in the long term in order not to provoke the majority population. The 1994 law aimed to create consensus among those subject to it, which is a general characteristic of Swedish corporate policy making and the strong influence of the labour market partners within it. We have argued that the character of the labour market positive action initiatives and their lack of attention to ethnic discrimination until the mid-1990s reflect the basic ideas of the 1994 legislation. The historical background of these initiatives, their low priority, their probable redistributive consequences, and the considerable discretion of gatekeepers in interpreting diffuse goals made all successful implementation difficult.

The absence until recently of ethnic discrimination as part of the explanation for the position of immigrants in the labour market, we have suggested, makes it difficult for the government and labour market organizations to define certain measures as positive action programmes, even when these address problems caused in part by ethnic discrimination. Similarly, ethnic monitoring presupposes the recognition of ethnic categories as significant workplace phenomena. But the labour market partners and the government, operating largely on the basis of a class-based model of working life, have, for the most part, been reluctant to do this. However, the government does routinely employ ethnic monitoring as part of its more general welfare planning.

Finally, we have examined the latest proposal for a new law against ethnic discrimination in the employment sector which is far more radical than its predecessor and represents a shift in how ethnic discrimination is understood. The earlier concentration on influencing attitudes has been replaced by demands for changes in behaviour. The new law moves the emphasis from top-down to bottom-up initiatives. Demands are made on employers in local workplaces thereby according the individual a central role. We have argued that these changes can be understood as a product of recent institutional developments – organizational and ideological – in the Swedish model. If effective, the changes that the new law requires will significantly alter the context in which future positive action measures adopted in the labour market will be introduced.

Notes

1. The public sector costs as a proportion of the gross national product rose to 20 per cent in 1965, to 40 per cent in 1980, and to 50 per cent in the beginning of the 1990s (SOU, 1997: 57). In the 1990s, public spending in the large European countries was around 50 per cent more than in the US, whereas the Scandinavian countries spent around twice as much (Rothstein, 1998).
2. On the distinction between positive action and positive discrimination see Jewson and Mason (1992).
3. Sweden is, of course, not alone in showing a greater reliance on non-intervention, neo-liberal solutions based on individual initiative and the ability of the market to meet demands. For varied disciplinary perspectives on these developments, see Keat and Abercrombie (1991).

–12–

The Integration of Immigrants and Refugees in European Societies
John Rex

The Meaning of Integration

The term 'integration' is used in various ways. Some take it to be identical with assimilation, which in its extreme form envisages the loss of all characteristics which distinguish a group from those of 'normal' members of a society or at least involves those characteristics being ignored for all practical purposes by their fellows. Others, however, see the term as opposite to this. A group that is integrated is quite different from one that is assimilated. In some sense its connection with mainstream society is asserted, but at the same time this connection is not seen as involving the loss of all distinguishing characteristics.

When groups are integrated in a society in this latter sense, the new situation is often referred to as one of 'multiculturalism', but this term itself involves difficulties. It usually refers to the co-existence on the one hand of a 'host' or mainstream culture and, on the other, of one or more minority cultures. Saying that a society is multicultural is to say either simply that these different cultures exist or that they are regarded as having a legitimate right to exist. If what is meant is the latter, there is a question of the particular areas of human activity in which one or other culture should prevail.

This, however, still involves oversimplification. The problem of a multicultural society is not simply one of different cultures confronting one another. A distinction has to be made between a 'civic' culture, which sets out the basic rules of citizenship, usually on a political and legal level, and the rules by which communities regulate everyday life. Thus, in European societies one would have to look at a set of rules and ideals thought to govern the interaction of all individuals regardless of their group membership; secondly, at the way of life in everyday things of the dominant or host group; and thirdly, at the ways of life of incoming minority groups. Being integrated into a society for a member of an incoming minority group would not mean abandoning the way of life of his/her own group and adopting that of the host group, but it would involve accepting the rules of citizenship or the civic culture.

Marshall, Citizenship and the Integration of Immigrants

The concept of citizenship implies consent by all individuals to the civic culture. Such consent may be given to rules imposed by a dominant group or in a democracy it may rest upon some concept of equality. It is this second concept to which Thomas. H. Marshall refers in his *Citizenship and Social Class* (1951). Marshall suggests that, historically, it involved first legal, then political, and, finally, social, rights – first equality before the law, then the right to vote and share in political decision making, and finally a bundle of social rights such as insurance against unemployment and ill health, a minimum standard of housing, education and healthcare and the right to collective bargaining over wages and conditions of work. When all of these rights are achieved, individuals may be expected to have a primary loyalty to the state rather than to such groups as social classes. Clearly this involves some concept of a welfare state.

Within this definition of citizenship there may be a range of interpretations. Marshall's concept of social rights implies action by the state in order to achieve a minimum degree of equality of outcome. Others, however, have insisted only on equality of opportunity, leaving the outcome to be determined by market competition. In either case, however, some concept of equality remains. What this democratic concept excludes is any concept of citizenship that does not require some kind of equality.

The basic question which Marshall addressed was that of the replacement of class loyalties by loyalty to the state. He does not consider other possible conflicting loyalties like the loyalty of incoming minorities to separate groups and their cultures. This is the problem to which European societies had subsequently to address themselves. Thus, in the UK, in defining 'integration', the former British Home Secretary, Roy Jenkins, saw it as implying the acceptance of 'cultural diversity', but as accepting 'equality of opportunity', this occurring 'in an atmosphere of mutual tolerance' (Rex, 1996).

The problem which we have to face in defining the integration of incoming minorities is that of relating this Jenkins formula to Marshall's conception of citizenship, particularly social citizenship. For these minorities integration into their societies of settlement implies their accepting the civic culture and having the rights that this civic culture guarantees including rights within the welfare state. This does not, however, exclude the maintenance of distinct cultures and a form of social organization that sustain them in any matters that do not challenge the civic culture, such as separate religions, languages, and family practices.

Some Recent Critiques of Policies of Multicultural Integration

Radtke

Radtke (1994) suggests that in the modern 'social democratic welfare state' a plurality of originally conflicting interests have been reconciled and all individuals should participate as individuals within this system. For him the suggestion that immigrant rights should be dealt with outside of this system by a 'multicultural bureau' is inconsistent with this. There is a danger, he believes, that the problems facing Turkish immigrants will be seen as arising from their cultural difference, and not being faced, as they should be, through the normal agencies of the welfare state.

Radtke's position is essentially an assimilationist one. He sees no place at all for a separate system for immigrants or for the recognition of their cultures and social organization. The view taken here in contrast is that, if the social rights of citizenship are guaranteed, there is a place none the less for the continuance of immigrant social organizations and culture if these are not in actual conflict with the culture of the welfare state.

Rath

A position similar to that of Radtke is taken up by Jan Rath in a thesis discussing the question of minorities (Rath, 1991). He sees the Dutch policy of multiculturalism as 'minorizing' minorities or marking them out for 'unequal' treatment. What he does not consider is the possibility that governments and the minorities might negotiate to produce an egalitarian and democratic form of multiculturalism in which the recognition of difference goes along with equal treatment for all.

Schierup and Alund

A final critique of multiculturalism is provided on the basis of Swedish experience by Schierup and Alund (1990). According to them the form of multiculturalism that has developed in Sweden involves an essentialist view of minority cultures, which are seen as represented by the views of elderly males who are manipulated so that they are subordinated to the purposes of the Swedish welfare state. This is a more radical critique than that of Radtke. Whereas, for him, the immigrants should accept and work within the institutions of the welfare state, Schierup and Alund are inclined to see these very institutions as a source of subordination and inequality. Their remedy for this is a non-essentialist view of minority cultures that sees them as flexible and changing, and, what is more, involving the formation of new synthetic cultures that cross the lines between separate ethnic groups, and between these ethnic groups and disadvantaged and dissident groups, reacting to their own position and fighting for rights within their society.

What Schierup and Alund are arguing for is absorbed in a wider argument about cultural hybridity. A number of authors have argued that the simple notion of host and immigrant cultures confronting one another is inadequate and that actual political processes are profoundly affected by cultural hybrids who are seen alternatively as being the agents through whom compromises and reconciliation are achieved or as wholly innovative and challenging both host culture and ethnic minority cultures. (Werbner and Modood, 1997). In my own work on ethnic mobilization the existence of such cultural hybrids is also recognized (Rex, 1996; 1999) as part of a study of the changing nature of minority cultures.

The question of minority rights has been taken up on a more abstract level by political philosophers and political theorists. For them the problem is essentially that of discovering the rights that are implied by the notion of a liberal society. Since, however, their argument dealt originally with the rights of individuals, the question that arises so far as minorities are concerned is whether they are also entitled to group rights. This is the problem that is addressed by Michael Walzer (1980), Charles Taylor (1992), Will Kymlicka (1995) and others who are concerned not simply with immigrant minorities but with national ones. Their complex arguments, focused particularly on the Canadian situation, seek to find a place for group rights but also to impose limitations on it.

International Debate about Integration

Globalization, Transnational Communities and Citizenship

Much of the discussion of integration has, in the past, dealt with integration into the nation state. The relevance of such discussion is now seriously questioned by the theory of globalization and discussion of human rights on an international scale. Yasemin Soysal (1994), for instance, has argued that we now live in a world in which universal human rights are more important than rights within national states and that there are now international courts that sustain these rights. This argument, however, is concerned only with the first of Marshall's three sets of rights, namely legal rights. It does not therefore cover the concept of integration in the sense in which we have been discussing it. Social rights still seem to depend upon the national welfare state. The only relevance of Soysal's argument is that it strengthens the claim of individuals in the nation state to legal rights or legal equality.

The Debate about Social Inclusion and Social Exclusion

Another form of the internationalization of the debate about integration occurs in discussions within the European Union. There it is suggested that the EU should do more than guarantee equality of opportunity, and that, whatever the outcome of such equality of opportunity, measures have to be taken to promote what is called social inclusion and to prevent social exclusion of individuals or groups of individuals. Prima facie this would seem to reproduce Marshall's notion that legal equality must be supplemented by political rights (through the right to vote) and social equality to at least a minimum level.

The concepts of social inclusion and social exclusion, however, are considerably less clear than those in Marshall's analysis. When any attempt is made to explain them the first emphasis is usually on employment/ unemployment and on levels of income. The unemployed and those receiving incomes below a certain level are the main categories of the socially excluded. It is usually implied, however, that the concept of inclusion/exclusion refers to something more and that is why debate is focussed on this something more rather than simply on questions of employment and income. Both the unemployed and the poor on the one hand and the employed and the better off on the other may also be excluded in other ways. They may lack political rights and may not share in the cultural and moral unity of their societies. The duty of the new supra-national entity is to promote this unity.

Of particular importance here are the rights of national and incoming ethnic minorities. In principle one might expect that the debate about inclusion and exclusion would have to face up to these questions. Clearly those who lack political rights, like guestworkers, may be said to be excluded, and steps also have to be taken to ensure that those who are culturally different and have separate communal organizations are not prevented from obtaining the equal treatment that comes from sharing in the civic culture. They should not be marked for inferior treatment. It must be said, however, that the use of the general terms inclusion and exclusion does not take on the full range of these problems and it would therefore be better to stick to the much clearer concepts suggested by Marshall and Jenkins.

The Means to Achieving Full Citizenship

The reasons why some individuals do not have equal rights are that they lack jobs, that their income is too low, that they lack the right to vote and that they are discriminated against because of their physical or cultural characteristics. If they are to attain these rights they must be able to obtain jobs, to have a minimum income, have the right to vote, and be protected against discrimination. This does not mean that they should be given special rights but simply that they should have equal rights.

So far as discrimination is concerned one important check on whether it exists can be provided by monitoring the percentages of those from various groups in varying types of employment, in various income groups, in different types of education, in the electorate (noting both those entitled to vote and those actually voting), and perhaps also in the cultural management of society. The aim of this monitoring would be to show the extent to which these forms of participation reflect the percentages of minorities in the total population.

What monitoring shows is the degree of disadvantage experienced by different groups, but there are two different interpretations of this disadvantage. One is that it is simply the product of unknown processes; the other that it is due to specific acts of discrimination. If the first interpretation is accepted, the state might intervene to demand quotas in such spheres as employment, housing and education. If, however, the second view is taken what it would have to do is to prevent acts of discrimination, by making them illegal and providing means of redress.

Unfortunately those who take the first view may actually help to conceal the fact of discrimination and provide cover for its continuance. This may not mean, as is sometimes said, 'blaming the victim', but it may involve excusing the discriminators from blame.

Affirmative Action

The setting up of and the attempt to achieve quotas is one, although only one, form of affirmative action. This wider concept includes any policy designed to compensate for disadvantage by giving special rights to minorities. It is common to all such policies that they assert the right of minorities to more than equal rights.

Such policies are always likely to result in a backlash amongst the majority who see the granting of special rights to the minorities as giving themselves less than equal rights. The policies are seen, that is to say, in zero-sum terms. These problems would not arise if disadvantage were seen as resulting from acts of discrimination that could be shown to be unfair.

One reason why the concept of affirmative action is being debated is that the question is being asked as to whether Europe can learn from American experience. It will therefore be necessary to look briefly at the substance and the context of the American debate in order to see whether a similar concept can be applied in Europe.

The American Debate

The American debate is focused on the position of the black population[1] thought to be of originally African descent, whose first ancestors in America had been slaves. Their legal status had first been changed by the ending of slavery, but they still lacked full legal rights and the right to vote. The intention of civil rights legislation in the 1950s and 1960s was to give them these rights. None the less when this programme was completed they still seemed to achieve unequally in all the major areas of life, especially in employment, housing and education. Some sought to explain this as being due to the character of the blacks and their institutions, particularly the matricental family. The Moynihan Report[2] (see Yancey and Rainwater, 1967) suggested that either these institutions had to be reformed or that their effect had to be compensated for by government social policies affecting the family. A more radical approach called for affirmative action to ensure that blacks had equal chances in the main areas of life. In my view the best discussion of these developments is to be found in Stephen Steinberg's book *Turning Back: The Retreat from Racial Justice in American Thought and Policy* (1995), but it is also the recurrent concern of other writers like Glazer (1983, 1987) and Wilson (1978, 1987).

A very important theme in all of this discussion is the relationship between class and 'race' as determinants of life chances. For Wilson the effect of affirmative action has been to enable some blacks to participate fully in American society, but the great majority of lower class blacks remain disadvantaged and segregated from mainstream society. Class or class within 'race' rather than 'race' itself then becomes the crucial factor and seems to point to the need for policies to deal with all the disadvantaged and the so-called 'underclass', regardless of 'race'. In opposition to this Steinberg (1995) argues that the actual structural position of blacks is such that separate policies of affirmative action are necessary quite apart from what might be done for all those in the so-called underclass. The structural position of the blacks results from the historic wrong involved in their ancestors' insertion into American society as slaves. Affirmative action involving additional rights for blacks is justified as being due to the need to rectify this historic wrong.

The concept of the underclass was introduced into American sociology by Myrdal in his *Challenge to Affluence* (1964). He referred to a group at the bottom of American society – mainly, but not only, blacks who were 'unemployed and increasingly unemployable'. To this notion others added the idea that the underclass lived in a 'culture of poverty' (Lewis, 1973) and a 'tangle of pathologies' (The Moynihan Report, see Yancey and Rainwater, 1967). Empirical approaches to the study of this underclass then established a number of quantitative indices through which it could be distinguished.

The Applicability of American Concepts in Europe

The first important point to notice when applying the notion of affirmative action in Europe is that those to whom it is directed have a quite different relationship to European society to that which American blacks have to American society. Their position results from the fact that they are guestworkers, immigrants, or refugees. None of these statuses is equivalent to that of slaves or their descendants. Guestworkers may have legal and social rights but lack the right to vote. Immigrants may, through naturalization, become full citizens. Refugees are entitled to acceptance if they are in personal danger in their countries of origin under the Geneva Convention. One cannot, therefore, simply apply to any of them policies that have been worked out to deal with the position of American blacks.

In the case of guestworkers it may well be shown that they are disadvantaged in their situation in employment, housing or education but it has to be asked why this is the case. Since, lacking a vote, they do not control these matters, they are dependent upon the benevolence of various organizations of the host society such as churches, trade unions and non-governmental organizations. For them to be offered affirmative action by a state that they do not control could only compound this situation and the suggestion that it might be the best means of integrating them could only serve to distract attention from their lack of political rights.

The alternative to affirmative action would appear to be giving them the right to vote so that they can protect themselves against injustice and ensure their equality.

Immigrants are in a different position. In principle they can readily become naturalized as citizens in their country of settlement and be in a position to control their own destiny winning positions of equality in the various institutional areas. It is, of course, to be expected that this position of equality may take a period of time to be realized, given a range of problems of adjustment that the immigrants might face, but what is usually at issue is whether they are entitled to settle in the first place and whether there are those in the host society who deliberately discriminate against them and prevent their gaining full equality. The first task of anyone seeking to facilitate their integration has to be to consider whether immigration controls are unfairly applied and whether there is subsequent discrimination preventing their gaining social equality. Here again the suggestion that they need the special rights offered by affirmative action distracts attention from the arbitrariness of immigration control and the fact of discrimination.

In fact in most countries there are varieties of different types of immigrants. Some are not seen as constituting special problems but others are. In the Netherlands for example, immigrants from Indonesia and Surinam have easier modes of entry and easier opportunities to achieve social equality than do Turks and Moroccans.

Refugees are entitled to special rights because of the Geneva Convention. If they can prove in their applications for asylum that they are in personal danger in the countries of origin, the state in the host society has an obligation to accept them. If they are so accepted they become to all intents and purposes like immigrants. Their case for asylum, however, has to be proved before representatives of the government in the country of refuge and these representatives have considerable discretion. Relatively few asylum applications are granted and it is frequently suggested that many of the applicants are bogus asylum seekers who are really economic migrants in disguise seeking to evade normal immigration controls. Far from enjoying a privileged position, these unsuccessful applicants are actually in a worse position than immigrants.

In fact the category of refugees is part of a wider category of political migrants, many of whom, though they are not in personal danger, come from intolerable situations of political conflict and ecological disaster. Such political migrants are therefore often not returned to their countries of origin until conditions there have changed. Their situation before any such return, however, is a highly ambiguous and precarious one. Their status is seen as temporary and they are even more likely to be objects of suspicion and hostility than actual asylum seekers or immigrants.

What this review of the position of guestworkers, immigrants, refugees and political migrants shows is that there are at present a number of categories of residents in European societies whose rights as citizens are non-existent or precarious, but the political discussion of their position is not usually even based upon an understanding of these distinctions. What commonly happens is that they are seen collectively as part of a general threat of immigration against which established societies have to protect themselves. Attacks on refugees in Rostock or Solingen are followed by attacks on Turkish families in West Germany and all the victims of these attacks are seen as part of a single group. Moreover all are liable to encounter the same prejudice and discrimination. Again in Britain or Ireland the discussion of the cases of specific groups of intending settlers, including Gypsies[3] from Romania, Slovakia and the Czech Republic, is in terms of a general problem of controlling a potentially bottomless pit of immigrants.

What does seem to be the case is that in contemporary Western Europe there is a fear of immigrants of any sort, they are subject to physical attack, barriers are thrown up against all of them, and they suffer discrimination in terms of social rights. Mainstream political parties are likely to say that these various developments are the result of the actions of extreme groups whom they denounce, yet at the same time they adapt their own policies to hold or win back votes that they would otherwise lose to the extremists.

In these circumstances any debate about affirmative action as a way of giving true citizenship or social inclusion to these various categories of residents can be very misleading. Those concerned are seeking not special rights to overcome an historical wrong as is suggested in the US. They are simply seeking to obtain equal rights as citizens.

In fact the term 'affirmative action' is very loosely used in the European debate. It may be taken to refer to all measures taken to overcome discrimination; it may refer to monitoring processes leading to the introduction of quotas; or it may refer to other special measures giving special additional rights to minorities. The central point being made here is that there is a danger that the term may often be used in the second or third sense and be taken to imply that minorities are already protected against discrimination and have equality and are to be given something more than this. This may then provoke resistance and a backlash on the part of the majority who then come to question all measures designed to combat discrimination. In this chapter, therefore, we need to address ourselves in the first place not to areas in which special rights need to be accorded but to all measures designed to combat unfair or unequal treatment of minorities.

The Main Institutional Areas within which the Effects of Discrimination Need to be Corrected

Minorities, consisting of guestworkers, immigrants, asylum seekers and political migrants and their descendants[4] have been shown to be disadvantaged in several institutional areas, the most important of which are the labour market, housing, education and family life.

Disadvantage in the Labour Market

In the labour market it can be shown in most countries of Western Europe that, even after several generations, members of some incoming minority communities are disadvantaged. They are more likely to be unemployed and, where they are employed, they are more likely to be concentrated in the least rewarding jobs marked by low status, low pay, and poor conditions. Such disadvantages can be monitored and corrected.

The process of monitoring itself can work to the disadvantage of incoming minorities if it is purely in the hands of government officials rather than based upon the recorded experience of the minorities themselves. Thus, an important recent report by social scientists to governments in the Netherlands attributes the poor employment record of Turkish and Moroccan youth to their failure to obtain qualifications and enter the labour market. It therefore proposes the withholding of benefit payments to those who are not taking courses or seeking employment. This appears to ignore the possibility that these failures may be the result not of the failure of the young people involved but from discrimination. Such attitudes are increasingly common in other countries too as is shown by recent arguments about moving from welfare to work in the UK. What seem to be required here are studies both of discrimination suffered and of the motivation of minority youth.

Disadvantage in Housing

In the sphere of housing it has been widely recognized that a free market in housing for purchase or rent leads to disadvantageous outcomes for some minorities. This is inevitable in that markets are influenced by the choices of the richest and most powerful members of the community.

What is less commonly recognized is that discrimination may also exist so far as social housing is concerned, particularly where this is provided by local government agencies (Rex and Moore, 1967).[5]

So far as other forms of social housing such as that provided by non-profit housing associations were concerned, we recognized that their effect upon the pattern of disadvantage and discrimination depended upon who controlled them. One should also note that in the private housing market estate agencies emerged that were run by immigrants and served to provide better housing for members of their own communities.

The debate about discrimination in the sphere of housing should not be confused with that about segregation. The existence of segregated ethnic communities does not necessarily result from discrimination alone. Members of ethnic minorities might well choose to live with their own group because of their need for places of worship, shops and other institutions. This does not mean, however, that they would choose to be segregated in the worst housing in the city. Existing patterns of segregation are the result of both choice and constraint.[6] What is involved here is the geographical expression of the general debate about multiculturalism. A segregated ethnic community provides for the continued existence of a private communal culture, but in an egalitarian multicultural society this does not mean that members of minority communities should not have the full rights of citizens including the right to buy or rent housing wherever they wish.

Disadvantage in Education

Education presents consequent problems. If ethnic communities are segregated, and if the notion of a local community school is upheld, then the schools in segregated areas of the city will themselves be ethnically segregated. Since, however, schools are differentially successful and the children of immigrants are concentrated in the least successful ones, the notion of the local community school may be called into question. The remaining middle classes in the host society will seek to move their children to suburban schools of their own choice and there will be a debate about whether the minority children should be given the opportunity of being bused to these schools (a particular form of affirmative action with many of the consequences that we have noted for affirmative action in its other forms).

A further question that arises in the schools concerns the syllabus in largely segregated schools. This is whether the syllabus should allow for education in minority cultures. Here again one should note that while minority parents may want their own cultures to be respected and fostered in the schools, they do not wish this to interfere with their children acquiring all the general skills that will enable them to compete equally in the employment market. In England one West Indian teacher has urged that supplementary schools should concentrate not on fostering minority cultures in order to increase self esteem, but on the basic skills of reading, writing, and arithmetic which all students need (Stone 1981).

Disadvantage in Relation to the Personal Social Services

So far as the personal social services focused on family problems are concerned some similar problems arise. A modern society does provide skilled social work offered by professionals to all families and it is important that the services offered to immigrant families are not inferior. Some argue, however, that such services may be insensitive to the special needs of different ethnic communities. What is necessary therefore is that either the professionally skilled social workers should be sensitized to minority needs or that social workers drawn from immigrant communities should be given the necessary general professional skills.

Conclusion

Summarizing what has been said above, there clearly is a need for action to be taken in these four institutional areas if immigrants of various kinds are to obtain their full rights as citizens. Many people, particularly in non-governmental organizations and amongst the immigrants themselves, feel that some action must be taken. This is also what leads to the ideological commitment in Europe to promote social inclusion and prevent social exclusion. In the looser usage of the term this is what is meant by positive or affirmative action. However, affirmative action is also thought to carry the implication of special extra rights and necessary policies to combat discrimination are often called into question. Still worse, commitment to affirmative action in the narrower sense diverts attention away from such discrimination.

It may still be asked, however, whether, if all forms of discrimination were actually overcome, there might not still be a case for positive or affirmative action in the narrow sense. The answer is that there might be because there may be undiscovered reasons for inequality. In America we saw that a radical case was argued for affirmative action on the grounds that the fact of slavery and its consequences left the descendants of slaves in a structurally distinct position from other members of excluded groups and the so-called 'underclass'. It was thought to be necessary in order to correct the historic wrong of slavery. The remaining question in Europe is that of whether the position of incoming minorities rests upon an equivalent historic wrong.

It can be argued that such an historic wrong is present in the poverty of the less-developed countries from which immigrants come and the political instability of these countries. Could it then be said that this constitutes a justification for affirmative action? Probably it does. The relative poverty of the less-developed countries and the political situations within them may be seen as historic wrongs that have some equivalence with slavery and a moral case can be made for the rectification of all three, but to say that there is such a moral case still leaves open the question of who is likely to argue for it. Governments responsive to majority pressure are unlikely to do so. Everything will therefore depend upon the capacity of the immigrants themselves and of the liberal minority in the host society acting through non-governmental organizations to compel or persuade the electorate of the necessity of such action. It is this process of resistance, compulsion and persuasion that is at the heart of the sociological problem of affirmative action.

Notes

1. In saying this I am conscious of the fact that some other groups, namely Hispanic immigrants and Native Americans are also brought into this discussion but the major debate has occurred in relation to the black population.
2. Yancey and Rainwater's book, 'The Moynihan Report and the Politics of Controversy' includes the text of the report together with a number of chapters on the ways in which it was taken up in American politics.
3. The term 'gypsy' is used here as a matter of convenience even though, like other terms such as 'Tsigan', it may have been used in a pejorative way. What does seem to be the case, however, is that there is a European-wide problem of dealing with minorities with a distinct Romany culture and this problem has recently been encountered in Britain and Ireland.
4. There is a real problem here in that, where there is a strong assimilationist ideology, as in France, there is resistance amongst policy makers

and social scientists to consider the position of descendants in the second and subsequent generations. Only in the UK has an ethnic question been included in the census. This question asks all respondents to indicate to which ethnic group they believe themselves to belong. The actual choices offered in this question are highly contentious, but, even if they were perfect, they would run into the objection that the very act of counting numbers in the second and subsequent generations denied their right to be treated as equal citizens.

5. One of the major themes of my research with Robert Moore in this book was discrimination by the local council in allocating tenancies in council-owned or council-built properties. This was not a popular view with our left-wing critics who wished to concentrate on the evils of a private market, although it was readily accepted by social scientists in some of the communist countries. We spoke of housing classes based upon differential access to different kinds of housing under any system whether a free market or a socialist bureaucratic one. This led to a considerable debate amongst urban sociologists (see Pahl, 1969 and Hancock, 1994).

6. When my book with Robert Moore was published we were criticized by Dahya (1973, 1974) for suggesting that segregation was the result of discrimination whereas he attributed it entirely to choice by the ethnic communities and the activities of their own housing entrepreneurs. In subsequent discussions, however, Dahya and I have been able to agree that segregation is the result of both constraint and choice.

13

'We Demand that the Foreigners Adapt to our Life-Style': Political Discourse on Immigration Laws in Austria and the United Kingdom

Ruth Wodak and *Maria Sedlak*

Introduction – The 'Big Change' ('Wende') 1989 and Problems of Immigration

In his introduction to the book *Racism*, Robert Miles states that

> migration . . . has been a precondition for the meeting of human individuals and groups over thousands of years. In the course of this interaction, imagery, beliefs and evaluations about the 'other' have been generated and reproduced amongst all the participants in the process in order to explain the appearance and behaviour of those with whom contact has been established and in order to formulate a strategy for interaction and reaction (Miles, 1991: 11).

Since 1989, and with the fall of the 'Iron Curtain', massive migration has taken place in Europe, and the strategies and reactions to cope with this phenomenon have been quite different for different countries, but in most of the Western European countries, racist practices against the migrants were and are observable. Thus, immigration is severely restricted in virtually all countries of the European Union and elsewhere in Western Europe, and the 'European Fortress' is no longer a rhetorical scare phrase, but begins to take on an increasingly concrete form. Besides these official political measures to 'curb' the immigration of unwanted others, each domain of European society shows signs of deteriorating human rights. Attacks on immigrants have become so widespread and common, and not only in Germany, that they are no longer routinely covered in the media. More-or-less subtle discrimination and everyday racism in housing, employ-ment, health care, legislation, policing, has become general practice.

The overall aim of the project 'Racism at the Top'[1] is to provide insight into the role of leading politicians in the reproduction of racism in Europe. More specifically, we want to know how political elites speak and write about 'ethnic' issues such as immigration, minorities, refugees, ethnic relations, prejudice, discrimination, and related topics. We have chosen parliamentary debates as our object of investigation in seven Western European countries (Germany, France, Netherlands, Italy, Spain, the UK, Austria). The project is concerned with the production and reproduction of racism and anti-semitism by politicians in debates, and our research combines qualitative and quantitative methods. In this paper, we focus on only one of the many possible topics – debates about immigration laws. After briefly presenting our approach to racism, elite racism and discourse and racism, we compare the laws on immigration of Austria and the UK and give a short description of political discourse in parliamentary context. Then, we describe a few important categories for analysis and apply these to some sequences out of Austrian and British parliamentary debates. Finally, we discuss the implications of such research.

Racism, Discourse and the Elites

Elite Discourse and Racism

The theoretical framework for this research project is guided by an ordered set of global hypotheses that link elite discourse with the reproduction of racism in European society.

1. Racism may be analysed into two main components: discrimination and its underlying, socially shared, ethnic prejudices. As far as our own definition of racism is concerned, we keep in mind Miles's (1991) caveat regarding hasty assumptions of a relationship between exclusionary practices and racist opinions. Nevertheless, we assume racism to be both an ideology of a syncretic kind and a discriminatory social (including discursive) practice which can be more-or-less institutionalized and which is more-or-less backed by hegemonic groups. Racism is based on the hierarchizing construction of groups of persons, which are characterized as communities of descent and that are attributed specific collective, naturalized or biologized traits that are considered to be almost invariable and negative. As an ideological *mixtum compositum*, racism combines different and sometimes contradictory doctrines, religious beliefs and stereotypes, thereby construct-

ing an almost invariable pseudocausal connection between – more or less fictitious – biological, social, cultural, and mental traits.
2. Ethnic prejudices are largely acquired and changed through public discourse. Discourse is seen as social practice, as constitutive and constituting interaction and society. Thus, racist attitudes can be co-constructed in an interaction, but they can also be more-or-less stable belief systems.
3. Leading politicians have preferential access to public discourse.
4. If elite politicians hold and express negative opinions about immigrants, the pervasive influence of their discourses on public opinion may significantly contribute to the formation, legitimization or confirmation of ethnic prejudices among the population at large, and thus play a role in the (re)production of racism in society.
5. Conversely, the same hypotheses also have a positive variant, which may be summarized as follows: if elite politicians hold and express clearly anti-racist opinions, these will positively affect public opinion on immigration and ethnic relations.

Some Additional Remarks about Racism

Racism is here understood as a historically developed system of ethnic or racial dominance (in this case of people of European descent over immigrants or minorities of non-European origin) resulting in social, economic, political and cultural inequality. That is, through a system of discriminatory practices (including inferiorization, marginalization and exclusion) dominant group members, organizations and institutions prevent equal access of dominated group members to valuable public resources, such as adequate forms of residence, housing, employment, income, education, knowledge, status, political representation, and human rights. These discriminatory practices are in turn based on, and legitimated by, shared social cognitions (beliefs, opinions, ideologies, norms and values) that basically establish a hierarchical relation between ingroup (Us) and outgroup (Them) by ascribing negative characteristics to Them, and positive ones to Us. Thus, positive self-presentation and negative other-presentation lie at the core of racist discourses with the specific attribution of traits and the use of pronouns becoming linguistically loaded markers of racist beliefs. The same is true for the denial of racism, because it is not possible in our countries to be explicitly racist. Many disclaimers are used, including the famous 'but': 'we have nothing against the Turks, Jews etc., but . . .' This system of ethnic dominance and inequality may become manifest under various guises in different historical and political contexts, viz., as (combinations of) ethnocentrism, eurocentrism, xeno-phobia, extreme nationalism, and anti-semitism. Following much of the scholarly and political literature, these various forms of ethnic dominance could simply be summarized under the label of 'racism'. We believe, the term 'ethnicism' would probably be more appropriate, given the largely ethnic-cultural nature of discrimination and prejudice in Europe. However, many forms of ethnicism are closely related to perceived (and negatively evaluated) differences of appearance of most immigrants and minorities, that is, to what is usually construed as racial differences, so that also for empirical reasons, the term 'racism' is not wholly misguided. Indeed, one may conveniently speak of different 'racisms' in Europe or, related to Richard Mitten's concept of 'syncretic anti-semitism', we would like to use the term 'syncretic racism' (Mitten, 1992). This means that, nowadays, the different distinctions between the different forms of ethnicism and racism have become blurred, and prejudices are functional-ized politically in every context where they apply best, neglecting their historical heritage and use. Thus, our use of the term 'syncretic racism' does not at all imply that ethnic dominance is blatant, direct, open, violent or extreme. On the contrary, it may often be covert, indirect, hidden, subtle and (therefore usually) denied. Neither does racism – as we understand it – apply only to extraordinary events and situations, such as lynchings, beatings, progroms, segregation, apartheid or killings. Although some of these extraordinary forms of racism in Europe do occur, and sometimes quite frequently, most – and the most pervasive – forms of racism in Western Europe are expressed in the many practices of everyday life, and in all social situations. Indeed, ethnic dominance is only possible when a majority of the majority engages in, condones or otherwise contributes to such dominance. This also means that we do not generally speak of racists, or simply distinguish between racist and non-racist people in society. Rather, we prefer to talk of racist (ethnicist) practices and prejudices as those that contribute to the reproduction of the system of ethnic inequality, and anti-racist ones as those that contribute to the challenge and breakdown of this system. Both may be widely distributed (even among the same people) within society, although at the moment the former apparently prevail, given the social position of immigrants and minorities in most countries of Western Europe.

Elite Racism

Relevant for this project is the further assumption that the social hierarchy of the dominant group plays a special role in the system of racism.

Powerful leaders, organizations, institutions, groups or classes, here conveniently summarized as the 'elites', are closely involved in the system of ethnic dominance. Although a full-scale analysis of their involvement (and hence of their very role as 'elites') would require extensive research for each group and social domain, earlier research allows us to conclude that the most consequential decisions and actions in the lives of minorities are taken by elites. This also applies to discriminatory social practices of which immigrants and minorities are the victims. That is, various elite groups are directly or indirectly responsible for unequal treatment or the unjust consequences of decisions, policies or activities related to immigration, residence, housing, employment, income, position, education, media coverage, health care, culture, religion, language, political representation, and so on. Again, such racism need not at all be overt, extreme or blatant. On the contrary, it may be quite ordinary, viz., as taken-for-granted and seemingly fair measures of everyday administration, bureaucracy and leadership of an organization, institution or the country as a whole. The crucial criterion, however, is based on the consequences on such everyday practices of the elites: immigrants and minorities receive less access to valued social resources than dominant group members. Against this theoretical background, we have a look at institutionalized racism, disguised in legal language and in the debates about legalese.

Legislation on Immigration in Austria and in the UK

For this chapter, we haven chosen two countries out of the seven Western European states to be investigated in the project: Austria and the UK: while both countries are members of the EU and share many general similarities, they also differ with respect to several important political, geographical and historical characteristics. Thus, for example, while Austria is a Schengen state at the core of Europe (without any colonial history), the UK is a non-Schengen state, an island, and once headed a vast colonial empire. In this context, then, it is interesting to compare their respective policies on immigration and asylum. To what extent are they different or similar?

For more than fifty years, Austria and the UK have been the destination of thousands of immigrants: Britain mainly for people from the Commonwealth and Austria for immigrants from Eastern Europe, ex-Yugoslavia and Turkey. In recent years, however, Austria and the UK have passed a number of new laws restricting immigration and asylum and regulating the residence of foreigners.[2] In the following section, we would like to discuss – though only roughly – some of the most important points of Austrian and British legislation on immigration, specifically the categorization of foreigners, the requirements for a residence permit, the occupation of foreigners and family reunion (see also Layton-Henry, 1994; Cinar, Hofinger and Waldrauch, 1995; Hödl and Winter, 1998).

Both the Austrian and British laws construe various categories of foreigners on the basis of their origin, family status, profession and intended length of stay and further assign different rights to each category. That is, citizens of a EU member state and family members of an Austrian or a EU citizen are clearly preferred under the Austrian laws. Likewise, in the UK, Commonwealth citizens with the right of abode, European Economic Area nationals, and the families of such nationals are privileged. Additionally, there are various other types of British citizens who differ with respect to the privileges they have (British Citizens by descent, British Citizens otherwise than by descent, British Dependent Territories citizens, British Nationals (Overseas, British Overseas citizens, British protected persons, British subjects)).

Any other foreigners, in other words, the majority of migrants, belong to the more or less 'unwanted' group of immigrants. In the UK, these are nonwhite immigrants from the Commonwealth, especially the West-Indies; in Austria, Turks, people from ex-Yugoslavia and Eastern Europe are no longer welcome. As the immigration of these groups is to be reduced, their access to either the UK or Austria has been increasingly restricted in the recent years in the form of visa regulations, including in the case of Austria, annual quotas and numerous of requirements that have to be met. Immigrants are required, among other stipulations, to (1) apply for a visa outside the UK (plus Islands) or Austria; (2) prove their identity and nationality; (3) register obligatorily with the police; (4) have adequate accommodations (in Austria, this means having at least 12 square meters for each person); (5) maintain themselves (i.e. financially) adequately without recourse to public funds; and, (6) in the UK, to medically tested.

In addition, there are several restrictions regarding the employment or occupations of foreigners in both countries: immigrants who want to work in the UK or Austria need a work permit. In general, such a work permit is valid only for specific labour (for example, seasonal work, au-pair work, paid employment) and is temporally limited. In Austria, for example, there are three types of work permits: 'Beschäftigungsbe-willigung', 'Arbeitserlaubnis' and 'Befreiungsschein'. The first two allow the holder to work for one year only and do not allow him/her to undertake any other employment except as specified in the permit. Only the 'Befreiungsschein' gives the holder somewhat more flexibility. Obtaining a work permit is also attached to a number of conditions: immigrants are only allowed to work in Austria or the UK, if

1. they have a job offer and their future employer is willing to apply for a work permit;
2. they are of an age eligible for employment;
3. they have the necessary qualifications for the job;
4. there is no resident of the country able to do this kind of work; and, in Austria, if
5. the annual quota for work permits has not already been filled.

The rules for family reunion in British and Austrian legislation are, likewise, restrictive and discriminating: immigrants settled in the UK or in Austria may bring only certain members of their family to join them: the spouse if they are legally wed and intend to live together and their children provided they are under the age of 18 years in the UK and under the age of 14 years in Austria. Under certain conditions, parents, grand-parents and financés are also allowed to immigrate to the UK. In any case, all immigrants must be able to support themselves and their families without recourse to public funds and have adequate accommodations where they can live. However, it is nowhere defined what 'adequate' means. Thus, these restrictions stay open for manifold interpretations (van Leeuwen and Wodak 1999). In both countries, a residence permit for a family member is first given only for a certain period of time (about one year) and, in general, does not give that individual permission to work during the first years after the immigration. In Austria, family reunion further depends on an annual quota, which has been continuously reduced in recent years.

Finally, the application for an entry clearance and a work permit, both in Austria and the UK, involves high fees, which have been raised continuously over the years, and thus are another way of reducing immigration.

Summing up this section, we can see that, on the whole, both the UK and Austria, despite certain historical differences (for example the UK as a former colonial power with an extensive Commonwealth), are rather similar in their legal practices concerning immigration: both Western European nations have a strong interest in keeping immigration to a minimum.

Political Discourse in the Parliamentary Context

At this point, we would like to turn to the linguistic analysis and to our notion of 'political discourse', as situated in the parliamentary context.

Politics and language are strongly linked to each other, because most political action and interaction is discursive (van Dijk, 1995). One need only to think about meetings, parliamentary sessions, election campaigns and press conferences to name but a few events, where an enormous amount of oral and written text is produced. Political action can be systematized into at least six fields of action (Girnth, 1996: 6; Reisigl and Wodak, 2000a). These fields are segments of the respective political reality which supply the frame of discourse and include (1) the legislative process; (2) internal party policy decisions; (3) public-political opinion making; (4) political propaganda; (5) political administration; and, finally, (6) political control. According to Girnth, prototypical text types can be related to each field, as shown in Figure 13.1.

In other words, we can speak of 'political discourse' as a form of political action, as a part of the political process. This view 'is perfectly compatible with the dominant paradigm in most social approaches to discourse, viz., that discourse is a form of social action and interaction' (van Dijk, 1995: 10). Both spoken interaction or dialogue and written texts, although this last category is not face-to-face, can thus be seen as a form of social and political action. Parliamentary debates are, besides propaganda leaflets, campaign speeches, party programmes, and so forth, one genre of political discourse.

The different discourse types and levels of discourse organization are linked to political situations and processes by specific intermediate levels, which Chilton and Schäffner (1997: 212ff.) have called 'strategic functions'. They distinguish four strategies, which are constitutive for political discourse: coercion; resistance, opposition and protest; dissimulation; and legitimization and delegitimization.

'Coercion' refers to speech acts like commands or laws, which are backed by sanctions:

> Political actors . . . often act coercively through discourse in setting agendas, selecting topics in conversation, positioning the self and others in specific relationships, making assumptions about realities that hearers are obliged to, at least temporarily, accept in order to process the text or talk. Power can also be exercized [sic] through controlling others' use of language – that is, through various kinds and degrees of censorship and access control (Chilton and Schäffner, 1997: 212).

Similarly, there are specific linguistic structures (such as petitions and appeals) specifically used for expressing resistance, opposition, and protest against power and coercion.

'Political control involves the control of information, which is by definition a matter of discourse control' (Chilton and Schäffner, 1997: 212). Preventing people from receiving information by secrecy or

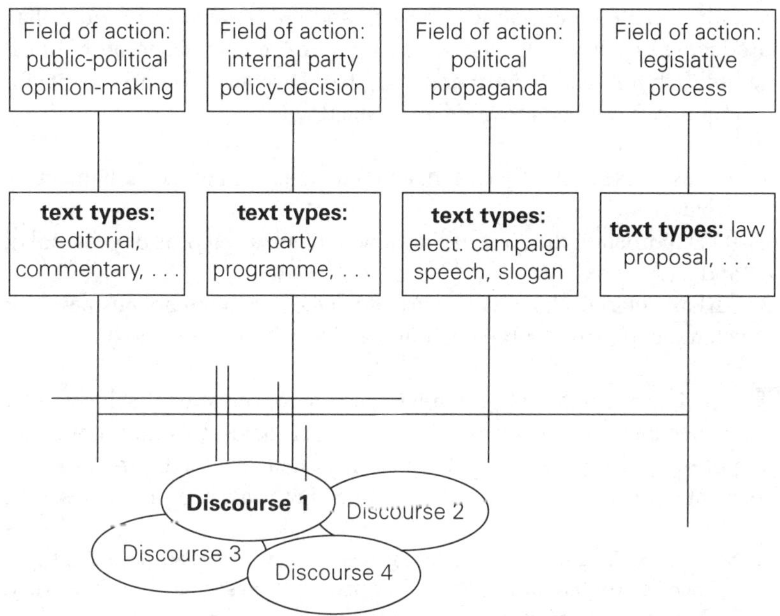

Figure 13.1. The relationship between field of action, text type and discourse (Source: Girnth, 1996: 69).

preventing people from giving information through censorship are two forms of such dissimulation. 'In another mode of dissimulation, information may be given, but be quantitatively inadequate to the needs or interests of hearers' (Chilton and Schäffner, 1997: 212f.). Dissimulation can also be achieved through various kinds of verbal evasion and denial, the omission of reference to actors by using euphemisms or implicit meanings, or by simply lying.

'Political actors, whether individuals or groups, cannot act by physical force alone' (Chilton and Schäffner, 1997:: 213). Thus, they must communicate reasons why people should listen to and obey them, linguistically either in form of overt statements or by implication (legitimization). In order to achieve this objective, they use, among other techniques, arguments about voters' wants and general ideological principles, project charismatic leadership, boast about performance and present themselves positively. At the same time, others have to be presented negatively. The use of ideas of difference and boundaries as well as speech acts like accusations, insults and blaming are typical techniques for delegitimization.

However, '"doing politics" by text and talk is obviously more than producing or perceiving discourse in political contexts and by political actors' (Chilton and Schäffner, 1997: 10). Discourse in parliament, for example, can only be regarded as political, when:

1. the discourse is overtly part of, and functional within the parliamentary debate;
2. it is recorded in the Acts of Parliament (such as records or protocols); and
3. parliamentarians intend to contribute to the parliamentary business (for example, debating a bill) (Chilton and Schäffner, 1997: 10).

Thus, when members of parliament have a conversational aside or talk about personal matters or other non-political topics, this does not count as political discourse at all, because it is neither 'for the record' nor relevant to the business at hand, as defined in the agenda. In other words,

> besides speaking publicly and for the record, they are thus expected to speak as member of parliament, and as member or representative of their party. Technically, a number of further conditions are required, such as speaking out loud, sometimes only when they have been allocated a speaking turn (expect in special cases, as in interruptions, where allowed), as addressing the assembly, and when speaking relevantly, i.e. 'on topic' (Chilton and Schäffner, 1997: 11).

In the following section, we would like to illustrate these theoretical assumptions by analysing two examples of parliamentary discourse on immigration in the UK and in Austria.

Some Important Linguistic Categories and their Application in the Analysis of Parliamentary Discourse

There are a number of central dimensions and categories, relating to the strategies mentioned above, which can be used to analyze parliamentary debates, focusing on racist argumentation and self- and other-presentation (for example, actor description, construction of Us versus Other, vagueness, metaphors, interaction). In this paper, however, we would like to focus only on the usage of disclaimers, pronouns, predications and topoi.

Referential Strategies/Nomination Strategies

Referential strategies are those strategies that are used in discourse for constructing and representing social actors and thus for forming ingroups and outgroups. Linguistically, these strategies can be realized – among others – in form of ethnonyms (the Austrians versus the Turkish, the Polish), toponyms (Austria versus Turkey) and orientational metaphors ('Inländer', natives versus 'Ausländer', foreigners). Table 13.1 illustrates this.

Table 13.1 Referential strategies

Referential Strategies (**Mainly reference to** **persons via nomination**)	*Examples for linguistic means and realizations*	
Reference to one's in-group(s)	– *deictis:*	we, us
	– *ethnonyms:*	Germans, Austrians (sometimes in form of synecdoches like 'the German', 'the Austrian')
	– *toponyms:*	Germany, Austria (very often used as personifications)
	– *reference based* *on local orientation*	natives (InländerInnen)
Reference to the out-group(s)	– *deictis:*	they, them
	– *ethnonyms:*	Turks, Romanians
	– *toponyms:*	Turkey, Poland
	– *reference based* *on local orientation*	foreigners (AusländerInnen), southerners (SüdländerInnen)
	– *explicitly dissimilating* *reference*	aliens (Fremde)

Pronouns

Among the referential strategies, pronouns like 'I', 'we', 'they'; 'my', 'our', 'their'; 'us' and 'them' play an important role in the construction and polarization of ingroups and outgroups. Especially the distinction between the inclusive and thus positive 'Us' and the exclusive, negative 'They' has become prototypical, both in political discourse and in discourse on immigration. Immigrants, for example, are usually referred to as 'they' and are thereby described as members of the outgroup. Since the use of 'we' and 'they' is contextually variable, these pronouns can refer to various ingroups and outgroups. For instance, 'we' may refer to any group with which the speaker identifies – 'we Austrians', 'we, members of our party', 'we German speakers' and so on. That is, according to their interests and the audience they address, speakers can create a number of personal and group identities in discourse.

Predication (Presentational Strategies)

Implicit or explicit predications belong to the set of presentational strategies and are one form of attributing stereotypically positive or negative traits to the social actors that have been identified before.

Topoi

By the use of topoi, speakers can plead for and justify social and political inclusion or exclusion, the discrimination or preferential treatment of the respective persons or groups of persons (Reisigl/Wodak 2000b). In argumentation theory, 'topoi' or 'loci communes' are content-related 'conclusion rules' that connect the argument/s with the conclusion (Kienpointner, 1992: 194). Previous research on discriminatory and racist discourse has shown that there are a number of topoi that are preferably employed in arguing for or against the discrimination of immigrants, refugees and minorities. For instance, immigrants or refugees are typically said to come in large numbers, which results in the conclusion that immigration must be reduced or even stopped. An argumentation schema like this one is defined as 'topos of number'. Another very common topos in discourse on immigration is that of 'culture'. Here the argumentation is, for example, the following: immigrants have another cultural identity than the one 'we' have. This causes cultural conflicts and threatens 'our' own culture. Thus, immigration policy has to be stricter, meaning immigrants have to adapt to 'our' culture if they want to live here.

Disclaimers

In discourse about immigrants and minorities, speakers often employ special semantic moves, so-called disclaimers, which express the contradiction between positive self-presentation and negative other-representation. That is, disclaimers allow speakers to formulate their actual negative opinions about others without at the same time offending their general norms and thus making a bad impression. Typical disclaimers are 'apparent denial'

(I have nothing against X, but . . .), 'apparent concession' (they are not all criminal, but . . .), 'apparent sympathy' (I like them, but . . .) and 'transfer' (not me, but my clients . . .), just to name a few.

Analysis of Excerpts of an Austrian and a British Parliamentary Debate

The Austrian Example

After this rather theoretical introduction, we would like to illustrate on the basis of two short excerpts — one taken from an Austrian parliamentary debate and the other from a British one — how racist tendencies in political discourse can be unveiled with the help of these categories. The first sequence we want to consider is part of a speech that was given by Helene Partik-Pablé, a delegate of the Austrian Freedom Party, at the beginning of a parliamentary session on 18 June 1996. This debate, which soon became very heated, took place within the frame of an urgent inquiry by the Freedom Party concerning foreigner policy and employment.[3] Partik-Pablé, being the first speaker in this debate, used the occasion to launch a massive attack on the governmental parties because of their foreigner policy. As we show in our analysis, Partik-Pablé's speech contains a number of features typical of explicit racist discourse:

> Can you imagine what kind of quality of life prevails in such a district, for example in the 16th and 17th district(s), where the Austrian population represents a minority, where so many foreigners live, who have a completely different conception of culture, who have a different way of life? — That's the place to start working, honourable Chancellor, for it is there that the Austrian population is so much pushed into the background, that it is no longer reasonable.
>
> As indicated, as Mayor Häupl has also said before, it is there that conditions beneath human dignity prevail, even if for the press these days he would like to distance himself from it.
>
> You always say the Austrians should adapt. We are not of the opinion that it is the Austrians who should adapt, but, to the contrary, we demand that the foreigners adapt to our life-style! [Applause among the FPÖ.]
>
> I have no sympathy at all for the fact that you, (of) the Social-Democratic Party and the Austrian People's Party with your overall immigration-policy, do not respect the desire of the Austrians to live the way they have been living for decades, but disregard it and even ridicule this desire.
>
> I recall that there was a celebration last year, a lamb-festival in a backyard, to which Mr Einem and Mr Scholten were invited, and also Mr Cap, I think,

was there. There they sneeringly ridiculed the population. They said: we wanted to show the people that it is not so bad. We wanted to stop the fear of contact! This is your way of dealing with that stratum of society that has to live with these circumstances: you have a lamb roasted by a chef, invite (people) to a well-tended backyard, and thus intend to familiarise the Austrian population with the culture of those countries, whose people you bring to Austria in such excessive numbers. That shows your policy of contempt for humankind, that shows your contemptuous way of dealing with the (Austrian) population.

In her speech, Partik-Pablé identifies a number of persons and groups of persons who are somehow involved in or concerned with immigration policy: the 'Austrians'; the chef; the 'foreigners'; the 'Austrian People's Party' (ÖVP) and the 'Austrian Social Democrats' (SPÖ) and the 'Austrian Freedom Party' (FPÖ). These persons and groups of persons are referred to in a specific way.

First, the 'Austrians': in the beginning, Partik-Pablé refers to a specific group of Austrians, namely the 'Austrian population living in the 16th and 17th district(s) of Vienna' (reference on the basis of the local orientation), but in the course of her speech, she tends to generalize from this specific group of 'Austrians' to all Austrians by speaking of 'the stratum of society', 'the Austrian residents', 'the population' and 'the Austrians' (the last one is what we call an ethnonym).

In contrast, Partik-Pablé uses mainly the label 'foreigner' (in German 'Ausländer') when she talks about immigrants. By doing so, she gives the impression that she means 'foreigners' in general. (Note that the German term 'Ausländer' itself is already problematic, as has been shown by Reisigl and Wodak, 2000b). Taking a closer look, by analysing the text in greater detail, however, we can see that the term 'foreigner' has a more restricted and specific meaning: it refers to immigrants with a different culture, a culture that is characterized by the cooking of lamb. In Austria, these are Turkish people and people from Arabic countries who are typically associated with the eating of lamb.

The governmental parties, especially the Austrian Social Democrats, are mainly represented by their members, that is, the Federal Chancellor Franz Vranitzky; the Minister of Domestic Affairs, Einem; the Minister of Education, Scholten; Cap, a high-level party member of the Social-Democrats; and the Mayor of Vienna, Michael Häupl. The Austrian Freedom Party, finally, is constructed more or less implicitly by the speaker herself in form of the pronouns 'I' and 'we'.

As a next step, we would like to analyse Partik-Pablé's use of pronouns: Partik-Pablé employs the pronouns 'they' and 'their' almost exclusively to refer to or address the governmental parties in general or to members of these parties and their political activities. Note, however, that in German, the polite form of address ('Sie') coincides with the third person plural of the personal pronoun ('sie'), and is distinguishable only in writing where, when used as a polite form of address, the pronouns are capitalized. Since Partik-Pablé's speech was oral, it is, therefore, not always clear if she is referring to or addressing a specific someone or if a plural 'they' was intended.

The case of 'we' is less ambiguous, with 'we' referring first to the members of the Austrian Freedom Party 'we are not of the opinion, we request' and second in a more generalizing way to 'we Austrians' ('our way of life'). Only once does the pronoun 'we' denote members of the government ('We wanted to show the people that it is not so bad. We wanted to stop the fear of contact!') A closer look, however, reveals that Partik-Pablé is quoting a speech by these members or, to be more precise, giving the impression of a quote.

Each of the above-mentioned social actors is presented and character-ized in a specific way.

The 'Austrians' are portrayed as 'a minority' that is driven out by the foreigners and forced to adapt to a foreign culture, although they 'have the desire to live as they have been living for decades'. Instead, they have to live under degrading conditions and their worries are not taken seriously. Thus, Partik-Pablé describes the 'Austrians' as the victims who need 'our' sympathy and help.

Responsible for the Austrians' misery are, according to Partik-Pablé, the 'foreigners' on the one hand and the government on the other. Both groups are therefore presented by the — more or less explicit — attribution of negative traits: the governmental parties want the 'Austrians' to assimilate to the culture of the foreigners. They do not respect the needs of the Austrians, but mock them, for instance, by going to parties where lamb is roasted. They bring masses of 'foreigners' with a different culture to Austria, and they pursue an inhumane immigration policy. Similarly, the 'foreigners' are also described negatively: they come to Austria and drive the 'Austrians' away. Because of their presence, the quality of living deteriorates. They have another cultural identity, another way of life. Partik-Pablé, however, does not specify in which sense their culture differs from the Austrian except for the cooking of lamb, which, according to her, is obviously not a positive trait. Clearly, these foreigners do not accept and assimilate to the Austrian culture.

To herself and the Austrian Freedom Party, Partik-Pablé assigns the role of the 'defender' of the 'Austrians': neither she nor the other members of her party agree that the 'Austrians' should be the ones that have to adapt ('We are not of the opinion', 'we demand'). None of them can understand the way the government treats the 'Austrians' ('I have no sympathy at all for the fact . . .'). To be more precise, they cannot accept the immigration policy of the government as it stands.

Summarizing our analysis of referential and presentational strategies, we can say that Partik-Pablé divides the social actors she speaks about into at least two groups: one group, the ingroup, consists of the 'Austrians', the 'Austrian Freedom Party', to some extent the chef, and herself and is represented in a positive way. The other group, to which the governmental parties and the 'foreigners' belong, is construed as the outgroup with negative features.

Let us now turn to the argumentation Partik-Pablé uses in her speech. Although this is only a short paragraph taken out of a longer speech, several topoi can be found here.

First, by using expressions like 'so many foreigners', 'the Austrian population is so much pushed into the background', 'whose people you bring to Austria in such excessive numbers', Partik-Pablé indicates that there are too many foreigners in Austria (topos of number). Therefore – is the implication – immigration policy has to change; that is, fewer immigrants should be let in. However, no concrete numbers are ever given in her speech.

Second, Partik-Pablé argues that the foreigners who live in Austria have a culture and way of life that is different from the Austrian way of life as is indicated by formulations like 'who have a totally different conception of culture', 'who have a different way of life'; 'to familiarize the Austrian population with the culture of those countries, whose people . . .'. This means that the 'Austrians' cannot live their own culture, but are forced to assimilate to that of 'the other'. In other words, a topos of culture is employed.

Both the topos of number and the topos of culture lead to another argumentative assumption, namely the topos of danger: the immigration policy of the governing parties results in a high number of foreigners with a different cultural identity in Austria. This is a dangerous situation, since the existence of the 'Austrians' and their culture are thereby threatened.

Partik-Pablé further speaks of 'conditions beneath human dignity', 'your policy of contempt for humankind' and 'your contemptuous way of dealing with the (Austrian) population', thus implying that the government pursues an immigration policy that does not conform with human rights and conventions. But whose human rights are offended? Who is forced to live under inhumane conditions? Partik-Pablé certainly does not mean the rights of the 'foreigners'. It is the 'Austrians' she refers to. In our opinion, this argumentation can be interpreted as a kind of a topos of humanitarianism, although this humanitarianism is restricted to 'Austrians' only.

Finally, Partik-Pablé refers to a so-called 'lamb festival' in a courtyard to which members of the government and other representatives of the Social-Democrat Party were invited. In this context, she accuses the government of mocking the 'Austrians', of not taking their needs and fears seriously. By giving this one example, she underscores her point that the government generally deals with the 'Austrians' in such a way (topos of example). Thus, the very conclusion we can draw from Partik-Pablé's speech is that foreigners are no human beings.

Summing up our analysis, Partik-Pablé not only completely distorts the immigration situation in Austria, she even goes so far as to deny that foreigners are human beings. And this is open racism.

The British Example

The second sequence that we would like to analyse is taken from a British parliamentary debate held on 11 December 1995. The central issue of the debate was the change of the British legal system and, again, immigration. Specifically, the then government was trying to install more restrictive measures to curb immigration and was using all possible kinds of arguments to legitimize its proposals. The debate was heated and polemical, and finally State Secretary Howard made a very rhetorical statement summarizing the position of the Tory government, a clear example of positive self-presentation. We thus confront this sequence with the one just discussed in order to illustrate the very different strategies politicians apply and the whole possible range of racist discourse and parliamentary political speak. The fact that the two sequences rely on different strategies is in part grounded in the fact that Partik-Pablé is a member of the right-wing populist opposition whereas Howard is a representative of the majority and the government that has to legitimate restrictive measures, while ostensibly maintaining the norms and values of democracy and tolerance.

Some have suggested that this is an immoral Bill, I reject that utterly. It is not immoral to protect our asylum procedures against the current massive level of abuse. It is not immoral to declare that, in our judgement, the conditions in some countries do not give rise to a serious risk of persecution. It is not immoral to insist that people arriving from other safe countries should return to pursue their claims there. It is not immoral to seek to protect employment opportunities for those entitled to live and work here, and it is not immoral to combat racketeering. Our position has always been clear. This country has a proud record on good race relations. I am determined to do everything that I can to maintain that record. Firm control of immigration is vital to achieve that objective. That involves a readiness to identify abuse and to take the action necessary to deal with it. The Bill is a measured response to the problems which we face. It is necessary, it is urgently needed and it deserves to reach the statute book as soon as possible. I commend it to the house.

Like in the sequence discussed above, several actors are identified by Howard: in his statement, Howard talks about himself ('I reject', 'I am determined', 'everything I can', 'I commend'), expressing his opinion about the Bill and the situation in Great Britain, and about 'us', that is, 'our asylum procedures', 'our judgement', 'our position', and of problems 'we face'. We can assume that he means here the government, of which he is a member and for whom he is speaking. Both the government and Howard as a member of this government form the we-group, although the reference of 'we' is not always completely clear: 'we' as in 'our asylum procedures' and 'problems we face' could also refer to someone else, such as the British population.

Also notable is that Howard actually speaks of several groups of 'others': Howard speaks of 'some' who considered the Bill immoral; he refers to 'those who are entitled to live and work here'; and finally there are people coming from 'some countries' and 'people arriving from other safe countries'. The use of vagueness in the construction of these 'others' is rather striking. No numbers are mentioned, no names of persons or countries are presented. Despite this vagueness, a more detailed analysis shows that Howard has mainly one specific group in mind when he talks about 'others': the immigrants, or to be more precise, the asylum seekers. It is this group that his statement focuses on.

As in the Partik-Pablé example, a positive presentation of the we-group is opposed to a negative construction of the 'others': the we-group, that is, the government and the speaker as a member of the government, is characterized positively, both lexically and syntactically. They fight against the abuse of the laws — the asylum procedures — and protect employment opportunities and combat racketeering. Furthermore, they are the ones judging whether a real risk of persecution exists. They have a clear position and are determined to act. To put it differently, the government is presented as moral, rational, tolerant and legal, working under the pressure of objective juridic and political conditions.

In contrast, the 'others', namely the foreigners, are portrayed as people who distort the conditions existing in their home countries and seek asylum in Great Britain on the basis of false claims, thus massively abusing the laws. They are racketeers and take jobs away from those whom the government deems as 'legitimate' job-seekers.

With regard to the structure of argumentation, this sequence consists of two parts.

In the first part of the statement, Howard brings forth numerous counterarguments in a negative mode: a whole chain of arguments is produced in a declarative fashion, none of which are proved valid at all. It is assumed, for example, that criminality is correlated to immigration: immigrants make false claims about the dangers in their countries, because there are no 'serious risks of persecution'; they abuse social security; and are involved in racketeering. It is also assumed that unemployment is increased by foreigners. In other words, a topos of danger is employed: immigrants threaten the British residents. Therefore, the government has to take certain measures, proposed in the Bill, in order to protect the British. All these are unproven and unjustified assumptions for which Howard does not provide any evidence. Instead they are legitimized with what van Leeuwen and Wodak (1999) call 'moral legitimization' by using very classical rhetorical devices like parallelisms ('it is not immoral') and are thus no longer open to questions and rational argumentation. These parallelisms are all constructed in the form of disclaimers. Denial of racism is the framework for this political position.

In the second part of the speech, Howard switches to a positive mode: he talks about the history of 'race' relations in Great Britain, which are claimed to be good and therefore have to be maintained.[4] Restrictive measures, for example 'firm control of immigration', as proposed in the Bill, are the means to achieve this objective. According to Howard, these measures are 'vital', 'necessary' and 'urgently needed', but a real explanation for their necessity is not given. They are positioned as the only possible way for the government to act, and no alternatives are discussed.

Summarizing our analysis, this whole statement is a perfect example of legitimization (Rojo and van Dijk, 1997; van Leeuwen and Wodak, 1999) and denial of racism (van Dijk, 1993). It is presented as a causal logic, in an almost scientific manner, and as a strategy of legitimization which we label as rational legitimization. Both strategies, denial and legitimization, are consistent with positive self presentation – the government has to present itself as tolerant, democratic and fully in favour of human rights despite proposing highly restrictive measures. The very clear message that we can extract from Howard's statement is that the government is protecting the country against illegal abuse on moral grounds, something every voter could identify with.

Conclusions

In this chapter, we have tried to present some important aspects of racism in Western Europe. Racism can present and manifest itself in different masks and guises: blatantly, aggressively, and explicitly as in the statement by Austria's right-wing opposition, or covertly in the mode of positive self-presentation and legitimization as in the speech by the British representative. Thus, we argue, exclusion and racism cannot be attributed to the populist and extreme right only; they are not marginal phenomena. Exclusion lies at that core of everyday politics in Western Europe today, and the mainstream parties are equally involved in restrictive and discriminatory practices, which are legitimized on moral and humanitarian grounds.

Critical discourse analysis is one way of combating racism. Many different strategies have to be considered: legal, caritative, bureaucratic and political. We claim that discourse is a central means of the production and reproduction of racism because communication is the instrument of political debate and the means through which beliefs and prejudices become manifest. Thus, the detailed analysis of the possible range of variation of linguistic realizations of racism is an important political task as it allows us to identify racist practices that would otherwise be covert. It is not difficult to recognize blatant racism, but it is difficult to identify latent racism, especially when it is masked as humanitarianism and as a necessity. Our project is a first step in making this whole range of possible discursive manifestations explicit. And consciousness is the first step to change. We hope to contribute to change at the end of the twentieth century for a more humanitarian society and politics.

Notes

1. We would like to thank our team members in this project – Teun van Dijk, Philomena Essed, Jessika Ter Wal, Ineke van der Valk, Tigrelle Uittjewal, Lena Jones, Luisa Martin Rojo and Martin Reisigl – for their support in the preparation of this paper.

2. The most important laws on immigration that have been passed in the UK are the: 1962 Commonwealth Immigrants Act; 1965 Race Relations Act; 1968 Commonwealth Immigrants Act; 1968 Race Relations Act; 1969 Immigration Appeals Act; 1971 Immigration Act; 1976 Race Relations Act; 1981 British Nationality Act; 1987 Immigration (Carrier's Liability) Act; 1988 Immigration Act; 1994 Race Relations (Remedy) Act; 1996 Asylum and Immigration Act. In Austria, these are the: 1991 Asylum Act; 1992 Immigration Law ('Residence Act'); 1995 First Amendment of the Residence Act; 1997 Second Amendment of the Residence Act.

3. The exact title of this debate is 'Urgent inquiry by Member of Parliament Dr Helene Partik-Pablé and fellow party members (FPÖ) to the Federal Chancellor concerning jobs – respectable foreigner policy, National Council session of 18.6.1996'.

4. Note, that it is not specified in which respect the 'race' relations are good or why their maintenance is important.

14

Equality as a Right: Lessons to be Learned from EC Sex Equality Law for a Multi-Dimensional EC Anti-Discrimination Law

Dagmar Schiek

Introduction

The European Commission is now considering the new legislation to be based on Article 13 EC Treaty after the coming into force of the Treaty of Amsterdam. Following the conference in Innsbruck in September 1998, the official policy has been presented to and debated at a political-legal conference in Vienna in December 1998. In his closing speech to this conference, Commissioner Padraig Flynn underlined the importance of 'our experience of gender legislation and action on the issue of equality' (Flynn, 1998) to the new anti-discrimination policy. Thus, it is more than appropriate that the achievements of EC sex equality law are scrutinized with a critical eye in order to avoid failures that may have hampered their effectiveness in other fields of anti-discrimination law. According to Commissioner Flynn, there will be a specific emphasis on racial discrimination in the new policy. Racial discrimination would be the only area outside the employment sector in which Community anti-discrimination law would be enacted. This specific emphasis on racial discrimination may colour the future of EC anti-discrimination law in the employment sector as well as in other fields of law. Thus, it appears important to consider the interrelation between gender and 'race' discrimination and discuss possibilities of addressing adequately both forms of discrimination and especially discrimination against ethnic minority women on both grounds in the new legal framework.

This chapter thus covers two different aspects of EC anti-discrimination law: the first part will analyse the legal concept of sex equality as mirrored in the European Court of Justice's (ECJ) jurisdiction with specific attention to the group dimension and the asymmetric dimension of sex discrimination. The second part will discuss how double discrimination can be addressed. The chapter will close with some remarks on the enforcement of equality law and an outline for a new concept of EC anti-discrimination law.

This chapter does not address the problems that may arise once equality law exceeds the boundaries of the employment market. This should not imply that a European policy to combat discrimination in the market place should not exceed these boundaries or that EC anti-discrimination legislation outside the employment market should restrict itself to racial discrimination. The chapter also starts from the assumption that the best way to fight (employment) market discrimination is to rely on private law remedies without repeating the well-known discussion of the effectiveness of criminal sanctions in this context.

Equality as Right in the Jurisdiction of the European Court of Justice

European Community policy on sex equality has been predominantly legal in character. Thus, the ECJ's concept of sex equality has been decisive for its successes. For quite a while the Court's jurisdiction furthered the development of a legal concept of sex equality in the workplace. Backing up the scarce secondary legislation in the field, the Court recognized sex equality as one of the fundamental rights of Community law.[1] It also developed the principle that equality rights must be effectively sanctioned in order for the member states to fulfil their obligations under the Sex Equality Directives.[2] However, in more recent cases the limits of this judge-made policy towards sex equality were highlighted (Ellis, 1998: 408). In particular, the Court's approach towards equality has been accused of not transcending the concept of an individual and negative right to equal treatment (Fenwick and Hervey, 1995). On close inspection, the Court's jurisdiction appears to mirror different approaches to equality, without allowing to conclude a monolithic conception.

Equality as a Right – Problems to be Addressed

Whoever attempts to legislate against discrimination on grounds of sex or 'race' in private (employment) law, has to answer a difficult question: can the quest for equality against the reality of asymmetrical, group-based discrimination be mirrored in individual rights to be enforced directly between private persons?

Formal Equal Treatment

The traditional response to this question is to further equality through formal non-discrimination. Under this perspective, equality as a right entitles a person not to be discriminated against purposely by others. Legal equality is thus limited to a right to be treated equally in a formal way. The ECJ jurisdiction mirrored this view in a number of decisions.

Thus, women cannot be barred from employment as social workers in a men's prison[3] or from occupations that require contact with foreign cultures[4] because of their sex; they are entitled to equal remuneration with male colleagues[5] or predecessors[6] doing like or comparable work. Equal treatment as a negative right also demands that men should not be barred from the profession of a midwife.[7]

Employers relied upon this concept to have a prohibition for women to work at night removed.[8] However, the interaction between traditional gender roles in families and women's weak labour market position led to dubious successes of this legal battle in terms of work place equality. Women's request for permanent night work in order to meet family plights during daytime and to earn a supplementary income at the same time enabled employers in Germany to replace male shiftworkers by women who worked a different rota and required much less remuneration (Schiek, 1996: 332).

This is one of many examples that demonstrate that the concept of equality as a right to formally equal treatment is an inadequate answer to (employment) market discrimination. In particular, it is neither responsive to the group-related dimension nor to the asymmetrical dimension of discrimination.

Group-related Dimension of Discrimination

Being group related is common to all forms of discrimination on grounds of an ascribed status, of which sex discrimination is only one example. I refer to discrimination on grounds of an ascribed status as discrimination against natural persons on grounds of personal characteristics ascribed to them as being permanent and as offering starting points for social exclusion. Examples for such characteristics are 'race', ethnic origin, disability and sex. Persons whose ethnic origin is ascribed as their personal characteristic are defined as belonging to a certain ethnic/racial group. The ascribed membership in this group results in racist discrimination. Persons to whom the status of a female is ascribed may suffer sexist discrimination.

Sex discrimination in the market place results from ascribing to women a set of characteristics, for example 'lack of bodily strength', 'lack of personal authority', or the willingness to pay a high price for a haircut. The belief that women lack bodily strength leads to their exclusion from paid occupations that are perceived as requiring muscle power and to perceiving occupations commonly taken by women as not requiring bodily strength. The assumption that women lack authority leads to hesitant acceptance of female applicants for managerial posts. Women's willingness to pay adequately for a haircut may lead hair stylists to gendered price lists and refusal to charge a woman a man's price for a man's haircut.

Consider, however, a hair stylist who just charges different prices for different hair styles without labelling these male or female hairstyles. He just happens to charge the highest prices for the styles customarily worn by women. Conceptualizing legal equality as a negative, individual right to equal treatment irrespective of sex, the lawyer would have difficulties in detecting sex discrimination. If the law is not responsive to this group dimension of sex discrimination, it cannot grasp the effects of seemingly neutral policies that still affect women more often than men. It also remains indifferent to the mutual reinforcement of the manifold forms of gender discrimination and sex discrimination.

Discrimination on grounds of characteristics or conditions typical to the group discriminated against is an aspect that can be captured by the prohibition of indirect discrimination. This concept enables the legal scholar and the European Court of Justice to see beyond intentional discriminatory acts and to perceive as discrimination some of the seemingly neutral employment strategies that serve to stabilize a gendered employment market.

Asymmetric Character of Sex Discrimination?

The single discriminatory acts and the less visible seemingly neutral policies towards stabilizing gendered behaviour are not just distinguishing between women and men, but involve disadvantage. The Canadian Supreme Court acknowledged this dimension of discrimination by characterizing discrimination as disadvantage rather than different treatment.

> Discrimination may be described as a distinction, whether intentional or not but based on grounds relating to the personal characteristics of the individual or group, which has the effect of imposing burdens, obligations or disadvantages

on such individual or group not imposed upon others, or which withholds or limits access to opportunities, benefits and advantages available to other members of society.[9]

This approach is to be complemented by the notion of group-specific disadvantages. The disadvantaging effects of discrimination are not spread out evenly between racial or ethnic majority and minority or between women and men. Thus, the very term 'sex discrimination' is misleading. It suggests that different treatment of women and men is as detrimental to one sex as to the other. Thus, it is more appropriate to speak of women's discrimination or – accordingly – of discrimination against racial or ethnic minorities. If the law does not respond to the asymmetric dimension of sex discrimination, the prospects for change through anti-discrimination legislation are very limited.

Steps Towards a Responsive Solution

The jurisdiction of the ECJ has already taken some steps towards recognition of the group-related and the asymmetric dimension of discrimination. However, the concept of equal treatment as a negative individual right being the main focus of that jurisdiction, these developments are severely hampered. The steps already taken call for a new conception of equality as a right, which should feed future Community policy towards sexual and racial equality.

The prohibition of indirect discrimination is an example of responses to group differences, while the limited acknowledgement of positive action in the recent *Marschall* decision (1997) hints towards a legal recognition of the asymmetric dimension of discrimination.

Acknowledging the Group Dimension of Sex Discrimination: Prohibiting Indirect Discrimination

Considering the hair stylist example, we would detect sex discrimination under the indirect discrimination test. The ECJ has developed the original definition of indirect discrimination 'European Style'.[10] This definition has now been summed up in the Burden-of-Proof-Directive as follows:[11]

> Indirect discrimination shall exist where an apparently neutral provision, criterion or practice disadvantages a substantially higher proportion of the members of one sex unless that provision, criterion or practice is appropriate and necessary and can be justified by objective factors unrelated to sex.

According to this definition, establishing indirect discrimination requires a two-stage test.

First, disparate impact has to be established. There is no need to isolate a special requirement or condition with which a considerably smaller proportion of women than men can comply. It suffices to demonstrate that an employment practice disadvantages women. Thus, the ECJ held in *Royal Copenhagen* (1995)[12] and *Danfoss* (1989),[13] that a remuneration scheme as a whole may be indirectly discriminatory. How disparate the impact must be is an unresolved question under EC law.

Secondly, it must be established that the condition or practice does not pass the objective justification test. If the condition or practice is objectively justified by factors unrelated to sex, there is no indirect sex discrimination despite the disparate impact of the policy. The objective justification test involves an application of the principle of proportionality.

The importance of a prohibition of indirect discrimination cannot be overestimated. While the formal approach to equality presupposes that formally equal rules of the game will guarantee equal opportunities, a prohibition of indirect discrimination elevates the game's results to the yardstick that measures equality. Thus, it transcends the formal and individualistic view of traditional equal treatment in favour of a substantive and collective view of equality while being sensitive to group disparity.

However, the concept may be more or less group directed. The key is the standard for objective justification. As long as detrimental stereotypes are allowed to feed seemingly gender-neutral differentiations, the prohibition of indirect discrimination will have little effect on gender barriers in the employment market.

Originally, the Court established that the objective justification test involved a strict proportionality standard. A criterion that produced disparate impact had not only to be 'appropriate with a view to achieving the objectives pursued' but also 'necessary to that end'.[14] Thus, a statistically discriminatory criterion could not be tolerated if and when there was a less discriminatory alternative. In addition (or above all), the seemingly neutral criterion must not be tainted by gender bias or 'unrelated to any discrimination on grounds of sex'.[15]

The court has rightly been criticized for deviating from this rather strict standard in several cases (Ellis, 1998; Wentholt, 1996). The decision in *Megner and Scheffel* (1995)[16] appears to be especially problematic. The issue was the legality of national legislation that excluded a specific section of part-timers, those in minor or short-term employment, from social security.[17] The Court ruled that in social security matters any reasonable policy could objectively justify disparate impact. Thus, the

Court allowed the German Government to justify the exclusion of a predominantly female part of the workforce from social security by reference to traditional principles of social security law. One of the principles in question was a special version of the principle of subsidiarity. According to this principle, social security may only be made available where there is no security through smaller units like the family. In effect, part timers were referred to an assumed 'family security'. This notion is far from being gender neutral. However, the Court did not investigate whether the justifying factor was tainted by gender bias.

The Directive's definition appears now to establish that the double test of strict proportionality has to be passed. It states that a criterion or practice has to be appropriate and necessary and capable of being justified by objective factors unrelated to sex in order not to violate the right to equal treatment despite having disparate impact. However, this important passage is far from clear. We can only hope that the future jurisdiction of the ECJ will respond to the group dimension of discrimination more adequately.

Acknowledging the Asymmetrical Dimension of Sex Discrimination: the Marschall Judgement

With regard to the acknowledgement of the asymmetric dimension of sex discrimination, the ECJ's decision in *Marschall* (1997)[18] gives some hope for a progressive development. This decision acknowledges positive action to a certain extent. The EC's policy towards positive action in favour of women has been rather cautious so far. While the council only issued a recommendation to that effect,[19] several Member States endorsed policies of positive action. Due to the differing national practices, the legal debate on preferential treatment used to be confined to the nation states. This changed as late as 1995, when the ECJ ruled the *Kalanke* (1995) case.[20] This judgement was followed by *Marschall* in 1997. In the *Badeck* case on slightly different forms of positive action, Advocate General Saggio has recently given his opinion,[21] which gives even more hope for progressive development.

The decision in *Marschall* involved a preferential rule. Mr Marschall's application for a promotion as a tenured teacher was denied, because the relevant District Authority decided to promote an equally qualified woman, who had reached tenure at a later date than Mr Marschall. This was in accordance with paragraph 25 (5) of the relevant Civil Servants' Code, which requires preference for women when deciding on promotion or employment to a grade post in a career bracket in which there are fewer women than men – 'unless reasons specific to an individual male candidate tilt the balance in his favour'.[22] The Verwaltungsgericht Gelsenkirchen (Administrative Court of Gelsenkirchen) referred to the ECJ the question of whether this kind of preferential rule was covered by Article 2 (4) of the Equal Treatment Directive. Answering this question in the positive, the Court acknowledged expressly that 'even where male and female candidates are equally qualified, male candidates tend to be promoted in preference ... because of prejudices and stereotypes concerning the role and capacities of women' (paragraph 29). Thus, the Court views preferential rules as a legitimate means to combat such structural discrimination – 'subject to the application of a "savings clause"' (paragraph 31).

This judgement clarified the regrettably short judgement in *Kalanke* and deviated from both Advocate General Tesauro's and Advocate General Jacobs's opinion on positive action. Both had assumed that a provision that goes beyond equal opportunities and pursues equality of results instead cannot be covered by Article 2 (4) of the Equal Treatment Directive. Going beyond Tesauro Jacobs acknowledged that equally qualified candidates of different gender may not have equal opportunities (paragraph 30 of his Opinion, 13 May 1997). He realized that traditional selection criteria may work to the detriment of women, especially referring to duration of service and the bread-winner concept (paragraph 39). However, he concluded that preferential treatment is not necessary to combat these structures and thus is not justifiable. Both Advocates General assumed that preferential treatment of women amounts to unjustifiable discrimination against men (paragraphs 32, 45). This argument arises from a symmetric view of the equality principle. Under this view the right of men to be treated formally equally competes with a right of women to be treated substantively equally. Thus, preferential rules require justification against the right of men to be treated formally equally in 'consideration of the question of proportionality' (Advocate General Tesauro, Opinion in *Kalanke*, paragraphs 6, 23) – a nearly insurmountable barrier for positive action to overcome.

Contrary to these opinions the Court upheld the specific form of preferential treatment in *Marschall*. Conceding, that indirect discrimination in personnel decisions has to be overcome, the Court also acknowledged that structural discrimination is not capable of being covered by the concept of indirect discrimination. Employment decisions consist of a number of subjective assessments, which may be tainted by conscious or unconscious prejudice. The ECJ acknowledges this reality (paragraph 29, cited above). Thus, it evades the assumption that social discrimination against women because of their gender happened only in the past. In this way the Court decides not to give women's right to substantial equality the second place behind men's right to formal equality, but considers the infringement of formal equality in order to achieve substantial equality admissible if balanced by a 'savings clause'. This conclusion is justifiable under a substantive approach to the principle of equal treatment as an asymmetric right.

The recent opinion of Advocate General Saggio in the *Badeck* case supports the view that equal treatment under Community law embodies the concept of substantive equality. The *Badeck* case involves binding goals and timetables, strict quotas for trainee positions and strict quotas for job interviews.[23] Advocate General Saggio concludes that all these measures are covered by Article 2 (4) of the Equal Treatment Directive. He refers to the alleged dichotomy between formal and substantive equality and submits that these two conceptions of equality are not as contradictory as is often asserted. According to Advocate General Saggio, both formal and substantive equality aim to achieve equality in fact, especially for groups of the populace who are being detrimented (No. 26). Thus he advocates the use of positive action measures in favour for individuals belonging to such groups, save these measures actually serve the goal of achieving social equality and do not detriment other groups disproportionally (No. 27). If the Court follows this opinion, this would be a huge step towards an asymmetric approach to the principle of equal treatment in Community law.

This asymmetric approach to the principle of equal treatment mirrors more precisely the special purpose of gender equality provisions (Sacksofsky, 1996; Hervey, 1996).[24] Equal treatment irrespective of one's sex has become a legal concept because of social discrimination against women. This is reflected in the UN Convention for the Elimination of All Forms of Discrimination against Women, which aims expressly at factual equality and thus authorizes the ratifying states to undergo specific measures to acquire *de facto* equality. The international perspective is similar with regard to racial discrimination. The Convention for the Elimination of All Forms of Racial Discrimination provides for positive measures as well. Thus, Community legislation on racial discrimination should respond to the asymmetrical dimension of racial discrimination as well.

Under Community law, the asymmetrical nature of sex equality has not yet been accepted wholeheartedly. The majority position is mirrored in the new subsection 4 of Article 119 of the EC Treaty as proposed by the Amsterdam Treaty (which would become Article 141 EC Treaty), according to which 'measures providing for specific advantages in order to make it easier to the underrepresented sex to pursue a vocational activity or to prevent or compensate for disadvantages in professional careers' shall not be precluded by the principle of equal treatment as embodied in the Treaty. In contrast to Article 2 (4) of the Equal Treatment Directive, this provision does not refer explicitly to women, but to the under-represented sex in a gender-neutral way. However, it is obvious that in gainful employment women are the underrepresented sex throughout the Community. This is acknowledged by a Declaration to the Final Act on Article 119 (4), according to which 'measures referred to in Article 119 (4) . . . should in the first instance aim at improving the situation of women in working life'.

Conclusion: Establishing a Group Sensitive and Asymmetric Notion of Equality

If EC anti-discrimination law is to respond adequately to the group-related and asymmetric dimension of discrimination, it should develop further towards a substantive and asymmetric concept of equality as a right. This requires a more positive approach towards preferential treatment and other forms of positive action in favour of women as well as a consequent opposition against indirect discrimination, outlawing any objective justification that relies on gender-specific notions that work to the detriment of women. The current fashion of gender-neutral devices, as in the new Article 141 of the EC Treaty, is of little help.

Positive Action, Indirect Discrimination and the Interrelation of Sex and Race Discrimination – Headscarves on Academics

However, if one regards the factual background of the ECJ's decision in *Kalanke* and *Marschall*, the model function of the positive action policy concerned becomes doubtful. In both cases, the preferential treatment rule in question effectively replaced the principle that promotions were to be awarded according to length of service. In the decision in *Gerster*[25] (1997) the ECJ held that calculation of length of service by German public employers may be indirectly discriminatory (critical analysis by Ellis, 1998: 382f.). Advocate General Jacobs' conclusions in *Marschall* high-lighted the interrelation of positive action and indirect discrimination. While the ECJ rightly rejected the view that preferential treatment can only be justified where eliminating indirect discriminatory criteria failed to achieve a better gender balance, it can still be a wise decision to tackle indirect discrimination along with instituting preferential treatment.

In the difficult context of positive action against racial or ethnic discrimination this might be even more important. Group sensitivity in this context requires a review of cultural standards that might exclude persons to whom minority status is ascribed from gainful employment or its more prestigious sectors. In this context an unbiased application of a prohibition of indirect discrimination appears to be specifically important. In addition the interrelation of sex and 'race' discrimination requires special attention.

Fereshta Ludin's Attempt to Become a Teacher

This may become decisive if indirect sex discrimination is intertwined with racial or cultural discrimination. Consider a recent German case that still awaits decision by the German courts. Fereshta Ludin, a German citizen of Afghan origin, used to wear a headscarf in the public in accordance with her religious convictions as a Moslem. After studying to become a teacher, she had to spend a two-year qualifying period at a school to complete her professional qualification. This required special admission from the Ministry of Education, because she refused to teach without a headscarf. Despite these difficulties her performance was rated as excellent, and she passed her examination with distinction. Normally, this would have secured her a post as teacher. However, this was denied because of the Islamic scarf. Women wearing headscarves in accordance with Christian customs – like nuns – are not prevented from teaching at public schools in Baden-Württemberg. On request from the Jewish Council, officials hastily ensured that men wearing a Jewish kipa would also be accepted. Thus, women displaying signs of minority creed face problems, whereas neither women's responsiveness to Christian dress codes nor men's responsiveness to any religious dress codes addressed to men lead to professional detriments.

The case of academically educated women seeking adequate employment while wearing headscarves is usually not considered as a case for women discrimination.[26] On the contrary, persons who are considered advocates of women's rights sided with Annette Shavan, the state Minister of Cultural Affairs in Baden-Württemberg in this case.[27] For example, the Women Committee of the most representative union in the field[28] was of the opinion that the headscarf represents the sexual status of a woman and, thus, is an obstacle to equality for women (Weltzel, 1998). In support they cite two women who prefer to wear headscarves in order to avoid sexual approaches from men. In contrast, the president of the same union defends the headscarf in the name of ethnic and religious tolerance (Dahlem, 1998).

However, under EC equality law as it stands the case would have to be treated as indirect discrimination on grounds of sex. The practice of excluding women who adhere to minority religious dress codes from employment will most certainly disproportionally disadvantage women. Under the test for indirect discrimination under EC law, this practice could only be regarded as lawful if it was objectively justified.

Thus, the motives for banning traditionally clad Islamic women from the profession become decisive. Ms Shavan's motives were made clear during the debate.[29] She considered the headscarf as a symbol of fundamentalism. She thus wanted to ban fundamentalism from German schools by outlawing a female dress code. She also wanted to prevent husbands and fathers form requiring wives and daughters to veil in public.

To pass the objective justification test under sex discrimination law, Minister Shavan's motives would have to be unrelated to any discrimination on grounds of sex. The urge to protect women from dominant male family members can hardly be so regarded. It operates on gender stereotypes that include the dependency of women from male family members. An unbiased analysis under sex discrimination law would consequently find sex discrimination in this case.

Ms Shavan also distinguished the traditional habit of Catholic nuns from the Islamic headscarf. Given the teaching of nuns in full religious habit in Baden-Württemberg's state schools, it is open to doubt whether the state Minister's reference to fundamentalism is to be taken seriously. An exclusive ban on Islamic fundamentalism would be tainted by ethnic stereotypes: in Germany, persons of Islamic creed are more likely to be ascribed minority status than persons who display behaviour that accords to Christian standards. Thus, a criterion that serves to deter Islamic fundamentalism especially will lead an employment policy to indirectly discriminate on grounds of 'race' or ethnic origin.

However, under current Community law the double discrimination inherent in the policy to ban academics[30] with headscarves from public schools could not be addressed.

Addressing 'Race' and Sex Discrimination Adequately

In the European Union, combating racial discrimination is discussed separately from measures against sex discrimination and discrimination of the disabled (Social Action Programme, 1998–2000 – Com (98) 259, 29 April 1998; Chopin and Niessen, 1998; Bell, 1998). However, a separate regulation will not address double discrimination adequately.

Some Differences between Racial or Ethnic and Sex Discrimination

The differences between racial or ethnic and sex discrimination cannot be denied. I would submit that it is in respect to the group dimension that sex discrimination differs from 'race' discrimination. Women do not form a social group; there is no 'essential woman'. To many women, their identification as members of other groups – be they ethnic, racial or religious – is more important than their identity as being female (Fredman, 1997: 146). Still, sex discrimination operates on the assumption that women share group characteristics. Of course, the group membership that is ascribed on racist grounds is as illusory as sex group membership. Both 'group memberships' are not open for choice by the persons affected. This involuntary group membership is common to racist and sexist discrimination.

However, in racist societies racial categories define social groups as well. The boundaries of 'race' often restrict persons, to whom minority status is ascribed, from social mobility. The interrelation of sex and 'race' discrimination may affect this form of discrimination in different ways. First, minority women show a greater social mobility to a certain extent. In Germany, for example, young women exceed their peers in the achievement of formal education. Young women from ethnic minorities are even more competitive in the schooling system compared to men from ethnic minorities. However, not all of them can use their relatively high education to study at an university or a polytechnic institution and to consequently achieve a secure position on the labour market (Mehrländer et al., 1996). British statistics show that the pay gap between men and women is much larger in the ethnic majority population than in minority population (Fredman, 1997: 147). The greater social mobility of ethnic minority women might contribute to this state.

Possible Effects of Isolated Policies

If sex and 'race' discrimination are addressed by different legal instruments and receive different levels of attention in the legal context, ethnic minority women may be forced to define their case along the lines of exclusive legislation. If, for example, remedies in cases of 'race' discrimination are inexistent and only remedies for sex discrimination are to be had, a case of double discrimination should be filed as a case of sex discrimination. As the law stands presently, this would probably be the most promising course of action for Ms Ludin. Her test case would thus not be a model case for other cases of ethnic discrimination. In addition, the school authorities could redefine their policies to effect male adherents to minority religions as much as females to evade illegality. This would be a bad service to integration of ethnic minorities.

If – on the other hand – Community legislation addressing discrimination in relation to provision of goods and services is restricted to racial discrimination, this might prove just as unsatisfactory. For example, acceptance policies for consumer credits are increasingly governed by 'credit scores'. These may prove indirectly discriminatory on grounds of 'race' as well as on grounds of sex. If, for example, ownership of a house and number of children are positive credit scores, the number-of-children-criterion might exclude ethnic minority applicants from cheap credit (Rodrigues, 1997: 150ff). The home ownership criterion may work to the detriment of women as well. An ethnic minority woman without children who is excluded because she owns no house might have a case under sex discrimination but not under 'race' discrimination law, depending on the specific national circumstances. If Community legislation only addresses 'race' discrimination, her case cannot be a model case for other cases of sex discrimination. In addition, banks could reshape their credit scores without eliminating sex discrimination.

In my view, any isolated equality policy will not respond adequately to discrimination against women, to whom the status of an ethnic minority is ascribed. This is demonstrated by the case of Fereshta Ludin. Even if becoming a teacher is still gendered female, ethnic minority women who achieve this aim exceed the confined space that society reserves for them. As in this case, sex and 'race' discrimination are intangible in most instances. Ignoring the interrelation of sex and 'race' discrimination might leave those worst off who need most protection: doubly discriminated ethnic minority women.

Enforcement of Equality Rights

Analysing the Community's experience in sex discrimination law, one cannot pass by the problem of enforcement. In this respect, the Community's policy has necessarily relied on an individual enforcement model. The EC's 'enforcement agency' in anti-discrimination matters has been the European Court of Justice. The most important decisions were taken in response to Article 177 references. It depends on the relevant national law whether proceedings are commenced by individuals,[31] by unions[32] or even by equality agencies.

While the 'individual enforcement model' has the advantage of empowering individuals who suffer from discrimination to take their own case to court, the disadvantages forbid reliance solely on this model. First of all, to rely on individual enforcement of anti-discrimination law alone means that legal action in the field is not the last resort, but the only way to bring about compliance with non-discrimination law. This is certainly not a sensible way to bring about social change. Secondly, individual parties may lack the resources to fight discrimination in court. This lack may be of a character that does not allow them to rely on the usual systems, like legal aid (McCrudden, 1998).

Thus, in a number of EU Member States, there are alternatives to the individual enforcement of equality law. For example, in the UK, the Netherlands and Austria the legislator relied on the agency approach in addition to individual enforcement. Equality agencies have different functions. They may investigate individual claims, issue strategic investigations, issue guidance and codes of practice for private parties and advise the government on law and practice (McEwan, 1997: 1–29). The Dutch and the Austrian Equality Commissions also fulfil para-judicial functions, giving 'decisions' on discriminatory practices (Heringa, 1994: 85ff).

A different possibility is to provide for other forms of court action. For example, in Dutch civil law group actions are well developed and can be used in anti-discrimination cases as well (Hondius, 1996: 357). Both strategies can serve to ease judicial protection against discrimination. The possibility of different approaches should also be used at the EC level.

In particular, it might be a sensible strategy to respond to the group dimension of discrimination with group remedies. The possibility of uniting individual claims in group actions or collective actions may also be a way of raising the price of discrimination. If an employer can realistically expect to be sued by all the victims of a discriminatory employment policy collectively, he may begin to value non-discriminatory employment policies as an economic advantage. As in the context of consumer protection, remedies aiming at prospectively establishing substantial equality are of equal importance. Such remedies are not covered by individual interests in litigation (Wilhelmsson, 1996: 385). Individuals cannot file a suit in order to force their employer to implement equality provisions effectively, for example by developing an equality plan. However, there may be some wisdom in providing just this kind of remedy – on action of associations, if necessary (Pfarr and Kocher, 1998).

Conclusion: Lessons to be Learned from the Experiences with EC Sex Equality Law

What lessons are to be learned for a more comprehensive EC policy towards sexual and racial equality from the EC model of legislating for sex equality in the workplace? My attempt to answer this is by no means exhaustive. I will rather try to give some hints for a better solution.

First of all it must be stressed that there is a need for a 'European' equality policy. Anti-discrimination policy has been characterized as one of the diffuse interests that require political entrepreneurship to be politically successful (Majone, 1996: 243). This explains why sex equality politics needed a European spur in most Member States and why a policy of racial equality will most probably need this spur as well. Thus, a European dimension to anti-discrimination policies appears especially important.

In addition I would suggest, that EC non-discrimination policy must not be restricted to an individual litigation approach. As it is sensible in a national context, the European dimension of anti-discrimination policy might need to be backed up by special structures. The advantages of the agency approach that have been acknowledged by national legislators should lead to an agency approach on the EC level as well. I do admit that this is contrary to the current policy of mainstreaming equality politics. However, mainstreaming needs an agent if the goal of sexual and racial equality is not to be dominated by 'more important' policies. A European agency could act in a more flexible and more comprehensive way than a collusion of national agencies. At the same time, it might serve as a safeguard against the danger of anti-discrimination policies being submerged by more urgent concerns. This stresses the importance of a European equality agency.

From this statement there is only a small step to the conclusion, that adequate enforcement of equality law should also have a European dimension. Even without requiring Member States to issue national legislation towards enforcement through agencies or through the possibility of litigation by associations and groups, it is possible to give associations and groups more importance in proceedings before the ECJ, as has been advocated for consumer and economic law cases (Hasselbach, 1998; Micklitz and Reich, 1996). It might also be possible to give a European equality agency para judicial powers or standing before the ECJ to invoke EC equality law.

It will come as no surprise if I conclude that this policy should be driven by an asymmetric and substantive approach to equality. This policy should comprise individual and group-related legal remedies. The empowering aspects of legal action against discrimination should not be underestimated. In addition, the European Community has been and continues to be a community of law. Thus, equality policy will be of little success if not shaped as legal policy.

Finally, EC policy has to respond adequately to multidimensional discrimination on grounds of sex and 'race'. Even if it is true that sex discrimination and 'race' discrimination are different, there is no such thing as women as group in an essential sense. Any policy that tries to separate sex and 'race' discrimination will most probably only benefit the most privileged 'members' of both protected groups. European Union anti-discrimination policy needs to embrace the many dimensions of discrimination as well as the cumulative effects of such discrimination to become really effective.

Notes

1. ECJ 43/75 (*Defrenne II*) 1976 ECR 455.
2. ECJ 14/83 (*Colson and Kamann*) 1984 ECR 1891; ECJ 79/83 (*Harz*) 1984 ECR 1921.
3. ECJ *Colson and Kamann*.
4. ECJ *Harz*.
5. ECJ *Defrenne II*.
6. ECJ 129/79 (*Smith*) 1980 ECR 1275.
7. ECJ 248/83 (*Commission/UK*) 1984 ECR 3431.
8. ECJ C-345/89 (*Stoeckel*) 1991 ECR I-4321.
9. *Andrews v. British Columbia*, 2 February 1989 – Dominion Law Report 1989, 4th Series, 1 (McIntyre Judge, 11).
10. Though this judicial development relied on the US-American model of disparate impact discrimination, which again spurred the British legislation and subsequent jurisdiction, the concept of European style indirect discrimination is different from the US-American concept of disparate impact in some aspects. For example, in US law there is much more discussion about less discriminatory alternatives, the existence of which renders any statistically discriminating practice illegal. However, in the last few years there has been some discussion about the question whether such less discriminatory alternatives may

or must not be more expensive to employers than the currently used discriminatory practices. Another difference, which the US American concept shares with its British equivalent, is the need for the plaintiff to isolate a specific requirement that leads to the disparate impact in question. The ECJ's recent decision in *Seymour-Smith & Perez* (9 February 1999, Case C-167/97, not yet reported) may serve as an example for the differences in approach. In that case it is disputed whether a statutory provision under which compensation for dismissals can only be granted to plaintiffs who have been in permanent employment for more than two years is indirectly discriminatory. Under English law, the plaintiffs have to show that the two-year-requirement is a specific barrier that they cannot mount due to reasons related to sex. Under Community law, the question to be answered is 'whether and to what extent a legislative provision, which, though applying independently of the sex of the worker, actually affects a considerably higher percentage of women than men, is justified by objective reasons unrelated to sex' (ECJ, No 68 of that decision). The differences between the US and the European approach are discussed by Selmi (1998) and Asscher-Vonk (1998).

11. Council Directive 97/80/EC of 15 December 1997 on the burden of proof in cases of discrimination based on sex, OJ L 14/6, 20 January 1998.
12. ECJ Case C-400/93, (1995) ECR I-1275.
13. ECJ Case 109/88, (1989) ECR 3199.
14. ECJ Case 170/84 – *Bilka* (1986) ECR 1620 at 1628.
15. Ibid.
16. ECJ Case C-444/93, (1995) ECR I-4741.
17. The relevant provision in the Social Security Law Book excludes persons working in minor occupations and those working in short-term employment from any social security insurance. Ms Nolte's claim only aimed at a specific pension for incapacity to work, whereas Ms Megner and Ms Scheffel strove for inclusion in the national insurance on illness, unemployment and incapacity to work on grounds of old age or health reasons. Persons working for fewer than 15 hours or for a wage of less than one-seventh of the average earned by those insured are regarded as being employed in minor occupations. One-seventh of the average monthly income earned by those insured was 630 DM in 1998 for West Germany. Persons employed for no more than 18 hours per week were except from unemployment insurance. Persons in minor employment and persons in short-term employment are predominantly female. The legislation on minor

occupations is presently under review. When the manuscript was finished the position of the German government was that incomes from minor employment would not be taxable in the future. Instead, persons in minor employment would be obliged to pay contributions to social security, while not earning rights to the equivalent benefits. Legal action against these plans, once they become law, has already been announced, because the constitutionality of the envisaged provisions is doubtful.

18. ECJ Case C-409/95, (1997) ECR I.
19. Council of Ministers: Recommendation of December 13 1984 on the promotion of positive action for women (84/635/EEC), O.J. No L 331/34 19.12.1984.
20. ECJ Case C-450/93, (1995) ECR I-3051.
21. On reference of the Hessen State Constitutional Court, registered with the ECJ under Case number C-158/97.
22. The quotations indicate the clause the ECJ refers to as 'savings clause'.
23. See in more detail Schiek, (1998: 149-52). The case also deals with quotas of committees, but these are not of interest in relation to employment equality, a fact that has been misunderstood by Advocate General Saggio.
24. I have cited only two voices of the emerging concert of European tunes on equality law. The asymmetric version of equality principles proposed against a European background differs from its US American counterpart, where the notion of an anti-domination principle as the groundwork for sex discrimination law was formulated by Catherine McKinnon. The term 'Antidominierungsprinzip' has also been used by Ute Sacksofsky, (1996) albeit with a different theoretical conception from Catherine McKinnon.
25. C-1/95, 1997 ECR I-5253.
26. There is no ban on part time cleaners in Baden-Württemberg's schools wearing headscarves. This heavily underpaid occupation is predominantly filled by ethnic minority women adhering to Muslim dress codes.
27. Interestingly Ms Shavan won wide public attention while excluding headscarves from qualified jobs; it secured her a post in the Christian Democrats 'shadow cabinet' for the elections in 1998.
28. The Union for Education and Science (Gewerkschaft Erziehung und Wissenschaft, GEW) is member of the German Trade Union Congress (Deutscher Gewerkschaftsbund, DGB) and organizes most teachers who are unionized. Ms Ludin herself is member of the less representative Association for Education and Training (Verband für Bildung

und Erziehung, VBE). The general position of the GEW was that Ms Ludin should take the case to court. The VBE did not utter comparable public support for the case. Ms Ludin's case, which is now represented by the VBE, had not been filed by the end of January 1999.

29. The relevant press release from Ms Shavan is still available on the Internet under http:/www.uni-tuebingen.de/uni/ukk/aktuell/kopftuch1.htm.

30. It has been noted in the German press that nobody objected to Turkish women wearing a headscarf as long as they sought employment as cleaning personnel.

31. As in *Colson and Kamann*, for example (ECJ Case 14/83, (1984) ECR 1891).

32. As in *Danfoss* (ECJ Case 109/88 (1989) ECR 3199) and *Royal Copenhagen* (ECJ Case C-400/93, (1995) ECR I-1275).

15

Combating Employment Discrimination in Europe: National Variation and the Dawn of 'Good Practice'

John Wrench

Introduction

This chapter starts with the evidence from recent European-wide reports that racial or ethnic discrimination in European labour markets is more common than is generally admitted. The chapter goes on to examine critically examples of initiatives in various EU countries that are designed to counter discrimination and further the integration into employment of Europe's post-war migrant population and their descendants. To do this it draws upon the 1997 *European Compendium of Good Practice for the Prevention of Racism at the Workplace*. Case studies are selected from this compendium to illustrate the kinds of initiatives against racism and discrimination in employment that have recently been introduced in both public and private sector organizations in various European countries. These examples show how the character and emphasis of anti-discrimination practices vary across EU member states. The chapter then attempts some explanation for this variation, in terms of factors including the difference in the character and legal status of the predominant post-war migrant groups and their differential participation in the labour market, as well as historically different national conceptions of racism and citizenship, and responses to immigration and ethnic diversity.

In the 1990s there were a number of international initiatives that helped to put employment discrimination against migrant workers and ethnic minorities on the European agenda. For example, the International Labour Organisation (ILO) programme 'Combating discrimination against (im)migrant workers and ethnic minorities in the world of work',[1] initiated a programme of 'situation testing' covering several countries of Western Europe.[2] This method utilizes two or more testers, one belonging to a majority group and the others to ethnic minority groups, all of whom apply for the same jobs, whether by letter, telephone or in person. The testers are matched for all the criteria that should be normally taken into account by an employer, such as age, qualifications, experience and schooling. If, over repeated testing, the applicant from the majority background is systematically preferred to the others, then this points to the operation of discrimination according to ethnic background (Bovenkerk, 1992: 6–7). Within the ILO programme, the Netherlands carried out the first national study (Bovenkerk et al., 1995), with others following in Germany, Spain, Denmark and Belgium (see Goldberg et al., 1995; Colectivo IOE, 1996; Hjarnø/Jensen, 1997).[3] The initial overall findings for discrimination testing in the various countries were summed up thus:

> The programme's findings show discrimination in access to employment to be a phenomenon of considerable and significant importance. Overall net-discrimination rates of up to 35 per cent are not uncommon, meaning that in at least one out of three application procedures migrants are discriminated against. In interpreting these results, it should be kept in mind that, as a consequence of the rigorous research methodology, the discrimination rates uncovered by the project must be assumed to be conservative estimates of what is happening in reality. Thus, discrimination constitutes a serious impediment for the migrants' chances of finding employment (ILO project Information Bulletin, No.4, May 1997, 2).

Further evidence on employment discrimination in Europe came from research commissioned by the European Foundation for the Improvement of Living and Working Conditions, Dublin, covering the fifteen European Union member states plus Norway (Wrench, 1996). From different EU countries came accounts of direct racial or ethnic discrimination, such as the refusal to employ people simply on the grounds of colour of skin or ethnic background, and indirect discrimination, such as restricting employment opportunities to the families of existing workers, or using questionable informal and subjective criteria in recruitment. From within the workplace came accounts of discrimination in access to promotion and training, and allocation of duties, as well as verbal harassment. The report also illustrated a widespread ignorance of the problems of racism and discrimination in employment on the part of European employers, trade unionists, labour inspectors, and so on.

Perhaps the most immediate implication of this evidence is that of the need to strengthen legal measures against discrimination. There have been several recent comparative analyses of the workings of national anti-discrimination law, and of enforcement agencies, in Europe in the 1990s (Forbes and Mead, 1992; CEC, 1993; MacEwen, 1995, 1997), highlighting the wide variation in the effectiveness of such laws between EU countries, and generally agreeing on the importance of strong legislation at both the national and EU level. In some cases there remains very little legal pressure on employers to avoid racial discrimination; in some others there is recently enacted legislation, the effects of which cannot yet be properly judged. In some European countries, legislation against employment discrimination does not cover the private sector. Even when strong law exists in theory, there can be problems in practice. The case of France is an example where a number of problems are experienced with the use of the criminal law against racism and discrimination. Cases of employment discrimination are seldom brought to court for lack of concrete evidence, and in practice employers are generally free to take on whoever they like (De Rudder et al., 1995). In France, in 1993, there were just two convictions for racial discrimination in employment (Banton, 1999), and in Sweden, during the year following the introduction of the 1994 law against employment discrimination, not one case of alleged discrimination found its way to a work tribunal, even though the Discrimination Ombudsman had received 75 complaints from members of the public (Graham and Soininen, 1998). In Britain, on the other hand, 2,324 cases under the Race Relations Act were received by Industrial Tribunals in 1994 (Banton, 1999). In the Netherlands a recent law commits companies with more than 35 employees to aim for the proportional representation of 'non-natives' in their workforces, and this puts pressure on them to formulate policies to achieve this. In theory, therefore, there is now more legal pressure in the Netherlands to institute such policies than in other EU member states. There is thus a great deal of variety between different EU countries in the degree of pressure to introduce policies for the prevention of racial discrimination and the promotion of equal treatment.

It is argued that an EU directive on racial discrimination would bring member states into line on this (Dummet, 1994; Mirza, 1995). However, action at the EU level has been slow to come, largely because of political opposition from various national governments. Less controversial have been policies against racism and discrimination at an organizational level, which are voluntarily introduced by private sector companies or public sector employers. One European initiative which attempts to stimulate this sort of activity is the Joint Declaration on the Prevention of Racial Discrimination and Xenophobia and Promotion of Equal Treatment at the Workplace, agreed by the European social partners in October 1995, at the Social Dialogue Summit in Florence. This sets out a range of means that can make a positive contribution towards preventing racial discrimination at the workplace, and encourages employers and trade unions to adopt such measures. Amongst other things, the Joint Declaration called for the compilation of a *Compendium of Good Practice.*

The European Compendium of Good Practice

Following the Joint Declaration, national researchers in each EU country were asked to produce a report covering cases of good practice in employment regarding immigrants and ethnic minorities within their own country, using a common methodology. The *European Compendium of Good Practice for the Prevention of Racism at the Workplace* (Wrench, 1997a) was compiled from these reports. It consists of 25 case studies from the fifteen countries of the European Union, encompassing private and public sector companies, trade unions, collective agreements, codes of conduct and national initiatives.

The single most common practice described amongst the 25 case studies in the *Compendium* was that of training. This training could be grouped under three main headings:

- training directed at the migrants/ethnic minorities themselves;
- training directed at the majority to produce attitude change;
- training directed at the majority to produce behavioural change.

Training Directed at the Migrants/Ethnic Minorities Themselves

Historically, in many countries training of the migrants themselves was the first type of activity adopted. Generally this was training for newcomers, teaching them the language, introducing them to important legal or cultural aspects of the new society, or showing them how to operate in the labour market. It was assumed that this would facilitate the integration of immigrants into society, and is still the sort of training given in many countries to refugees and other newcomers. In the *Compendium* there were also examples of training for an older and more established immigrant population, in two contexts: (1) where restructuring of the economy has led to the closure of old industries and heavy unemployment amongst immigrant workers, who had been overrepresented in these employment sectors (Martens and Sette, 1997), and (2) where restructuring within a firm has adversely affected the existing immigrant workforce by requiring from them new skills or language abilities that they do not possess (Gächter, 1997).

However, although providing training for migrants is an important activity, the question has to be asked as to whether it is contributing to, in the words of the Joint Declaration, 'the prevention of racism and xenophobia'. Perhaps it might be argued that if these measures help to reduce the overrepresentation of immigrants and ethnic minorities amongst the unemployed, or promote their broader and better employment, then they are tackling the roots of racism by undermining the idea that 'visible minorities' are second-class citizens, naturally suited for second-class jobs. This, however, is at best only indirectly confronting racism.

There are problems in overemphasizing the role of training of immigrants, or as seeing it as sufficient in itself. For one thing, training directed at immigrants carries with it the assumption that the problems they encounter are a result of their own deficiencies. Yet there is a great deal of evidence that well-educated migrants and ethnic minorities with no language problems at all suffer discrimination and exclusion from opportunities for which they are well qualified. It can therefore be argued that if you are aiming to counter racism, discrimination and xenophobia, then your training should logically be directed at those whose attitudes and actions cause the problem – members of the white majority population. There are several different examples of this in the *Compendium*, and these can be divided into those initiatives which aim to change attitudes, and those which attempt to change behaviour.

Training Directed at the Majority: Attitude Change

An example of an initiative to change majority attitudes is the 'Living with Foreigners' campaign set up jointly by the German social partners, the Deutsche Gewerkschaftsbund (DGB) and the Bund Deutscher Arbeitgeber (BDA) (Brüggemann and Riehle, 1997). This is targeted at around one million apprentices in German industry, using training packages and media materials aimed at countering attitudes of intolerance and xenophobia. The assumption behind this sort of campaign is that educational material and greater contact with people from other cultures can help to break down attitudes of racism and prejudice, and thereby reduce discrimination. Another example of the provision of educational material or information for the white national employees is the local authority in Århus, Denmark's second largest city. All employees were sent a newspaper *På Lige Fod* (*On an Equal Footing*), which presented success stories of ethnic minorities employed in the council, the positive benefits of working with others from different cultures, and so on (Wrench, 1997b).

The implicit assumption here is that the production of this sort of information will help to reduce racist attitudes and thereby reduce resistance to employing migrants. It is assumed that attitudes can be changed in this way, and that attitude change will lead to changes in behaviour and practices. However, this assumption may well be naive. For one thing, racist attitudes and prejudices are unlikely to be changed simply by the provision of training and information. Secondly, it is quite possible for practices of racial discrimination to be carried out by someone who does not have racist attitudes. Therefore, it can be argued that attempts to produce changes in people's behaviour are more fruitful than trying to change people's attitudes.

Training Directed at the Majority: Behavioural Change

A number of initiatives in the *Compendium* place a greater importance on changing individual behaviour than attempting to change attitudes. These initiatives can be divided into two sorts: those that can be categorized as 'multicultural' in their approach or those that work from an 'anti-discrimination' perspective.

Examples of initiatives with a 'multicultural' emphasis are those which provide training for managers and supervisors in 'inter-cultural management', or training workers in 'inter-cultural cooperation' or how to work in multicultural teams. For example, the Thyssen Stahl steel company in Germany provides training in leading multicultural teams, as well as providing Turkish courses for German workers wishing to learn the language either for job-related or personal reasons (Brüggemann and Riehle, 1997). Similarly in the Netherlands the Dr Sarphatihuus nursing home introduced mandatory 'inter-cultural management' courses for middle and senior managers to help counter their ignorance about the implications of working with a multicultural staff (Abell, 1997).

Again, although these initiatives are undoubtedly valuable, they are still only indirectly addressing racism and discrimination. A more direct approach calls for an 'anti-discrimination' rather than a 'multicultural' emphasis. An example of this kind of training would be that introduced in Belgium as a result of the 'Code of Conduct' for temporary employment agencies, signed by employers and trade unions in the temporary employment agency sector (Martens and Sette, 1997). A survey of agency staff had revealed that most received discriminatory requests from employers, ranging from requesting perfect bilingualism for manual occupations[4] to explicit requests not to be sent any foreigners. Both trade union and employers representatives admitted that the temporary employment sector is indeed beset with problems of racial discrimination. The training aimed to make staff aware of the problem of racial discrimination, and instructed them how to respond to employers who made discriminatory requests, and how to ensure that only functionally relevant requirements are taken into account when selecting temporary staff.

There were other examples in the *Compendium* of the anti-discrimination training of gatekeepers and others whose activities could have a direct effect on the opportunities of ethnic minorities. Measures included training on fair recruitment and selection procedures, and how to comply with anti-discrimination legislation. Generally speaking, these initiatives work from the assumption that 'measures to prevent racism and xenophobia and promote equal treatment at the workplace' are to be directed at members of the majority society, not at the migrants themselves, given that problems of racism, xenophobia and unequal treatment are the product of the attitudes and practices of the majority, and the workings and structures of the majority institutions of society.

Positive Action

Many of the initiatives listed in the *Compendium* are aimed at providing equal treatment by attempting to change attitudes and practices, and removing discriminatory barriers, so as to produce a 'level playing field'. However, there is also a strong argument that these are not enough, and that action is needed over and above the simple provision of equal rights and the removal of discrimination. A further range of measures is needed where the targets are the migrants themselves, and these fall under the heading of positive action (CRE, 1985). They are based on the assumption that equal treatment is not going to be much use if migrants are starting from very different and disadvantaged positions, sometimes because of the operation of racism and xenophobia in the past. Positive action goes further than equal treatment. Whereas equal treatment would mean treating people who apply for jobs without discrimination, positive action means, for example, making an extra effort to encourage groups who might not normally apply. Therefore, positive action is in fact doing something extra for previously excluded minorities, something you are not doing for the national majority (Blakemore and Drake, 1996; Moore, 1997).

Positive action still arouses negative reactions in some quarters, but in its weakest sense, positive action could simply mean devoting extra resources to language and other training for immigrants in order to better equip them for work. This type of initiative is probably the single most common amongst all the case studies in the *Compendium*, and seems to arouse the least controversy. Indeed, such measures might not even be called positive action at all, but simply varying the distribution of resources according to need. Other measures that go further than equal treatment are those that accommodate the specific religious or cultural needs of minority groups within the organization. Again, these are not uncommon amongst the case studies. Stronger forms of positive action might include special recruitment initiatives, such as translating job advertisements into ethnic minority languages, placing advertisements in the ethnic minority press, or using statements to encourage applicants from minorities. An increasingly used measure is that of mentoring. This is intended to increase the retention of minorities once they have been recruited into the organization.

Only a minority of case studies operated a whole package of equal opportunities measures, covering, for example, the range of suggested initiatives in the Florence Joint Declaration, as well as others, combined with some positive action. Examples of these in the *Compendium* included the case studies from the Netherlands and the UK, and these could be called 'organizational equal opportunity policies'.

Organizational Equal Opportunity Policies

The first example is that of Virgin Our Price (UK), whose 'High Street' stores sell a wide range of goods including music CDs and cassettes, videos, games, books, T-shirts, chart music and other such accessories (Virdee, 1997). Management decided to carry out an employee profile audit of the workforce, and personal information forms, including a request to self-nominate their ethnic origin, were issued to all employees. The audit showed that although the proportion of ethnic minorities employed was broadly in line with the size of the ethnic minority population nationally (just over 5 per cent), ethnic minorities were underrepresented in middle management and senior positions.

Virgin Our Price made an explicit commitment to redressing past disadvantage through the adoption of positive action measures. Recognizing that certain groups within the community may be underrepresented in the business as a whole or in particular parts of it, it made special efforts to ensure that opportunities are made known to those groups, and where appropriate that training is provided to enable members of those groups to compete on equal terms for the opportunities available. To ensure that interview panels operate according to the company equal opportunity policy, all individuals who sit on recruitment and selection panels receive anti-discriminatory training, and one personnel representative is present at all interviews. Virgin Our Price also introduced an anti-harassment policy. It states that a single serious incident of harassment can result in summary dismissal for gross misconduct.

The company states that its policy has a number of advantages, including:

- attracting the best from the pool of skills and talent that is becoming increasingly diverse and using people's potential to the full;
- ensuring that the company meets the needs of its current and potential customers effectively through a workforce that reflects the make up of the communities which it serves, and providing a competitive edge in reaching and attracting alternative new markets;
- avoiding incurring the direct costs of racial discrimination: financial, reduced employee morale and commitment, and cost to the image of the organization resulting from adverse publicity (Virdee, 1997).

A second example of an organizational equal opportunity policy is that of the North Holland Department of the Directorate-General for Public Works and Water Management, part of the Ministry of Transport, Public Works and Water Management, which is the third largest ministry in the Netherlands. It is responsible for flood defences and water management, traffic, transport and communications (Abell, 1997).

The head of personnel believed that an organization like the North Holland Department could not 'stand apart from society'.[5] At the end of 1991, the Ministry of the Interior called upon all parties to add extra wording to advertisements recruiting personnel from outside to the effect that, all other things being equal, priority would be given to ethnic minorities, as well as to women and disabled people. However, applications to the organization from ethnic minorities were low, and a survey revealed that disillusionment was one of the main reasons for the low response to advertisements. The study also showed that recruitment of ethnic minorities required a less conventional approach, such as the use of informal networks. Contacts were then initiated with migrant organizations and other relevant bodies to stimulate applications. Agreements were also concluded with temporary employment agencies that requests for temporary staff would be met in the first instance by candidates from one of the ethnic minorities.

In addition to diversifying the recruitment procedures, the Department held preliminary interviews with applicants of minority ethnic origin to ensure that they met the requirements of the job. During the preliminary interview information was given about the organization and the procedure, and applicants were advised on how to improve their letters of application and CVs. Preliminary interviews created a relationship of trust, so that contact was maintained after the initial application and feedback was obtained on the progress of the procedure. During selection, personnel officers were careful to see that the correct procedures were followed in the case of applicants of minority ethnic origin and that no improper arguments were used to reject them. Line managers also underwent training in selection skills to avoid bias in selection interviews, and there were information campaigns and meetings with Dutch non-immigrant staff to convey the message of the initiative, and to reduce any potential hostility to it. By 1 January 1996 the percentage of employees of minority ethnic origin was seven per cent, two per cent higher than the recommended target set by the national Civil Service Plan. It was interesting that this policy was introduced through the commitment of senior staff using arguments of a social and moral nature. Unlike the previous example, this organization was not trying to increase its appeal to a multicultural clientele.

These organizations in the UK and the Netherlands had policies of a greater variety and strength than the case studies from other countries.[6] Between them they operated a whole range of different practices, including special advertisements, allowances for cultural difference, positive action training for immigrants, training for staff on how to recruit and select without discrimination, and procedures for sanctioning harassment, with progress reviewed and monitored by statistics, and targets set relating to the long term proportional representation of minorities. The accurate monitoring of their workforces over time allowed these organizations to review their progress and make appropriate policy changes and, indeed, the monitoring was able to demonstrate that they had progressed significantly towards a greater representation of ethnic minorities amongst their employees.

However, in some EU countries the sorts of policies described above are quite unknown. This might be because of differences in national ideologies or in national circumstances.

Differences in National Ideologies

There are clearly great differences, historically and culturally, in national responses to immigration and ethnic diversity. Castles (1995) provides a categorization of such responses, which includes:[7]

- differential exclusion: immigrants are seen as guestworkers without full social and political rights (for example, Germany, Austria, Switzerland, Belgium);
- assimilation: immigrants are awarded full rights but are expected to become like everyone else (for example, France, the UK in the 1960s);
- pluralism/multiculturalism: immigrants have full rights but maintain some cultural differences (for example, Canada, Australia, Sweden, the UK more recently).

The differential exclusion model was based on the desire to prevent permanent settlement, and has proved hard to maintain because it leads to social tension and contradicts the democratic principle of including all members of civil society in the nation state. The case of Germany fits this model, although there has been a shift to assimilation policies in some areas, and some multicultural policies in education.[8] In France, probably the best example of the assimilation model with its republican tradition of equal treatment for all, there has been a move to some elements of the pluralist model, and this has led to some difficulties because of contradictions between explicit goals and actual policies. In the UK in the 1950s and 1960s there was a sort of *laissez-faire* assimilation that moved to pluralist and multicultural models in the 1970s. There is now a mixture of assimilationist and pluralist policies, without a clear overall objective (Castles, 1995).

These contrasting national approaches provide very different contexts in which the case studies are located. Often, the ideologies relating to these ideal types remain in official discourse, and are directly reflected in how policies on the treatment of migrants and ethnic minorities are expressed. Furthermore, different conceptions of racism are emphasized in different European countries, and these have corresponding implications for the character of measures to counter racism and discrimination. We can illustrate this by considering the cases of the UK and France. For example, it is suggested by Michael Banton that policies in France start with the assumption that the causes of racism lie within the realm of ideas, and that the first priority is therefore to penalize incitement to racial hatred. Official discourses on racism are concerned with phenomena such as racial attacks, attack on mosques or Jewish cemeteries, or the incitement to racial hatred. Correspondingly, the policing of the press and publications regarding racism is much stricter than it is in Britain. In Britain, official policy makes no similar usage of the concept of racism but emphasizes action against discriminatory behaviour in a rather pragmatic approach (Banton, 1999). There are also differences in the degree to which policies against racism and discrimination have as part of their approach a practical recognition of ethnic categories. The French idea of its national community does not sit well with the recognition of ethnic or immigrant minorities within it. According to Michael Banton, 'The French see their country as a political community which could be undermined were they to recognize differences based on ethnic origin in the relations between citizen and the State' (Banton, 1999). Thus, in France, the emphasis is on broader equal rights policies as a means of avoiding discrimination for all citizens and workers, and initiatives to encourage the recruitment of migrants have been phrased not in terms of anti-discrimination or anti-racism policies for migrants, but as egalitarian approaches guided by a universalistic ideology (De Rudder et al., 1995).

To talk of measures in Anglo-Saxon equal opportunities terms runs counter to established philosophies of universalistic treatment, with a resistance to dividing up the targets of policies by ethnic background. Therefore, in France, practices that benefit ethnic minorities are more likely to do so indirectly, without being designed in ethnically specific forms. The British, on the other hand, have a much weaker and more complicated conception of citizenship and the national community, which has not been threatened by the recognition of ethnic categories or ideas of multiculturalism. Discussions on the forms that multiculturalism might take are a regular part of public debate in some sectors, and equal opportunities policies often operate in ways that take practical account of categories of ethnic difference (Jenkins and Solomos, 1987). There is also a difference in the readiness to record and use data according to ethnic minority background. In the UK a question on ethnic background forms part of the official census, and ethnic monitoring within organiza-tions is often used to evaluate the progress of policies, whereas in France as in other countries, the recording of 'racial' or ethnic origin in official or private registration is legally proscribed.

Therefore, an important question is whether the sorts of policies discussed earlier – equal opportunity policies at an organizational level, positive action, celebrating diversity – are only compatible with the 'pluralist' or 'multicultural' approach. In the light of this question, it is interesting to consider the French case study.

The French Case

The French case study in the *Compendium* is of a very different character to the others. This case covers the staff recruitment and training policy of the Continent hypermarket in a large shopping complex recently opened in an urban area in Marseilles (Quartiers-Nord) suffering from many social problems: unemployment and insecure employment, low incomes, a high proportion of people on benefit, a high percentage of young people without any qualifications or training, and so on (De Rudder et al., 1997). There is a high percentage of foreigners and French citizens of foreign origin in this area. However, acknowledging ethnic origin in the context of social policy contradicts the predominant 'republican model' in France, and so in this case this is side-stepped by applying measures based on a territorial definition of social problems.

A policy of 'local preference for recruitment' in the shopping complex was initiated after vociferous lobbying (and even occasional acts of violence) during the construction phase by local people, who had felt that they were going to receive no benefit from the new shopping complex. A *charte emploi* (employment charter) was drawn up, in which all retailers wanting to open outlets at the centre were asked to sign, and under which they undertook to give priority for jobs to people living in districts close to the shopping centre ('provided they have the appropriate skills and abilities'). A training programme for Continent managers was instituted, entitled 'Sensibilisation à la problématique des Quartiers-Nord de Marseille' (Raising awareness of the problems of Marseilles' Quartiers-Nord). The idea was to make managerial staff familiar with the hyper-market's economic, social and cultural context, and also with its future employees. An agreement was made with a local agency to select particu-larly disadvantaged people from the Quartiers-Nord, provide them with initial training to improve their chances of being employed at Continent. The agreed selection criteria for these people were that the person must otherwise have 'little hope of getting a job', and that priority should be given to those persons resident in one of the four public housing estates closest to the shopping centre.

Ninety people followed an 'initial skills/employability' training programme and individual 'mentoring' of trainees was also provided. Altogether, Continent took on 58 of these 90 people 'blind' – without having to undergo any further selection tests, before the store opened; they were employed under permanent contracts, albeit only part time, after receiving a further two to three months' training from the enterprise. An agreement was made with the Agence Locale pour l'Emploi to make provision for the establishment of a 'one-stop-shop' for recruitment, and this was followed by a local public information campaign to announce the availability of the jobs. At the end of this process, more than 450 people, including 220 cashiers, were recruited and began the training provided by Continent in August and September 1996. When the store opened, a total of 489 new staff had been hired, and 95 per cent of locally recruited employees were, by February 1997, covered by permanent contracts of employment.

Thus, in this French case there was something very similar to what the British or Dutch would call positive action – a policy targeted at an excluded group. Training was directed at local disadvantaged people to improve their chances of employment at the hypermarket, and when this was combined with the policy to give priority for jobs to people living in the districts close to the shopping centre – provided that they had 'appropriate skills and abilities' – this formed a strong and effective positive action policy that bordered on positive discrimination. This was less controversial than it might have been because it was not openly framed as positive action for ethnic minorities, but for local people. Supporters of this approach might argue that if this policy produced benefits for a previously excluded group, it was of no importance that the policy was not 'ethnically specific'. Opponents might argue that the 'hiding' of the ethnic factor in such policies is disingenuous and unsatisfactory. Not specifying 'race' or ethnicity allows in theory for the repetition of such a policy in an area where a new enterprise is located within a population of the white majority. Restricting recruitment to a primarily white catchment area has long been seen as a way of indirectly but intentionally discrimination against ethnic minorities (Lee and Wrench, 1983).

Differences in National Circumstances

The working population of the EU can be divided into five main categories in terms of legal status (Wrench, 1996: 3):

1. citizens living and working within their own country of citizenship;
2. citizens of an EU Member State who work in another country within the Union (EU denizens/citizens);
3. third country nationals who have full rights to residency and work in a Member State (non-EU denizens);
4. third country nationals who have leave to stay on the basis of a revocable work permit for a fixed period of time;
5. undocumented or 'illegal' workers.

The above five categories reflect formal status, and a continuum of rights ranging from full rights and privileges of citizenship in group (1) to virtually no rights in group (5). It is clear that the problem of discrimination in the labour market of countries in the EU differs according to which categories most of its migrant and minority ethnic workers fall into. This will have corresponding implications for policies and practices on discrimination and equality.

In countries of Northern Europe, migrants and ethnic minorities are more likely to be skewed towards the top groups of the five legal categories of workers. Here, migrants are longer established and issues of the second generation are important, with concern over the unjustified exclusion of young people of migrant descent from employment opportunities by informal discrimination on 'racial' or ethnic grounds, and their over-representation in unemployment. In the UK, for example, most migrants and their descendants are found in group (1); the legal status of migrant workers is generally not a problem, and a major part of equal opportunities activity concerns tackling the informal discrimination that, in practice, reduces the opportunities of minority ethnic workers, either at the workplace or within a trade union. In other countries of Northern Europe, a higher proportion of workers fall into group (3), suffering not only informal racial discrimination but also formal legal discrimination. For example, nationals of non-EU countries, even when legally resident and lawfully employed within an EU member state, are excluded from a whole range of jobs, and may be entitled to lower levels of unemployment benefit, or even inferior rights to representation on works councils. In this context, the first stages of any initiatives are more likely to concern themselves with the sorts of exclusion related to naturalization and citizenship issues. This has implications for the overtones of the concept of discrimination itself. For example, in the UK the use of a broad definition of discrimination allows for measures that tackle indirect, institutional or unintentional discrimination, whereas in Germany, avoiding discrimination is more likely to be seen more narrowly as working to ensure equal employment rights, and paying equal wages for equal work, through formal agreements between the social partners.

In countries of Southern Europe immigrants are likely to be over-represented towards the bottom of the five groups. Workers of groups (4) and (5) are actively preferred and recruited because they are cheaper, more vulnerable, and more pliable — they are less able to resist over-exploitation in terms of work intensity or working hours, in conditions which indigenous workers would not tolerate. Anti-discrimination activities in these circumstances are initially more likely to emphasize measures to empower such workers and reduce their vulnerability to exploitation, with, for example, initiatives to unionize, regularize and train them.

Thus, a practice within one context might carry different overtones to the same practice in another. For example, in Southern European countries where migrants are severely exploited in illegal work because they do not have the power to resist or to seek alternative employment, providing language training for them in the national language might be seen to be part of anti-discrimination activity because it empowers them and enables them to resist such discrimination. In Northern Europe where migrants have more legal rights and are longer established, including a second generation, the provision of language training is less likely to be seen as countering discrimination, and might even be interpreted as an alibi for the absence of stronger measures.

In Northern European countries, where most immigrants might have full citizenship rights, a knowledge of the language from the colonial links, and are relatively long established in the country, then equal opportunities policies and tackling 'informal' discrimination directed at the second generation are logical priorities. However, such instruments are less relevant for countries of Southern Europe where a newer migrant population is concentrated more towards the bottom groups – many are on restricted work permits, many are 'illegal', and most are relatively recent. To talk about 'ethnic monitoring' or 'targets' in an environment where large numbers of undocumented workers suffer great exploitation would be inappropriate. Here, simply implementing equal treatment would bring considerable improvements.

This difference in emphasis was borne out in the *Compendium* case studies from Southern Europe, where many of the initiatives were directed to countering the inequality that is rooted outside the organization, in broader society. Hence in Greece and Portugal the case studies consisted of initiatives against the illegal exploitation of immigrants (Fakiolas, 1997; Palma et al., 1997). In an Italian case study employers directed some of their measures outside the organization with interventions to counter discrimination in the housing market on behalf of their employees (Carrera et al., 1997), whilst in Spain the unions became concerned with broader welfare issues outside the workplace (Cachón, 1997). Anti-discrimination initiatives in the forms found in, for example, the UK and the Netherlands, are less appropriate for these circumstances. Having said this, there was evidence of a growing realization that in the future, employers and unions will need to take on board some of the ideas current further north in Europe. At the moment, immigrants in the southern countries of Europe are not generally in competition with native workers for their jobs. However, a whole new set of problems will arise when second-generation immigrants with better academic qualifications and aspiring to more skilled work start to compete with the majority population in the 'normal' labour market.

Conclusion

The Joint Declaration on the Prevention of Racial Discrimination and Xenophobia and Promotion of Equal Treatment at the Workplace, signed in 1995 by EU workers' and employers' organizations, has had an educational impact and has helped to put the issue of racism and discrimination at work onto national agendas, in some countries for the first time. The 1997 European Year Against Racism provided a further stimulus to awareness of these issues. Nevertheless, it is clear that specific initiatives and measures by employers to counter racism, discrimination and the exclusion of migrants and their descendants are still not accorded the legitimacy they deserve in member states of the EU. The European *Compendium* gives some examples of positive practices, demonstrating the sorts of measures that might be adopted by others. However, when these are set in a broader EU context they remain untypical.

One of the problems in furthering action against discrimination across the EU is the differing conceptions of, and assumptions about, racism and discrimination that exist in different European countries. In many countries people are uncomfortable with the usage of the term 'racism', particularly those whose histories give them most cause to remember the suffering caused by the doctrines of Nazism. In Germany, for example, a reluctance to use the term 'racism' in regard to events of everyday life is understood to be a reflection of the recent historical experience of this extreme form of racism, but is also interpreted by some scholars as a way of playing down the seriousness of recent events, such as the arson attacks on refugee hostels (Piper, 1998).

In many countries, the term 'racism' is often seen to cover only pathological forms of racial hatred and extremist behaviour. This view is associated with the assumption that discrimination must be a product of racist attitudes. Therefore, the fact that such attitudes are by definition held only by an extremist minority in a society leads to the assumption that discrimination must be equally untypical. This particular conventional wisdom underlies one commonly heard rationalization for inaction, frequently encountered at European meetings, namely that within a particular member state the problem of racism and discrimination in employment is 'abnormal' and not widespread enough to justify the introduction of special measures. There is a common attitude of 'no problem here', an attitude that is, however, expressed uncommonly, each manifestation being culturally and historically specific to each member state. Examples of such national arguments which have expressed in recent years by employers' representatives, trade unionists, civil servants and officials are as follows.

- In Spain there is no racism towards migrants because Spain has traditionally been a country of emigration, and therefore its population understands well the problems faced by immigrants.
- Racism is not a normal part of Italian culture. This is apparent for two reasons: firstly, because Italian fascism, unlike German fascism, was never anti-Semitic, and secondly, because Italy had the largest communist party in Europe, reflecting a culture of international brotherhood and solidarity.
- In Germany racism is no longer a problem. Germany had been the most institutionally racist state in Europe under the Nazis, and therefore, racism was removed when the Nazi state was abolished.
- Racism is absent from French culture because since the 1789 revolution and the institutionalization of 'liberty, equality and fraternity' into French society, France is the only European country that exhibits the true republican spirit of universalism.
- Racism is not a part of Swedish society because Sweden, unlike the major migrant-receiving countries of Europe, has never been a colonial power ruling over non-white peoples.
- In the Netherlands, racism is not a normal part of the national character because, in comparison to other European colonial powers, the Dutch operated a more benevolent form of colonialism. This is illustrated amongst other things by a high rate of intermarriage between Dutch and ex-colonial peoples.
- Attitudes of racism are alien to the Portuguese character because Portugal was the first country to open up new lands with its voyages of discovery to Africa and India, thus exposing the Portuguese people to non-Europeans earlier than other countries, and laying the foundations of universalism and tolerance in the national character.

Participants in international meetings have even heard the observation that the absence of legislation against racial discrimination in a particular country is in itself a convincing demonstration that the problem does not exist in that country.[9]

The research evidence quoted at the beginning of this chapter counters the assertion that there is 'no problem here', as well as showing that routine normal and institutional discrimination is not simply the result of extremists and right-wing racists but is found quite commonly within the organizations of society. There is clearly a need to get racism and discrimination further on the European agenda, with specific measures to tackle them, even if the exact character of these measures will vary between different national contexts.

The European Compendium of Good Practice was not in any way a survey, but simply a collection of case studies that act as examples of some of the practices at work. Therefore, it cannot taken as providing an overview of the state of action on this issue across the EU. Nevertheless, it does give us some indication of the character of this action. It was significant that sometimes national researchers had to look rather hard to find their case studies of good practice for the *Compendium*.

Some of the cases that feature in the *Compendium* reveal the continuance of the assumption that measures to promote equal treatment in the labour market are to be directed at the migrants themselves, and that employers and other interested parties seem to be far more comfortable with this approach. For example, in Belgium, recent attempts to move the emphasis of anti-discrimination training away from training directed at migrants to training aimed at representatives of the societal majority met with significant resistance, countering some of the potential effects of anti-discrimination training measures and leading to some initiatives being discontinued (Castelain-Kinet et al., 1998; *ILO Project Information Bulletin*, No. 5, August 1998, 5). Furthermore, those initiatives that are directed at the white majority frequently work from the assumption that racism and discrimination can be addressed simply by 'attitude change' measures such as information provision, or a modicum of 'inter-cultural contact'. Stronger anti-discrimination or anti-harassment measures that have implications for organizational practice are relatively rare.

One problem is that, on the whole, employers and their organizations remain ideologically unsympathetic to stronger measures to counter discrimination and to further equal opportunities. Receptivity to them seems to be greater in the public sector, and in the retail part of the private sector where a pay-off in terms of broader customer appeal is recognized. The business case for such measures remains unrecognized in some member states. Yet the business case itself can be overstated (Rubenstein, 1987), and will not alone provide sufficient incentive for change. Where a 'business pay-off' is not immediately obvious, extra pressure will need to be applied via the legal framework, and where legal arrangements at a national level are inadequate, it is likely that pressure from the European level will improve this. Even in Sweden, which has often been held up as a model for others in the rights and protection it grants to immigrants, the impetus to introduce legislation against ethnic discrimination in employment originated not from within the country itself but from the external pressure of international organizations and agreements (Graham and Soininen, 1998: 536). In the 1997 Treaty of Amsterdam there was included for the first time an article which condemns discrimination based on criteria that include racial or ethnic origin. Ratification of this treaty will empower the European Commission to propose specific action, such as a directive to cover racial and ethnic discrimination at the workplace in all EU member states.

Notes

1. The ILO initiative also included Canada and the United States, but in this chapter, discussion is restricted to the European countries.
2. 'Situation testing' is sometimes known as 'discrimination testing' or 'practice tests', see Banton (1997).
3. The UK was not included in this exercise because evidence for discrimination had already been established there using this method (see for example Hubbuck and Carter, 1980; Esmail and Everington, 1993; Simson and Stevenson, 1994).
4. Regarded in the temporary staff sector as a kind of secret code for the exclusive selection of Belgian workers.
5. The Department is located within a highly multiethnic part of the Netherlands.
6. These two countries plus Sweden were described as 'frontrunners' in the development of anti-discrimination legislation in a 1991 ILO report (Zegers de Beijl 1991: 2).
7. These are 'ideal' types, and in reality there have been some tensions within them.
8. For a recent discussion of how German conceptions of citizenship and national ethnic community similarly discourage official recognition of immigrants as distinct ethnic minority groups, see Piper (1998).
9. The above arguments have all been heard by the author expressed at international conferences and meetings over recent years, apart from the Italian case, which was taken from documentary sources.

Relevant Legal Instruments

US

Fifth Amendment of the US Constitution (1791)
Thirteenth Amendment of the US Constitution (1865)
Fourteenth Amendment of the US Constitution (1868)
Fifteenth Amendment of the US Constitution (1870)
Civil Rights Act (1886)
Civil Rights Act (1964) – Title VI and Title VII
Civil Rights Act (1991)
Civil Rights Restoration Act (1997)
Age Discrimination in Employment Act (1974)
Equal Employment Opportunity Act (1972)
Equal Pay Act (1963)
Executive Order 10,925 (1961)
Executive Order 11,246 (1965) as amended by Executive Order 11,375,
    as amended by Executive Order 12,086 and Revised Order 4
Executive Order 8,802 (1941)
Homestead Act (1865)
Pregnancy Discrimination Amendments (1978)
Proposition 209 (1997)
Public Works Employment Act (1977)
Race Relation Act (1976)
Sex Discrimination Act (1975)
The Americans with Disabilities Act (1990)
Title IX of the Education Amendments (1972)
Vietnam-era Veterans Readjustment Act (1966, 1974) (GI Bill)
Voting Rights Act (1965)
Wagner Act (1935)

Canada

Constitution Act (1981)
Canadian Human Rights Act. Revised Statutes of Canada (1985)

Employment Equity Act. Revised Statutes of Canada (1986–87–88)
Employment Equity Act (1996). Statutes of Canada (1995)
Individual Rights Protection Act, Alberta (1990)
Barristers and Solicitors Act, British Columbia (1979)
Employment Equity Act, Ontario (1993)

United Nations

Convention on the Elimination of All Forms of Racial Discrimination (1965)
Convention on the Elimination of All Forms of Discrimination against Women (1979)

European Union

EC Treaty (1992)
Treaty of Amsterdam (1997)
Equal Pay Directive – Directive 75/117
Equal Treatment Directive – Directive 76/207
Burden-of-Proof-Directive – Directive 97/80
Florence Declaration on the Prevention of Racial Discrimination (1995)
Joint Declaration on the Prevention of Racial Discrimination and Xenophobia and Promotion of Equal Treatment at the Workplace (1995)
Recommendation of December 13 1984 on the Promotion of Positive Action for Women

Relevant Cases

US

Adarand Constructors Inc. v. Pena 115 S. Ct. 2097 (1995)

Bazemore v. Friday 478 U.S. 385 (1986)

Boston Superior Officers Fed'n v. City of Boston 6/22 (1988) No. 97-1880

Brown v. Board of Education 347 U.S. 483 (1954)

City of Richmond v. J.A. Croson Co. 488 U.S. 469 (1989)

Contractors Ass'n of Eastern Penn. v. Secretary of Labor 442 F.2d 159 (3d Cir. 1971)

De Funis v. Odegaard 416 U.S. 312 (1974)

Firefighters Local Union No. 1794 v. Stotts 467 U.S. 561 (1984)

Fullilove v. Klutznick 448 U.S. 448 (1980)

Hopwood et al. v. State of Texas et al. 78 F.3d 932 (5th Cir. 1996) cert. denied 116 S.Ct. 2582 (1996)

Internat.'l Brotherhood of Teamsters v. U.S. 431 U.S. 324 (1971)

Johnson v. Santa Clara County Transportation Agency 480 U.S. 616 (1987)

Lau v. Nichols 414 U.S. 563 (1974)

Local 28 of the Sheet Metal Workers' International Assoc. v. EEOC 478 U.S. 421 (1986)

Local No. 93 International Assoc. of Firefighters v. City of Cleveland 478 U.S. 501 (1986)

McLaughlin v. Florida 379 U.S. 184 (1964)

Metro Broadcasting v. FCC 110 S.Ct. 2297 (1990)

Muller v. Oregon 208 U.S. 412 (1908)

Plessy v. Ferguson 163 U.S. 537 (1896)

Podberesky v. Kirwan 38 F.3d 147 (4th Cir. 1994) cert. denied 115th Ct. 2001 (1995)

Regents of the University of California v. Bakke 438 U.S. 265 (1978)

Shaw v. Reno 113 S.Ct. 2816 (1993)

Swann v. Charlotte-Mecklenburg Board of Education 402 U.S. 1 (1971)

Sweatt v. Painter 339 U.S. 629 (1950)

Taxman v. Board of Education of the Township of Piscataway 91 F.3d 1547 (1996)

United Jewish Organizations v. Carey 430 U.S. 144 (1977)
United States v. Montgomery County Board of Education 395 U.S. 225
(1969)
United States v. Paradise 480 U.S. 149 (1987)
United Steelworkers of America AFL-CIO v. Weber 443 U.S. 193 (1979)
Wygant v. Jackson Board of Education 476 U.S. 267 (1986)

Canada

Action Travail des Femmes v. Canadian National Railway Co. (1987) 1
S.C.R. 1114
Andrews v. Law Society of British Columbia (1989) 10 C.H.R.R. D/5719
NCARR v. Health Canada (1997) 28 C.H.R.R. D/179
Re Athabasca Tribal Council v. Amoco Canada Petroleum Company Ltd.
(1981) 1 S.C.R. 699
The Ontario Court of Appeal in Lovelace v. Ontario (1997) 33 O.R. 3d.
735, under appeal of the SCC
Weatherall v. Canada (Attorney General) (1993) 1 S.C.R. 872

European Union

Badeck (Case C-158/97) pending
Bilka-Kaufhaus GmbH v. Karin Weber von Hartz (Case 170/84) (1986)
ECR 1607
Colson v. Kalmann (Case 14/83) (1984) ECR 1891
Commission v. United Kingdom (Case 248/83) (1984) ECR 3431
Danfoss (Case 109/88) (1989) ECR 3199
Defrenne v. SABENA (Defrenne II) (Case 43/75) (1976) ECR 455
Gerster v. Freistaat Bayern (Case C-1/95) (1997) ECR I-5253
Harz v. Deutsche Tradax (Case 79/83) (1984) ECR 1921
Kalanke v. Freie Hansestadt Bremen (Case C-450/93) (1995) ECR I-3051
Marschall v. Land Nordrhein-Westfalen (Case C-409/95) (1997) ECR
Megner and Scheffel v. Innungskrankenkasse Vorderpfalz (Case C-444/
93) (1995) ECR I-4741
Royal Copenhagen (Case C-400/93) (1995) ECR I-1275
Seymour-Smith and Perez (Case C-167/97) 9 February 1999, not yet
reported
Smith (Case 129/79) (1980) ECR 1275
Stoeckel (Criminal Proceedings v. Stoeckel) (Case C-345/89) (1991) ECR
I-4321

Bibliography

Abell, Paul (1997). Case Studies of Good Practice for the Prevention of Racial Discrimination and Xenophobia and the Promotion of Equal Treatment at the Workplace: The Netherlands, Dublin: European Foundation for the Improvement of Living and Working Conditions, WP/97/44/EN.

Abram, Morris B. (1986). Affirmative Action: Fair Shakers and Social Engineers, in: Harvard Law Review, 100.

Alexander, Larry (1997). Affirmative Action and Legislative Purpose, in: Yale Law Journal, 107.

Allen, Anita (1996). Affirmative Action, in: A. Saltzman, D. Smith and C. West (eds), Encyclopedia of African-American Culture and History, New York: Macmillan.

Antoniolli Deflorian, Luisa (1996). The Dilemma of Affirmative Actions: A Comparison of European Community Law and the American Experience, in: I. Cameron and A. Simoni (eds), Dealing with European Integration, Uppsala: Iustus.

Antoniolli Deflorian, Luisa (1997). Breve quadro ricostruttivo delle azioni positive nel sistema giuridico statunitense, in: S. Scarponi (cur.), Le pari opportunità nella rappresentanza politica e nell'accesso al lavoro, Trento: Dip. Scienze Giuridiche.

Appelt, Erna (1998). Combating Racial Discrimination: 'Affirmative Action' as a Model for Europe? Innsbruck: Department of Political Science, University of Innsbruck, Austria.

Asscher-Vonk, Irene (1999). Towards One Concept of Objective Justification, in: Titia Loenen and Peter R. Rodrigues (eds), Non-Discrimination Law: Comparative Perspectives, The Hague: Kluwer.

Bäck, Henry and Maritta Soininen (1998). Immigrants in the Political Process, in: Scandinavian Political Studies, 21.

Banton, Michael (1997). The Ethics of Practice-Testing, New Community, 23 (3).

Banton, Michael (1999). National Variations in Conceptions of Racism, Migration, Vol. 38.

Bauböck, Rainer (1995). The Integration of Immigrants, Council of Europe, Reprint No.15. Wien: Institut für höhere Studien.

Bell, Derrick (1992). Faces at the Bottom of the Well: The Permanence of Racism, New York: Basic Books.

Bell, Mark (1998). EU Anti-Discrimination Policy: From Equal Opportunities between Women and Men to Combating Racism, European Parliament, Directorate General for Research, Working Document LIBE 102 EN, Luxembourg: Office for Official Publications of the European Communities.

Belz, Herman, (1984). Affirmative Action from Kennedy to Reagan: Redefining American Equality, Washington.

Berman, Harold J. (1983). Law and Revolution – The Formation of the Western Legal Tradition, Cambridge, Ma.: Harvard University Press.

Berry, Mary Frances (1997). Pie in the Sky? Clinton's Race Initiative Offers Promise and Potential Perils, Emerge, 9.

Berry, Mary Frances (1999). The Pig Farmer's Daughter and Other Tales of American Justice, New York: Knopf.

Berry, Mary Frances and John W. Blassingame (1982). Long Memory: The Black Experience in America, New York: Oxford University Press.

Blakemore, Ken and Robert Drake (1996). Understanding Equal Opportunity Policies, Harvester Wheatsheaf: Prentice Hall.

Blumrosen, Alfred W. (1993). Society in Transition IV: Affirmation of Affirmative Action under the Civil Rights Act of 1991, in: Rutgers Law Review, 94.

Bonacich, Edna (1972). A Theory of Ethnic Antagonism: The Split Labor Market, in: American Sociological Review, 37.

Bovenkerk, Frank (1992). Testing Discrimination in Natural Experiments: A Manual for International Comparative Research on Discrimination on the Grounds of ‚Race' and Ethnic Origin, Geneva: International Labour Office.

Bovenkerk, Frank, Mitzi Gras and D. Ramsoedh (1995). Discrimination against Migrant Workers and Ethnic Minorities in Access to Employment in the Netherlands, Geneva: International Labour Office.

Bowen, William G. and Derek Bok (1998). The Shape of the River: Long Term Consequences of Considering Race in College and University Admissions, Princeton, NJ: Princeton University Press.

Boxhill, Bernard (1984). Blacks and Social Justice, Totowa, New Jersey: Rowman & Littlefield.

Bronner, Ethan (1999). Conservatives Open Drive against Affirmative Action, in: New York Times, January 26.

Brüggemann, Beate and Rainer Riehle (1997). Case Studies of Good Practice for the Prevention of Racial Discrimination and Xenophobia and the Promotion of Equal Treatment at the Workplace: Germany,

Dublin: European Foundation for the Improvement of Living and Working Conditions, WP/97/39/EN.

Cachón, Lorenzo (1997). Case Studies of Good Practice for the Prevention of Racial Discrimination and Xenophobia and the Promotion of Equal Treatment at the Workplace: Spain, Dublin: European Foundation for the Improvement of Living and Working Conditions, WP/97/46/EN.

Cahn, Steven M. (ed.) (1995). The Affirmative Action Debate, New York: Routledge.

Capaldi, Nicholas (1985). Out of Order: Affirmative Action and the Crisis of Doctrinaire Liberalism, Buffalo, New York: Prometheus Books.

Carens, Joseph H. and Melissa S. Williams (1996). Muslim Minorities in Liberal Democracies: The Politics of Misrecognition, in: Rainer Bauböck, A. Heller and A. Zolberg (eds), The Challenge of Diversity: Integration and Pluralism in Societies of Immigration, Aldershot: Avebury Press.

Carrera, Francesa, Francesco Ciafaloni and Maria I. Mirabile (1997). Case Studies of Good Practice for the Prevention of Racial Discrimination and Xenophobia and the Promotion of Equal Treatment at the Workplace: Italy, Dublin: European Foundation for the Improvement of Living and Working Conditions, WP/97/42/EN.

Carter, Steven L. (1991). Reflections of an Affirmative Action Baby, New York: Basic Books.

Cashman, Sean D. (1990). African Americans and the Quest for Civil Rights, 1900-1990, New York: New York University Press.

Castelain-Kinet, F., S. Bouquin, H. Delagrange and T. Denutte (1998). Pratiques de formations antidiscriminatoires en Belgique, Geneva: International Labour Office.

Castles, Stephen (1993). Migrations and Minorities in Europe. Perspectives for the 1990s: Eleven Hypotheses, in: John Wrench, John Solomos (eds). Racism and Migration in Western Europe, Oxford/Providence.

Castles, Stephen (1995). How Nation-States Respond to Immigration and Ethnic Diversity, New Community, Vol. 21 (3).

CEC (Commission of the European Communities) (1993). Legal Instruments to Combat Racism and Xenophobia, Luxembourg: Commission of the European Communities, Office for Official Publications of the European Communities.

Chavez, Lydia (1998). The Color Bind: California´s Battle to End Affirmative Action, Berkeley: University of California Press.

Chilton, Paul and Christina Schäffner (1997). Discourse and Politics, in: Teun van Dijk (ed.), Discourse as Social Interaction. Discourse Studies: A Multidisciplinary Introduction, Vol. 2, London: Sage.

Chopin, Isabelle and Jan Niessen (eds) (1998). Proposals for Legislative Measures to Combat Racism and to Promote Equal Rights in the European Union, London: The Commission for Racial Equality.

Cinar, Dilek, Christoph Hofinger and Harald Waldrauch (1995). Integrationsindex. Zur rechtlichen Integration von AusländerInnen in ausgewählten europäischen Ländern, Reihe Politikwissenschaft, Bd. 25, Wien: IHS-Publikationen.

Cohen, William and Jonathan D. Varat (1997). Constitutional Law – Cases and Materials, Westbury, Conn.: Foundation.

Colectivo IOE: Miguel A. de Prada, Walter Actis, Carlos Pereda and Pérez R. Molina (1996). Labour Market Discrimination against Migrant Workers in Spain, Geneva: International Labour Office.

Cooper, Kenneth J. (1998). Where Quotas Work Some Countries Mandate Affirmative Action, Emerge IX, May.

CRE (Commission for Racial Equality) (1985). Positive Action and Equal Opportunity in Employment, London: Commission for Racial Equality.

Crenshaw, Kimberle (1992). Whose Story Is It, Anyway? Feminist and Antiracist Appropriations of Anita Hill, in: Toni Morrison (ed.), Race-ing Justice, En-gendering Power: Essays on Anita Hill, Clarence Thomas, and the Contraction of Social Reality, New York: Pantheon.

CUCO (Commission on University Career Opportunity) (1994). A Report on Universities' Policies and Practices on Equal Opportunities in Employment, London: CUCO.

CUCO (Commission on University Career Opportunity) (1996). Equality Targets – Action Planning and Monitoring in Universities and Colleges, London: CUCO.

Cunningham, Frank (1987). Democratic Theory and Socialism, Cambridge, Ma.: Cambridge University Press.

Cunningham, Frank (1994). The Real World of Democracy Revisited, Atlantic Highlands, NJ: Humanities Press.

D´Souza, Dinesh (1996). The End of Racism: Principles for a Multiracial Society, New York: Free Press.

Dahlem, Rainer (1998). Verbote stärken den Fundamentalismus, Frankfurter Allgemeine Sontagszeitung, 19.7.1998.

Dahya, Bhadra (1973). Pakistanis in Britain: Transients or Settlers, in: Race, No. 14.

Dahya, Bhadra (1974). The Nature of Pakistani Ethnicity in Industrial Cities in Britain, in: Abner Cohen (ed.), Urban Ethnicity, ASA Monograph, No. 12, London: Tavistock.

Daniel, Jack and Anita Allen (1988). Newsmagazines and the Black

Agenda, in: G. Smitherman-Donaldson and Teun van Dijk (eds), Discrimination and Discourse, Detroit: Wayne State University.

Day, S. (1990). Equality Seekers Troubled by Affirmative Action Rulings, 6 Can. Human Rights Advocate, 1.

De Rudder, Véronique, Christian Poiret and François Vourc'h (1997). Case Studies of Good Practice for the Prevention of Racial Discrimination and Xenophobia and the Promotion of Equal Treatment at the Workplace: France, Dublin: European Foundation for the Improvement of Living and Working Conditions, WP/97/38/EN.

De Rudder, Véronique, Maryse Tripier and François Vourc'h (1995). Prevention of Racism at the Workplace in France, Dublin: European Foundation for the Improvement of Living and Working Conditions.

Diskriminerings Ombudsman (1990). De fyra första åren: en redovisning, Motala: Borgströms Tryckeri.

Drake, W. Avon and Robert D. Holsworth (1996). Affirmative Action and the Stalled Quest for Black Progress, Urbana: University of Illinois Press.

Dummett, Ann (1994). Citizens, Minorities and Foreigners: A Guide to the EC, London: Commission for Racial Equality.

Dworkin, Ronald (1977). Umgekehrte Diskriminierung, in: Beate Rössler (ed.) (1993). Quotierung und Gerechtigkeit. Eine moralphilosophische Kontroverse, Frankfurt/New York: Campus Verlag.

Dworkin, Ronald (1986). Law's Empire, Cambridge, Ma.: Harvard University Press.

Dworkin, Ronald (1987). Taking Rights Seriously, London: Duckworth (first ed. 1977).

Dworkin, Ronald (1996). Freedom's Law. The Moral Reading of the American Constitution, Oxford: Oxford University Press.

Dworkin, Ronald (1998). Is Affirmative Action Doomed? In: The New York Review, November 5.

Eastland, Terry and William Bennett (1979). Counting by Race: Equality from the Founding Fathers to Bakke und Weber, New York: Basic Books.

Economic Report of the President (1998). Economic Report of the President Transmitted to the Congress, February 1998 together with the Annual Report of the Council of Economic Advisers, Washington DC: US Government Printing Office.

Edelman, Murray (1988). Constructing the Political Spectacle, Chicago: University of Chicago Press.

Edley, Christopher Jr. (1996). Not All Black and White: Affirmative Action, Race and American Values, New York: Hill & Wang.

Ellis, Evelyn (1998). Recent Developments in European Community Sex Equality Law, in: Common Market Law Review, 35.

Employment Department (1993). Equal Opportunities: Ten Point Plan for Employers, Sheffield.

EOR (Equal Opportunities Review) (1987). Achieving Equal Opportunity Through Positive Action, No. 14.

EOR (Equal Opportunities Review) (1990). Positive Action in the West Midlands, No. 30.

EOR (Equal Opportunities Review) (1991). Ethnic Minorities in Finance: a Sheffield Initiative, No. 35.

EOR (Equal Opportunities Review) (1994). Positive Action for Race: Madness, Positive Discrimination or a Sound Business Approach, No. 58.

Erzorsky, Gertrude (1991). Racism and Justice: The Case for Affirmative Action, Ithaca, New York: Cornell University Press.

Esmail, Aziz AND S. Everington (1993). Racial Discrimination against Doctors from Ethnic Minorities, British Medical Journal, 306 March.

Eurobarometer (1998). Report Number 48, ed. by European Commission, Brussels.

European Commission (ed.) (1997). The European Institutions in the fight against racism: Selected texts, Brussels.

European Parliament (1995). Confronting the Fortress. Black and Migrant Women in the European Union, Luxembourg/Brussels.

Fakiolas, Rossetos (1997). Case Studies of Good Practice for the Prevention of Racial Discrimination and Xenophobia and the Promotion of Equal Treatment at the Workplace: Greece, Dublin: European Foundation for the Improvement of Living and Working Conditions, WP/97/40/EN.

Farber, Daniel A. (1994). The Outmoded Debate over Affirmative Action, in: Californian Law Review, 82.

Faundez, Julio (1994). Affirmative Action: International Perspectives, Geneva: International Labour Office.

Fenwick, Ellen and Tamara Hervey (1995). Sex Equality in the Single Market: New Directions for the European Court of Justice, Common Market Law Review, 32.

Finch, Minnie (1981). The NAACP: Its Fight for Justice, Metuchen, New Jersey: Scarecrow.

Flynn, Padraig (1998). Speech: Anti-Discrimination: The Way Forward. Conference on Anti-discrimination, Vienna, December 4 1998. (http://europa.eu.int/rapidsta..oc=SPEECH/98/282/0/RAPID&lg=EN).

Forbes, Ian and Geoffrey Mead (1992). Measure for Measure, London: Employment Department Research Series, No. 1.

Franklin, John H. (1959). Jim Crow Goes to School. The Genesis of Legal Segregation in Southern Schools, South Atlantic Quarterly LVIII.

Franklin, John H. (1989). Race and History: Selected Essays, 1938–1988, Baton Rouge: Louisiana State University Press.

Fraser, Nancy (1997). Justice Interruptus: Critical Reflections on the ‚Postsocialist' Condition, New York: Routledge.

Fredman, Sandra (1997). Women and the Law, Oxford: Clarendon Press.

Fried, Charles (1989). Affirmative Action after City of Richmond v. J.A. Croson Co.: A Response to the Scholar's Statement, in: Yale Law Journal, 99.

Fullinwider, Robert (1977). On preferential hiring, in: Mary Vetterling-Braggin, Frederick Elliston, Jane English (eds). Feminism and philosophy, Totowa, NJ: Littlefield, Adams Totowa.

Fullinwider, Robert K. (1980). The Reverse Discrimination Controversy: A Moral and Legal Analysis, Totowa, NJ: Rowman & Littlefield.

Gächter, August (1997). Case Studies of Good Practice for the Prevention of Racial Discrimination and Xenophobia and the Promotion of Equal Treatment at the Workplace: Austria, Dublin: European Foundation for the Improvement of Living and Working Conditions, WP/97/34/EN.

Girnth, Heiko (1996). Texte im politischen Diskurs. Ein Vorschlag zur diskursorientierten Beschreibung von Textsorten, in: Muttersprache, 106/1.

Glazer, Nathan (1964). Negroes and Jews: The New Challenge to Pluralism, Commentary, December.

Glazer, Nathan (1981). The United States, in: Robert G. Wirsing (ed.), Protection of Ethnic Minorities: Ethnic Perspectives, New York: Pergamon Press.

Glazer, Nathan (1983). Ethnic Dilemmas 1964 to 1982, Cambridge, Ma.: Harvard University Press.

Glazer, Nathan (1987). Affirmative Discrimination: Ethnic Inequality and Public Policy, Cambridge, Ma.: Harvard University Press.

Glazer, Nathan (1997). We Are All Multiculturalists Now, Cambridge, Ma.: Harvard University Press.

Glazer, Nathan (1998). In Defense of Preference, in: The New Republic, April 6.

Glazer, Nathan (1999). The Public Interest, 135, Washington: Winter.

Goldberg, Andreas, Dora Mourinho and Ursula Kulke (1995). Labour Market Discrimination against Foreign Workers in Germany, Geneva: International Labour Office.

Goldberg, David T. (1993). Racist Culture: Philosophy and the Politics of Meaning, Oxford: Blackwell.

Goldberg, David T. (1997). Multiculturalism: A Critical Reader, Boston, Ma.: Blackwell Publishing.

Goldman, Alan (1979). Justice and Reverse Discrimination, Princeton: Princeton University Press.

Gould, Carol (1996). Diversity and Democracy: Representing Differences, in: Seyla Benhabib (ed.), Democracy and Difference, Princeton, NJ: Princeton University Press.

Graham, Mark and Maritta Soininen (1998). A Model for Immigrants? The Swedish Corporate Model and the Prevention of Ethnic Discrimination, in: Journal of Ethnic and Migration Studies, Vol. 24 (3).

Greenawalt, Kent (1983). Discrimination and Reverse Discrimination, New York: Knopf.

Greene, Kathanne W. (1989). Affirmative Action and Principles of Justice, New York: Greenwood Press.

Greenhouse, Linda (1998). Supreme Court Weaves Legal Principles From a Tangle of Litigation, in: New York Times, June 30.

Gutmann, Amy and Dennis Thompson (1996). Democracy and Disagreement, Cambridge, Ma.: Harvard University Press.

Hancock, Lynn (1994). Tenant Participation and the Housing Class Debate, Ph. D. Thesis: University of Liverpool.

Hasselbach, Kai (1998). Der Schutz von Verbandsinteressen vor dem EuGH, Zeitschrift für Zivilprozeßrecht, 109.

Heckmann, Friedrich (1992). Ethnische Minderheiten, Volk und Nation. Soziologie inter-ethnischer Beziehungen, Stuttgart.

Heringa, Alt W. (1994). Algemene wet gelijke behandeling, Deventer: Kluwer.

Herring, Cedric and Sharon M. Collins (1995). Retreat for Equal Opportunity? The Case for Affirmative Action, in: M. P. Smith and J. R. Feagin (eds), The Bubbling Cauldron: Race, Ethnicity, and the Urban Crisis, Minneapolis: University of Minnesota Press.

Hervey, Tamara (1996). The Future for Sex Equality Law in the European Union, in: Tamara Hervey and David O'Keefe, Sex Equality Law in the European Union, Chichester: Wiley.

Hill, Michael (1997). The Policy Process in the Modern State, Harvester Wheatsheaf: Prentice Hall.

Hill, Robert B. (1988). Structural Discrimination: The Unintended Consequences of Institutional Processes, in: H. J. O'Gorman (ed.), Surveying Social Life: Essays in Honor of Herbert H. Hyman, Middletown, Ct.: Wesleyan University Press.

Hjarnø, Jan and Torben Jensen (1997). Diskrimineringen af unge med invandrerbaggrund ved jobsøgning, Esbjerg: Migration Papers, No. 21, South Jutland University Press.

Hödl, Gertraud and Petra Winter (1998). Auf der Suche nach einem sicheren Hafen. Zur rechtlichen Stellung und Lebenssituation von Fremden in Österreich, Wien: International Helsinki Federation for Human Rights.

Hondius, Ewoud (1996). The Dutch Act on Group Action/Consumer Protection as a Catalyst of Law Reform, in: Hans-Wolfgang Micklitz (ed.), Rechtseinheit oder Rechtsvielfalt in Europa? Rolle und Funktion des Verbraucherrechts in der EG und den MOE-Staaten, Baden-Baden: Nomos.

Horne, Gerald (1992). Reversing Discrimination: the Case for Affirmative Action, New York: International Publisher.

Horwitz, Morton J. (1992). The Transformation of American Law, 1870–1960, New York: Oxford University Press.

Hubbuck, Jim and Simon Carter (1980). Half a Chance? A Report on Job Discrimination against Young Blacks in Nottingham, London: Commission for Racial Equality.

Human Resources Development of Canada (1997). Annual Report: Employment Equity (1997), Ottawa: Minister of Supply and Services, Canada.

Ignatiev, Noel (1996). How the Irish Became White, New York: Routledge.

Institut für Migrations- und Rassismusforschung (1992). Rassismus und Migration in Europa. Beiträge des Hamburger Kongresses "Migration und Rassismus in Europa" (26. bis 30. September 1990), Hamburg/Berlin: Argument-Verlag.

Jacobson, Matthew F. (1998). Whiteness of a Different Color, Cambridge, Ma.: Harvard University Press.

Jenkins, Richard and John Solomos (1987). Racism and Equal Opportunity Policies in the 1980s, Cambridge: Cambridge University Press.

Jewson, Nick and David Mason (1992). The Theory and Practice of Equal Opportunity Policies: Liberal and Radical Approaches, in: Peter Braham, Ali Rattansi and Richard Skellington (eds), Racism and Anti-Racism, Inequalities, Opportunities and Policies, London: Sage/Open University Press.

Jewson, Nick, David Mason, Alison Drewett and Will Rossiter (1995). Formal Equal Opportunities Policies and Employment Best Practice, Department for Education and Employment Research Series, No. 69, Sheffield.

Johnson, Alex M. (1992). Defending the Use of Quotas in Affirmative Action: Attacking Racism in the Nineties, University of Illinois Law Review, 43.

Johnson, Lyndon B. (1967). Commencement Address, Howard University,

June 1965, in: William L. Yancey and Lee Rainwater (eds), The Moynihan Report and the Politics of Controversy, Cambridge, Ma.: MIT Press.

Joint Statement (1989). Constitutional Scholars' Statement on Affirmative Action after City of Richmond v. J.A. Croson Co., in: Yale Law Journal.

Jones, Augustus J. (1991). Affirmative Talk, Affirmative Action: a Comparative Study of the Politics of Affirmative Action, New York: Praeger.

Kahlenberg, Richard (1996). The Remedy: Class, Race and Affirmative Action, New York: Basic Books.

Keat, Russell and Nicholas Abercrombie (eds) (1991). The Enterprise Culture, London: Routledge.

Kennedy, Randall (1986). Persuasion and Distrust: A Comment on the Affirmative Action Debate, in: Harvard Law Review, 100.

Kerner Commission Report (1968). The Report of the National Advisory Commission on Civil Disorders, New York: Bantam.

Kienpointner, Manfred (1992). Alltagslogik. Struktur und Funktion von Argumentationsmustern, Stuttgart, Bad Cannstatt: frommann-holzboog.

King, Martin L. (1964). Why We Can't Wait, New York: Signet.

Kovig, David (1996). Explicit and Authentic Acts: Amending the US Constitution, 1776–1995, Lawrence: University Press of Kansas.

Krouse, Richard (1983). Classical Images of Democracy in America: Madison and Tocqueville, in: Graeme Duncan (ed.), Democratic Theory and Practice, Cambridge, Ma.: Cambridge University Press.

Kull, Andrew (1992). The Color-Blind Constitution, Cambridge, Ma.: Harvard University Press.

Kymlicka, Will (1995). Multicultural Citizenship, London: Oxford University Press.

Lawrence, Charles R. and Mari J. Matsuda (1997). We Won't Go Back: Making the Case for Affirmative Action, Boston: Houghton Mifflin.

Layton-Henry, Zig (1994). Britain: The Would-be Zero-Immigration Country, in: Wayne Cornelius, Philip L. Martin and James F. Hollifield (eds), Controlling Immigration. A Global Perspective, Stanford, Ca.: Stanford University Press.

Lee, Gloria and John Wrench (1983). Skill Seekers — Black Youth, Apprenticeships and Disadvantage, Leicester: National Youth Bureau.

Lewin, Tamar (1998). American Colleges Begin to Ask, Where Have All the Men Gone? In: New York Times, December 6.

Lewis, Oscar (1973). Five Families: Mexican Case Studies in the Culture of Poverty, London: Souvenir Press.

Lindbeck, Assar (1997). The Swedish Experiment, Stockholm: SNS Förlag.

Lipsky, Michael (1980). Street-Level Bureaucracy, New York: Russell Sage Foundation.

Livingston, John C. (1979). Fair Game? Inequality and Affirmative Action, San Francisco: W.H. Freeman.

Loury, Glenn (1988). Why Should We Care About Group Inequality? In: Social Philosophy and Policy 5.

Loury, Glenn (1995). One By One From the Inside Out: Essays on Race and Responsibility, New York: Free Press.

Lowi, Theodore (1972). Four Systems of Policy, Politics and Choice, in: Public Administration Review 32.

Lustgarten, Laurence and John Edwards (1992). Racial Inequality and the Limits of the Law, in: Peter Braham, Ali Rattansi and Richard Skellington (eds), Racism and Antiracism: Inequalities, Opportunities and Policies, London: Sage/Open University Press.

MacEwen, Martin (1995). Tackling Racism in Europe, Oxford: Berg.

MacEwen, Martin (ed.) (1997). Anti-Discrimination Law Enforcement: A Comparative Perspective, Aldershot: Avebury.

Majone, Giandomenico (1996). Sozialregulative und distributive Politik, in: Markus Jachtenfuchs and Beate Kohler-Koch (eds), Europäische Integration, Opladen: Leske und Budrich.

Marshall, Gordon (ed.) (1994). The Concise Oxford Dictionary of Sociology, New York: Oxford University Press.

Marshall, Thomas H. (1951). Citizenship and Social Class, Cambridge, Ma.: Cambridge University Press.

Martens, Albert and Katia Sette (1997). Case Studies of Good Practice for the Prevention of Racial Discrimination and Xenophobia and the Promotion of Equal Treatment at the Workplace: Belgium, Dublin: European Foundation for the Improvement of Living and Working Conditions, WP/97/35/EN.

Mattei, Ugo (1992). Common Law, in Trattato di diritto comparato, Torino: UTET.

Mattei, Ugo (1994). Etnocentrismo, neutralità e discriminazione. Tensioni nel diritto occidentale, in: Giur. It., 11, IV.

Mattei, Ugo (1996). Il modello di common law, Torino: Giappichelli.

Mayer, Jane and Jill Abramson (1994). Strange Justice: The Selling of Clarence Thomas, New York: Houghton Mifflin.

McCrudden, Christopher (1999). Specific Problems Regarding Enforcement of Anti-Discrimination Law and Strategies to Overcome them, in: Titia Loenen and Peter R. Rodrigues, Non-Discrimination Law: Comparative Perspectives, Dordrecht: Kluwer.

McGary, Howard Jr. (1977–78). Justice and Reparations, in: Philosophical Forum 9.

McWhirter, Darien A. (1996). The End of Affirmative Action, New York: Birch Lane Press.

Mehrländer, Ursula et al. (1996). Repräsentativuntersuchung 95: Situation der ausländischen Arbeitnehmer und ihrer Familienangehörigen in der Bundesrepublik Deutschland, Bonn: Forschungsbericht des Bundesministeriums für Arbeit und Soziales, Sozialforschung, Nr. 263.

Micklitz, Hans-Wolfgang and Norbert Reich (eds) (1996). Public Interest Litigation before European Courts, Baden-Baden: Nomos.

Miles, Robert (1991). Rassismus. Einführung in die Geschichte und Theorie eines Begriffs, Hamburg: Argument.

Mills, Charles (1997). The Racial Contract, Ithaca: Cornell University Press.

Mirza, Qudsia (1995). Race Relations in the Workplace, London: The Institute of Employment Rights.

Mitten, Richard (1992). The Politics of Anti-Semitic Prejudice. The Waldheim Phenomenon in Austria, Boulder: Westview Press.

Moens, Gabriel A. (1997). Equal Opportunities not Equal Results: ´Equal Opportunity´, in: European Law after Kalanke, 23 Journal of Legislation, 43.

Montgomery, Edward (1996). A Look at Affirmative Action and Reparations in the United States, in: International Policy Review, 6 (1).

Moore, Robert (1997). Positive Action in Action, Aldershot: Ashgate.

Mosley, Albert G. (1992). Affirmative Action and the Urban Underclass, in: The Underclass Question, Philadelphia: Temple University.

Mosley, Albert G. and Nicholas Capaldi (1996). Affirmative Action: Social Justice or Unfair Preference, Lanham, Rowman & Littlefield.

Münz, Rainer (1996). A continent of migration: European mass migration in the twentieth century, New Community, 21 (3).

Myrdal, Gunnar (1964). Challenge to Affluence, New York: Macmillan.

Nager, Glen D. (1993). Affirmative Action after the Civil Rights Act of 1991: The Effects of a 'Neutral' Statute, in: Notre Dame Law Review, 68.

Newton, Lisa (1973). Reverse Discrimination as Unjustified, in: Ethics, 83.

Nicolodi, Camilla (1994). 'Affirmative Action' – Un dilemma americano, Graduate Dissertation, University of Trento: Faculty of Law.

O'Brien, David M. (1997). Constitutional Law and Politics, Vol. 2, New York: Norton.

Okin, Susan M. (1989). Justice, Gender and the Family, New York: Basic Books.

Oppenheim, Felix (1971). Democracy – Characteristics Included and Excluded, in: The Monist, Vol. 55 (2).

Pahl, Raymond (ed.) (1969). Readings in Urban Sociology, London: Pergamon Press.

Palma, Carlos, Maria Leonor and Carlos Dias da Silva (1997). Case Studies of Good Practice for the Prevention of Racial Discrimination and Xenophobia and the Promotion of Equal Treatment at the Workplace: Portugal, Dublin: European Foundation for the Improvement of Living and Working Conditions, WP/97/45/EN.

Pateman, Carole (1988). The Sexual Contract, Stanford: Stanford University Press.

Patterson, James (1996). Grand Expectations: Postwar America, 1945–1974, New York: Oxford University Press.

Pentney, W. (1985). Discrimination and the Law, Canada: Thomson Professional Publishing.

Pfarr, Heide and Eva Kocher (1998). Kollektivverfahren im Arbeitsrecht: Arbeitnehmerschutz und Gleichberechtigung durch Verfahren, Baden-Baden: Nomos.

Piper, Nicola (1998). Racism, Nationalism and Citizenship: Ethnic Minorities in Britain and Germany, Aldershot: Ashgate.

Player, Mack A., Elaine W. Shoben and Risa L. Lieberwitz (1995). Employment Discrimination Law – Cases and Materials, St. Paul, Minn.: West.

Plous, Scott (1996). Ten Myths about Affirmative Action, in: Journal of Social Issues, 52 (4).

Pollert, Anna and Teresa Rees (1992). Equal Opportunity and Positive Action in Britain: Three Case Studies, Warwick Papers in Industrial Relations, No. 42, Coventry: University of Warwick.

Porter, Aaron (forthcomming). W.E.B. DuBois and Social Responsibility: An Essay on Leadership in Social and Political Context, in: Clark Cunningham (ed.), (forthcoming), New York: Oxford University Press.

Posner, Richard (1979). The Bakke Case and the Future of 'Affirmative Action', in: California Law Review.

Premfors, Rune (1996). Reshaping the Democratic State: Swedish Experience in a Comparative Perspective, Stockholm: Center for Organisational Research.

Radtke, Frank-Olaf (1994). The Formation of Ethnic Minorities and the Transformation of Social into Ethnic Conflicts in the So-Called Multicultural Society – The German Case, in: J Rex. and B. Drury (eds) (1994). Ethnic Mobilization in a Multicultural Europe, Aldershot: Avebury Press.

Rae, Douglas et al. (1981). Equalities, Cambridge, Ma.: Harvard University Press.

Rath, Jan (1991). Minosering: De social constructe van ethnische Minderheden, Ph.D. Thesis: University of Utrecht.

Rawls, John (1971). A Theory of Justice, Cambridge, Ma.: Harvard University Press.

Reisigl, Martin and Ruth Wodak (2000a). The Linguistic and Rhetorical Analysis of Racism and Anti-Semitism, in: Ruth Wodak and Martin Reisigl (eds). Discourse and Discrimination. The Rhetorics of Racism and Antisemitism (in print).

Reisigl, Martin and Ruth Wodak (2000b). 'Austria First.' A Discourse-Historical Analysis of the Austrian 'Anti-Foreigner-Petition' in 1993, in: Ruth Wodak and Martin Reisigl (eds), The Semiotics of Racism, Vienna: Passagen Verlag (in print).

Rex, John (1996). Ethnic Minorities in the Modern Nation State, New York: Macmillan, Basingstoke and St. Martin' s Press.

Rex, John (1999). Political Sociology and Cultural Studies in the Study of Migrant Communities in Europe. Paper delivered to a Conference on 'Pluralisme culturale, mettisage ed identita miste', organized by the Commune di Firenze and The University of Florence, September 1997 (in print).

Rex, John and Robert Moore (1967). Race. Community and Conflict, London: Oxford University Press and the Institute of Race Relations.

Riksrevisionsverket (RRV) (1996). Förvaltningspolitik i förändring: en kartläggning och analys av regeringens styrning av statsförvaltningen, Stockholm.

Rodrigues, Peter (1997). Anders Niets? Discriminatie naar ras en nationaliteit bij consumententransacties, Leylystaad: Koninglijke Vermande.

Roediger, David S. (1991). The Wages of Whiteness: Race and the Making of the American Working Class, New York: Verso.

Rössler, Beate (ed.) (1993). Quotierung und Gerechtigkeit. Eine moralphilosophische Kontroverse, Frankfurt/New York: Campus Verlag.

Rojo, Luisa M. and Teun van Dijk (1997). 'There Was a Problem and It Was Solved!' Legitimating the Expulsion of 'Illegal' Migrants in Spanish Parliamentary Discourse, in: Discourse & Society, 8 (4).

Rosenfeld, Michel (1991). Affirmative Action and Justice – A Philosophical and Constitutional Enquiry, New Haven, Conn.: Yale University Press.

Rossum, Ralph A. (1980). Reverse Discrimination: The Constitutional Debate, New York: M. Decker.

Rothstein, Bo (1986). Den socialdemokratiska staten: Reformer och förvaltning inom svensk arbetsmarknad- och skolpolitik, Lund: Arkiv.

Rothstein, Bo (1994). Vad bör staten göra? Stockholm: SNS Förlag.

Rothstein, Bo (1998). Just Institutions Matter: The Moral and Political Logic of the Universal Welfare State, Cambridge, Ma.: Cambridge University Press.

Rotunda, Ronald D. (1993). The Civil Rights Act of 1991: A Brief Introductory Analysis of the Congressional Response to Judicial Interpretation, in: Notre Dame Law Review, 68.

Rubenfeld, Jed (1997). Affirmative Action, in: Yale Law Journal, 107.

Rubenstein, Michael (1987). Modern Myths and Misconceptions: 1 'Equal Opportunities Makes Good Business Sense', in: Equal Opportunities Review, No. 16, November–December.

Sabatier, Paul (1986). Top-Down and Bottom-Up Approaches to Implementation Research: a Critical Analysis and Suggested Synthesis, in: Journal of Public Policy, 3.

Sacco, Rodolfo (1991). Legal Formants: A Dynamic Approach to Comparative Law, in: American Journal of Comparative Law.

Sacksofsky, Ute (1996). Das Grundrecht auf Gleichberechtigung, Baden-Baden: Nomos.

SAF (Svenska arbetsgivareföreningen) (1994). December, SAF tidning: Invandrad kompetens.

SAF (Svenska arbetsgivareföreningen) (1995). March, SAF tidning: Tema: Företagande invandrare.

Schiek, Dagmar (1996). Lifting the Ban on Women's Night Work in Europe – A Straight Road to Equality in Employment? Cardozo Women's Law Journal.

Schiek, Dagmar (1998). Sex Equality Law after Kalanke and Marschall, European Law Journal, 4.

Schierup, Carl-Ulrik and Alexandra Alund (1990). Paradoxes of Multiculturalism, Aldershot: Gower.

Schnapper, Eric (1983). The Perpetuation of Past Discrimination, Harvard Law Review, 96.

Schwartz, Bernard (1988). Behind Bakke: Affirmative Action and the Supreme Court, New York: New York University Press.

Selmi, Michael (1999). Indirect Discrimination. A Perspective from the USA, in: Titia Loenen and Peter R. Rodrigues (eds), Non-Discrimination Law: Comparative Perspectives, The Hague: Kluwer

Sher, George (1997). Approximate Justice: Studies in Non-Ideal Theory, Lanham: Rowman & Littlefield.

Simms, Margaret C. (ed.) (1995). Economic Perspectives on Affirmative

Action, Washington, DC: Joint Center for Political and Economic Studies.

Simpson, Alan and John Stevenson (1994). Half a Chance, Still? Nottingham: Nottingham and District Racial Equality Council.

Skrentny, John D. (1996). The Ironies of Affirmative Action. Politics, Culture and Justice in America, Chicago, London: The University of Chicago Press.

Smeets, H. et al. (1997). Jaarboek Minderheden 1998: Beleidsontwikkelingen – feiten en cijfers – feestdagen – adressen, Houten, Lelystad: Bohn Stafleu van Loghum, Koninklijke Vermade.

Sniderman Paul S. and Edward G. Carmines (1997). Reaching Beyond Race, Cambridge, Ma.: Harvard University Press.

Sniderman, Paul S. and Thomas Piazza (1993). The Scar of Race, Cambridge, Ma.: Harvard University Press.

Socialstyrelsen (SoS) (1995). Invandrares hälsa och sociala förhållanden, Stockholm: Socialstyrelsen.

Soininen, Maritta and Mark Graham (1995). Persuasion contra Legislation: Preventing Racism at the Workplace: Sweden, Dublin: European Foundation for the Improvement of Living and Working Conditions, WP/95/53/EN.

Soininen, Maritta and Mark Graham (1997). Case Studies of Good Practice for the Prevention of Racial Discrimination and Xenophobia and Promotion of Equal Treatment in the Workplace: Sweden, Dublin: European Foundation for the Improvement of Living and Working Conditions, WP/97/47/EN.

SOPEMI (1997). Trends in International Migration: Continuous Reporting System on Migration. Annual Report 1996, Paris: Organisation for Economic Cooperation and Development in Europe.

SOU (Statens offentliga utredningar) (1995). Arbete till invandrare, Stockholm: Fritzes.

SOU (Statens offentliga utredningar) (1996). Sverige: framtiden och mångfalden, Stockholm: Fritzes.

SOU (Statens offentliga utredningar) (1996). Sverige: framtiden och mångfalden. Stockholm: Fritzes.

SOU (Statens offentliga utredningar) (1997). Räckna med mångfald: förslag till lag mot etnisk diskriminering i arbetslivet, Stockholm: Fritzes.

SOU (Statens offentliga utredningar) (1997). I medborgarnas tjänst: en samlad förvaltningspolitik för staten, Stockholm: Fritzes.

Sowell, Thomas (1975). Affirmative Action Reconsidered: Was it Necessary in Academia, Washington: American Enterprise Institute for Public Policy.

Sowell, Thomas (1981). Ethnic America, New York: Basic Books.

Sowell, Thomas (1983). The Economics and Politics of Race. New York: W. Morrow.

Sowell, Thomas (1984). Civil Rights: Rhetoric or Reality? New York: W. Morrow.

Soysal, Yasemin (1994). Limits of Citizenship: Migrants and Post-National Membership in Europe, Chicago: University of Chicago Press.

Spann, Girardeau (1993). Race Against the Court: the Supreme Court and Minorities in Contemporary America, New York: New York University Press.

Steele, Shelby (1994). A Negative Vote on Affirmative Action, in: N. Mills (ed.), Debating Affirmative Action: Race, Gender, Ethnicity, and the Politics of Inclusion, New York: Delta.

Steele, Shelby (1998). Dream Deferred: the Second Betrayal of Black America, New York: Harper Collins.

Steinberg, Stephen (1995). Turning Back: The Retreat from Racial Justice in American Thought and Policy, Boston: Beacon Press.

Stone, Maureen (1981). The Education of Black Children in Britain: the Myth of Multicultural Education, London: Fontana Books.

Symposium (1995). Race and Remedy in a Multicultural Society, in: Stanford Law Review.

Taylor, Charles (1992). Multiculturalism and the Politics of Recognition, Princeton, NJ: Princeton University Press.

Taylor, Gill (1992). Equal Opportunities: A Practical Handbook, London: The Industrial Society.

Taylor, Paul (1996). Race for Opportunity: Market Leaders in the West Midlands. Unpublished Research Report, Centre for Research in Ethnic Relations, Coventry: University of Warwick.

Taylor, Paul, Diana Powell and John Wrench (1997). The Evaluation of Anti-Discrimination Training Activities in the United Kingdom, Geneva: International Labour Office.

tenBroek, Jacobus (1969). Equal under Law, New York: Collier.

Tesser, P. et al. (1996). Minderhedenbeleid 1997: Rapportage minderheden 1996 – Bevolking, arbeid, onderwijs, huisvesting, Rijswijk: Sociaal Cultureel Planbureau.

Theodorson, George A. and Achilles G. Theodorson (eds) (1969). A Modern Dictionary of Sociology, New York: Thomas Y. Crowell Co.

Thernstrom, Stephan (1997). The Scandal of the Law Schools, in: Commentary, December.

Thernstrom, Stephan and Abigail Thernstrom (1997). America in Black and White: One Nation, Indivisible, New York: Simon & Schuster.

Thomson, Judith J. (1977). Preferential Hiring, in: Marshall Cohen, Thomas Nagel and Thomas Scanlon (eds), Equality and Preferential Treatment, Princeton, NJ: Princeton University Press.

Tilton, Tim (1990). The Political Theory of Swedish Social Democracy, Oxford: Oxford University Press.

Traub, James (1998). Nathan Glazer Changes His Mind, Again, in: New York Times Magazine, June 28.

Ura – Report series Arbetsmarknad och arbetsmarknadpolitik: 1997, 1998.

van Dijk, Teun (1993). Elite Discourse and Racism, Newbury Park, CA: Sage.

van Dijk, Teun (1995). What is Political Discourse Analysis? Unpublished Manuscript.

van Leeuwen, Theo and Wodak, Ruth (1999). Legitimizing Immigration Control, in: Discourse Studies (in print).

Vedung, Evert (1997). Public Policy and Program Evaluation, New Brunswick: Transaction Publishers.

Veenman, J. (1995). Onbekend maakt onbemind: Over selective van allochtonen op de arbeidsmarkt, Assen: Van Gorcum.

Ventura, Caterina (1995). From Outlawing Discrimination to Promoting Equality: Canada's Experience with Anti-discrimination Legislation, Geneva: International Labour Office.

Virdee, Satnam (1997). Case Studies of Good Practice for the Prevention of Racial Discrimination and Xenophobia and the Promotion of Equal Treatment at the Workplace: The UK, Dublin: European Foundation for the Improvement of Living and Working Conditions, WP/97/48/EN.

Vizkelety, B. (1990). Affirmative Action, Equality and the Courts: Comparing Action Travail des Femmes v. CN and the Manitoba Rice Farmers Association v. The Manitoba Human Rights Commission, 4 CJWL 1990.

Wakolbinger, Eva (1995). Austria: The Danger of Populism, in: B. Baumgartl and A. Favell (eds), New Xenophobia in Europe, London: Kluwer Law International.

Walzer, Michael (1980). Pluralism: A Political Perspective, in: Harvard Encyclopaedia of Ethnic Groups, Cambridge, Ma.: Harvard University Press.

Wasmuth, Ulrike C. (1996). Rechtsextremismus. Bilanz und kritische Würdigung sozial-wissenschaftlicher Erklärungsansätze, SOWI-Arbeitspapier Nr. 96, Strausberg: Sozialwissenschaftliches Institut der Bundeswehr.

Welsh, Colin, James Knox and Mark Brett (1994). Acting Positively:

Positive Action under the Race Relations Act 1976, Employment Department Research Series, No. 36, Sheffield.

Weltzel, Dorothe (1998). Kopftuch-Symbol hinderlich auf dem Weg in gleichberechtigte Gesellschaft, in: bildung & wissenschaft, September 1998, 14.

Wentholt, Klaartje (1996). (In)compatibility of the Legal and Feminist Debate, in: Yota Kravaritou (ed.), The Sex of Labour Law in Europe, The Hague: Kluwer Law International, 1996.

Werbner, Pnina and Tariq Modood (1997). Debating Cultural Hybridity, London, New Jersey: Zed Books.

Wildman, Stephanie M. et al. (1996). Privilege Revealed: How Invisible Preference Undermines America, New York: New York University Press.

Wilhelmsson, Thomas (1996). Public Interest Litigation on Unfair Terms, in: Hans Wolfgang Micklitz and Norbert Reich (eds), Public Interest Litigation before European Courts, Baden-Baden: Nomos.

Williams, Melissa S. (1998). Voice, Trust, and Memory: Marginalized Groups and the Failings of Liberal Representation, Princeton, NJ: Princeton University Press.

Williams, Patricia J. (1995). The Rooster's Egg: On the Persistence of Prejudice, Cambridge, Ma.: Harvard University Press.

Williams, Patricia J. and Kimberley Crenshaw (1989). Demarginalizing the Intersection of Race and Gender in Antidiscrimination Law, Feminist Theory and Antiracist Politics, in: Chicago Legal Forum, 139.

Wilson, William J. (1978). The Declining Significance of Race, Chicago: University of Chicago Press.

Wilson, William J. (1987). The Truly Disadvantaged, Chicago: University of Chicago Press.

Wing, Adrienne K. (1997). Critical Race Feminism: A Reader, New York: New York University Press.

Winkelman, Christina Smith, Faye J. Crosby and Ronald L. Cohen (1994). Affirmative Action: Setting the Record Straight, in: Social Justice Research 7 (4).

Wrench, John (1996). Preventing Racism at the Workplace: A Report on 16 European Countries. Luxembourg: Office for Official Publications of the European Cummunities.

Wrench, John (1997a). European Compendium of Good Practice for the Prevention of Racism at the Workplace, Luxembourg: Office for Official Publications of the European Cummunities.

Wrench, John (1997b). Case Studies of Good Practice for the Prevention of Racial Discrimination and Xenophobia and the Promotion of Equal

Treatment at the Workplace, Denmark, Dublin: European Foundation for the Improvement of Living and Working Conditions, WP/97/36/EN.

Wrench, John and John Solomos (eds) (1993). Racism and Migration in Western Europe, Oxford/Providence: Berghahn Books.

Wrench, John and Paul Taylor (1993). A Research Manual on the Evaluation of Anti-Discrimination Training Activities, Geneva: International Labour Office.

Yancey, William L. and Lee Rainwater (eds) (1967). The Moynihan Report and the Politics of Controversy, Cambridge, Ma.: MIT Press.

Young, Iris M. (1990). Justice and the Politics of Difference, Princeton, NJ: Princeton University Press.

Zack, Naomi (1997). Race and Philosophic Meaning, in: Naomi Zack (ed.), Race/Sex: Their Sameness, Difference, and Interplay, New York: Routledge.

Zegers de Beijl, Roger (1991). Although Equal before the Law . . . . The Scope of Anti-Discrimination Legislation and its Effects on Labour Market Discrimination against Migrant Workers in the United Kingdom, the Netherlands and Sweden, Geneva: International Labour Office.

Zegers de Beijl, Roger (1997). Combatting discrimination against migrant workers: International standards, national legislation and voluntary measures – the need for a multi-pronged strategy, Geneva.

http://www.civilrights.org.
http://www.uni-tuebingen.de/uni/ukk/aktuell/kopftuch1.htm.
http://www.whitehouse.gov.